THE HA

**Statement by An Taoiseach, Charles J. Haughey TD
30 January 1992**

"I have today informed the Parliamentary Party of
my decision to retire as leader of the party, as President of
Fianna Fáil and as Taoiseach. I am sincerely grateful to the
many thousands of people at home and abroad who
have sent me messages of support and urged
me to remain in office …"

**With these words Charles J. Haughey announced his resig-
nation after an astonishing career in Irish politics, spanning
many years, with innumerable disputes, controversies and
debates, and unprecedented about-turns and policy
changes. His reign was extraordinary, unlike any since the
founding of the state.**

Stephen Collins has followed the career of Charles J. Haughey since
he began to report on Irish politics in 1976. Since then he has been
building up a file on the Haughey career, and in this book he takes
that story right up to date. This book offers a complete and insightful
account and interpretation of the Haughey career. It deals with the
years of power, with the achievements, intrigues and surprises that
characterise the Haughey era.

"the Harry Truman of Irish politics"
Hugh Carey, Governor of New York

• AN O'BRIEN PRESS BOOK •

Charles Haughey leaving the Taoiseach's Department on the day he
announced his resignation, 30 January 1992

What they said after Haughey's resignation

Senator Edward Kennedy
"A great personal friend"

*Tom Foley, Speaker of the US
House of Representatives*
"He has been both an Irish and a
European leader"

*Bob Hawke, former Australian
Prime Minister*
"There is life after politics"
(in message to Haughey)

Lord Fitt
"Whoever replaces Haughey ... is
bound to be an improvement"

Dr Ian Paisley
"His general attacks and attempts to
undermine the Union showed him to
be a public enemy of our state"

*Desmond O'Malley, Leader
Progressive Democrats*
"His career has been marked by a
mixture of outstanding achievements
and profound controversy"

Peter Bottomley, former NI Minister
"He's a bit like Margaret Thatcher,
he's quitting while he's ahead"

The
HAUGHEY
FILE

*The Unprecedented Career and Last Years
of The Boss*

STEPHEN COLLINS
Illustrated

THE O'BRIEN PRESS
DUBLIN

For Jean

First published 1992 by The O'Brien Press,
20 Victoria Road, Dublin 6, Ireland
Copyright © text Stephen Collins
© Design and typesetting The O'Brien Press

10 9 8 7 6 5 4 3 2 1

ISBN 0-86278-298-8

British Library Cataloguing in Publication Data
A catalogue reference for this book is available
from the British Library
Typesetting and design: The O'Brien Press
Cover separations: The City Office Ltd., Dublin
Printing: Guernsey Press Co., Ltd

Acknowledgements
I would like to thank my family for their help and support in writing this
book and one friend in particular who read the manuscript and provided
valuable advice. To the politicians who helped me with information and
anecdotes I owe a debt of gratitude. I am also grateful to the editor of the
Sunday Press, Michael Keane, and the deputy editor, Andrew Bushe, for
giving me the opportunity to write about politics. To the Irish Press Group
Ltd. and the photographers of the three papers thanks for the illustrations.
Thanks also to the staff of the Oireachtas Library who were always
courteous and helpful. I am indebted to my political correspondent
colleagues in Leinster House for their advice and their fund of political
wisdom. Finally I would like to thank Michael O'Brien and Ide O'Leary
of the O'Brien Press for their encouragement and professionalism.
Stephen Collins

Contents

The Final Curtain – Resignation

When Charles Haughey rose to his feet to address the Fianna Fáil parliamentary party just after 11.30 on the morning of 30 January 1992, none of the deputies and senators present was surprised to hear him announce his resignation, nonetheless they found it difficult to comprehend. After all the drama, the controversies, the splits, the sackings and the sheer excitement of his twelve-year reign, it was hard to believe that it was all over.

Even though his departure had been inevitable for a week, following Seán Doherty's bombshell and the ultimatum from the Progressive Democrats, a lot of people both inside Fianna Fáil and outside it had a lingering suspicion that he would launch yet another fight back from the brink of defeat. Given his amazing record of survival, many were inclined to share Conor Cruise O'Brien's warning that until a stake had been driven through Haughey's heart, politically speaking, it would be wise to wear a clove of garlic.

Yet again Haughey confounded his critics, this time by the manner of his departure. People waited in vain for the fireworks to begin, for another roller-coaster political drama, but it didn't happen. Haughey went quietly and calmly, in obedience to the political imperative at the heart of the final drama in which he held centre stage.

When Brian Lenihan was sacked fourteen months earlier, Kildare TD Seán Power had asked Haughey if he would similarly sacrifice himself if the PDs came looking for his head at some future stage. Haughey now answered that question by stepping down in order to avoid an unnecessary general election. At the end of a such a rumbustious political life he went so quietly that it took some time for the full import to sink in, among friends and enemies alike. The method of his departure indicated that what his friends said was true: that he had intended all along to step down by June of this year at the latest.

Though he was deeply hurt at being pushed he was in a situation somewhat similar to that of Jack Lynch in December 1979. Having made up his mind that he was going in a few months, there was no point in fighting one last battle, which he couldn't win in any case because this time his future was in the hands not of Fianna Fáil TDs but of another party

It was ironic that Haughey had to resign at the behest of Des O'Malley, whom he had drummed out of Fianna Fáil seven years earlier. But there was a much deeper irony in the fact that Haughey's woes resulted from the actions of Seán Doherty who had been such a staunch supporter in his early years as Taoiseach. It wasn't his old enemies who ultimately brought Haughey down, but his old friends.

Right up to the time he entered the party rooms on the fifth floor of Leinster House to announce his intentions, Haughey continued to show the Dáil the political flair that had characterised his career as Taoiseach. The day before his announcement, he put John Bruton in his place when the Fine Gael leader claimed that the political insta-bility could lead to difficulty in getting the budget through the Dáil. Haughey immediately pounced to remind Bruton of his own disas-trous budget defeat which brought down the Fine Gael-Labour gov-ernment in 1982.

Even less than half an hour before telling his party of his plan to resign, Haughey handled the order of business in the Dáil with his usual panache. In the light of the expected announcement, Proinsias De Rossa of the Workers' Party was the only Opposition leader to snipe at Haughey. "Perhaps he and I could get together and I could advise him how to safeguard his own position," remarked Haughey apropos the continuing divisions in the Workers' Party.

After that Haughey went off to his parliamentary party to give them the news they all expected. He reminded them that he had outlined a programme of work the previous October which he had wished to complete, the Maastricht summit, the budget, the renegotiation of the Programme for Economic and Social Progress and the formulation of new plans to try and deal with unemployment. He said he had now completed that agenda. Avoiding a direct reference to the Progressive Democrats or Seán Doherty, he spoke about the uncertain political situation which was very unhelpful to Fianna Fáil and the country. He said that in view of that uncertainty and the fact that he had completed his agenda of work, he had decided to resign.

In a short speech he also called on the Fianna Fáil party to select a new leader in an orderly and dignified manner and he urged all those present to unite behind that new leader. He said that he would not take sides in that leadership contest.

After Haughey's announcement there was an outpouring of tributes. A total of eighty-four TDs and senators eulogised his leadership, including some of those who had bitterly opposed him at different stages of his career. Haughey sat impassively through the flowery tributes. According to a close associate he didn't enjoy a minute of it and just wanted to get out of the room as quickly as possible. However, it was one of his last duties to sit and listen to praise, sincere and insincere, being heaped upon his head for more than three hours.

Both outside and inside the room people were trying to come to terms with the thought of life without Charlie. Even though he has stepped down as Taoiseach, he has no intention of becoming some "elder statesman" figure in the Dáil. He often expressed puzzlement at why Garret FitzGerald insisted on staying on as a Dáil deputy, making occasional interventions in the chamber. Haughey regarded such activity as pointless and he does not intend to appear very often for the remainder of the life of the twenty-sixth Dáil and will not stand at the next election.

What he will do without politics, which has been his life for thirty-five years, it is hard to imagine. Former Australian Prime Minister Bob Hawke, with whom he had a very good relationship, sent him a telegram on the morning of his resignation announcement. The message from Hawke, who was ousted in not dissimilar circumstances, was "There is life after politics". Haughey is now finding out what that life is like.

Prologue – "Coalitions just don't work"

Exasperation spread across the face of Government Press Secretary P.J. Mara as a journalist expressed his disbelief at the impending Dáil announcement confirming that Fianna Fáil was about to enter a coalition government with the Progressive Democrats.

"Look, do you not know one of the oldest rules of politics?" snapped Mara. "Sometimes you have to sacrifice your friends to placate your enemies."

It was just after lunchtime on the afternoon of 12 July 1989, and Mara had formally announced in the political correspondents' room in Leinster House that his boss, Charles Haughey, the Taoiseach and leader of Fianna Fáil, had agreed terms on the formation of a coalition government with the Progressive Democrats. Not only that but the smaller party was getting two seats at the Cabinet table.

Downstairs in one of the Dáil corridors PD Mary Harney had just heard the news and she burst into tears. Her tears of joy and relief were a response to the emotion of the situation and to the fact that she was to become a junior minister. Her reaction was widely misinterpreted and rumours swept the House to the effect that the coalition talks had broken down or that Harney was bitterly disappointed at not getting a Cabinet post.

The reality of the situation was difficult to believe – Charles Haughey had just agreed to abandon Fianna Fáil's sixty-year-old policy of refusing to enter coalition. He had also agreed to share power with his deadliest political enemies, the Progressive Democrats. To cap it all he had given in to their demand for two Cabinet posts even though they were, strictly speaking, only entitled to one, on a proportional basis.

It was one of the most astounding developments in modern Irish politics and one which deeply traumatised the Fianna Fáil party whose activists were adamantly opposed to coalition with anyone, but particularly the PDs.

Looked at from Haughey's point of view the decision was laden with irony. The PDs existed as a political party only because their leader, Desmond O'Malley, had been driven out of Fianna Fáil by

Haughey. That expulsion followed three attempts by O'Malley in the early 1980s to oust Haughey from the leadership of the party. After his expulsion O'Malley had gone on to found the PDs with a rump of anti Hagheyites from his old party.

Those in Fianna Fáil who had stood by Haughey in the internal battles against O'Malley were stunned by their leader's decision to share power with his mortal political enemy, particularly as only a little over a week earlier the acting Taoiseach had airily dismissed the likelihood of Fianna Fáil ever entering a coalition arrangement.

"Coalitions just don't work. They can't give effective, decisive government. The proof of that was the last coalition government," he told the nation just forty-eight hours before phoning Des O'Malley to offer him a coalition deal.

Ministers like Albert Reynolds, Pádraig Flynn and Bertie Ahern, who had stood by Haughey against O'Malley during all the heaves, were sent out in the intervening period to give media interviews ruling out coalition, only to find that their leader had reversed engines. These ministers who had stood by Haughey through thick and thin felt betrayed by the fact that their leader had come to terms with people they regarded as little better than traitors.

That sense of betrayal, among the people who had stood by him for a decade, was ultimately to erode Haughey's authority as the life of the coalition government wore on, but in July 1989 he was able to dance rings around them.

On top of everything, Haughey had made the decision to go into coalition behind their backs. Even as his ministers stoutly maintained an anti coalition stance in public, and defended their position as a "core value", the Taoiseach had already formed the basis of a coalition agreement with O'Malley. Haughey's decision, and the way he made it without consulting them, baffled and angered his supporters but they were afflicted with a political paralysis and were unable to intervene to stop him doing a deal with his, and their, enemies.

Haughey himself suffered no such agonies. O'Malley and the PDs may have been his enemies but he had one simple calculation to make: how best to retain the Taoiseach's job? Once it became clear in the aftermath of the 1989 election that no one would support a Fianna

Fáil minority government from the outside, the inevitable conclusion was that coalition was the price of power. At that stage all Haughey's instincts for self preservation and his immense political skill came to the forefront. He abandoned his party's "core value" without a backward glance.

"Nobody but myself could have done it," he remarked with a beam on his face as he shook hands on the deal with Bobby Molloy that hot afternoon in July 1989.

All along he had out-manoeuvred the majority of his Cabinet colleagues and the bulk of the parliamentary party, who were opposed to the coalition and who would have favoured another election instead. Haughey manipulated his Cabinet and his party so that they never got to the stage of giving him a clear directive, either on the issue of coalition or on the number of Cabinet seats for the PDs.

"He is absolutely brilliant and he is only at his best when his back is to the wall," said Fianna Fáil TD Charlie McCreevy, when the deal was announced, lost in admiration despite all his rows with Haughey over the years.

Most Fianna Fáil deputies were annoyed not just at the fact of coalition but that the PDs were perceived as the clear victors in the negotiations. There were also some people in the smaller party who had qualms about the whole idea of supporting Haughey as Taoiseach, good bargain or not. After his expulsion from Fianna Fáil in 1985 had not O'Malley himself expressed the opinion that Haughey was unfit to govern?

Following the foundation of the PDs, Mary Harney had said that she would never vote for Haughey as Taoiseach. In view of all that had happened between Haughey and O'Malley over the years it was remarkable to hear the two of them announce the coalition deal to the Dáil that evening.

"I want to acknowledge the courage and skill exhibited, particularly by Deputy Haughey in recent weeks, courage and skill which I know he possesses in abundance and which has been utilised in the national interest during this time," the PD leader told the Dáil.

After his election, Haughey responded : "I want to say about them all, particularly Deputy O'Malley, that I was able to conduct my conversations with them in a way that was always not just courteous but constructive, and I shall always remember that as one of the most important developments in this new Dáil as it went about its arduous and complicated business."

The coalition deal was certainly the most remarkable feature of the twenty-sixth Dáil. Whatever about the deep hostility of the majority of Fianna Fáil TDs and party members to the arrangement and the grave suspicions of many PDs, it marked a critical stage in the modernisation of Irish politics.

While Fianna Fáil members found the idea of a coalition difficult to take, the general public was more than happy at the arrangement. An MRBI opinion poll conducted before agreement was reached and published at a critical stage in the Fianna Fáil-PD negotiations showed that a decisive majority of the electorate favoured the formation of a power-sharing administration under Haughey's leadership.

After the formation of the government on 12 July there was a broad welcome from the media. *The Irish Times* praised the agreed programme for government and even brought itself to utter some words of praise for the Taoiseach.

"Mr Haughey has added to his own stature and has enhanced his own reputation in coming to terms with a set of circumstances which he found utterly unpalatable and by pressing ahead — albeit when other avenues were closed to him — with the task of forming a government."

Despite the welcome by the media and by a public relieved at avoiding another election, the sullen resentment in Fianna Fáil to the whole concept could not be disguised. It might not have come as such a shock if they had taken notice of a jibe by the late Frank Cluskey who died shortly before the campaign got underway. Back in the election campaign of 1981, when he was Labour leader, he referred during a press conference to the possibility of going into coalition with Fianna Fáil at some stage.

"Surely you are aware that Fianna Fáil are on record as saying they will never enter coalition," said John Bowman of RTE.

"Yeah, but Fianna Fáil are also on record as saying they would never enter Dáil Eireann," replied Cluskey, as quick as a flash.

1 – Rise and Fall

The antipathy between Charles Haughey and the Progressive Democrats went back a long way. The expulsion of Des O'Malley from Fianna Fáil in 1985 followed O'Malley's three attempts to depose Haughey. They in turn arose out of the bitter leadership contest of 1979 when Haughey succeeded Jack Lynch. That leadership contest itself was just a stage in a power battle which stretched back to the Arms Crisis of 1970 and ultimately to the leadership struggle of 1966 when Haughey and George Colley first squared up to each other.

The fallout from the Colley-Haughey contest hung like a poisonous cloud over Fianna Fáil for more than two decades. The resulting division of the party into struggling factions and the personal bitterness which that engendered provided the backdrop to the political history of the era. At the heart of the internal conflict was not just a power battle but a struggle for the soul of Fianna Fáil.

"The public view of the 1966 contest was that it had really been between Colley, as the clean-cut, Irish-speaking representative of old values, and Haughey, as the high flying spokesman of business and financial interests," wrote Dick Walsh in his book *The Party*.

While Haughey was the ultimate victor, that victory came only after a series of traumas. He was fired from the government, charged in open court with importing arms, and forced to embarrass himself by voting confidence in those who had fired him, before he could begin to crawl humiliatingly back up the ladder of party hierarchy to put himself in a position to contest the leadership in 1979. That experience left scars which could never be healed and merely fueled his determination to take over the leadership of Fianna Fáil no matter how hard he had to drive himself to achieve that goal.

Charles Haughey followed a well-travelled route towards involvement in politics. He was born in Castlebar, County Mayo, in September 1925, the third child of a Free State army officer. Haughey senior resigned from the army three years later and tried his hand at farming in County Meath, but he developed multiple sclerosis and the family moved to Belton Park Road in Donneycarney in the early 1930s. With a family of seven children to support on his army and Old IRA pensions, things were not easy.

Coming from this lower middle class background, Charles Haughey was educated by the Christian Brothers at St Joseph's in Fairview where he was a brilliant student and an enthusiastic GAA player. It was only logical that he would progress as an adult to join the great national family of Fianna Fáil. Though his father's role as an officer on the Free State side in the Civil War was unusual for a Fianna Fáil member, Haughey's class and cultural milieu led almost inevitably into political support for the party.

After secondary school Haughey went on to UCD, where he studied commerce – Garret FitzGerald was a contemporary at college, but the two mixed in very different circles. The university was dominated by a bourgeois Fine Gael tradition but in the mid-1940s it was opening up to lower middle class Catholics, many of whom came to resent the middle class ethos of the institution. That resentment was to surface again and again during Haughey's political career. No matter what he achieved he was always regarded as an outsider by certain sections of the rich and the powerful in Irish society.

This attitude to Haughey was not displayed by rich Fine Gaelers only. Many in the establishment of his chosen party, Fianna Fáil, also came to regard him as an outsider, and a dangerous one at that, but not before he had insinuated himself into the party's complex hierarchy.

A clue to Haughey's character was provided by an escapade he got involved in as a student at UCD. On VE day in 1945, Trinity College, which along with *The Irish Times* represented the last vestiges of the Act of Union, flew the Union Jack and other Allied flags over the entrance to the college. When some passersby objected, Trinity students took down the Irish tricolour, which was also flying over the college, and burned it. Word travelled quickly to UCD, then in Earlsfort Terrace nearby. A group of UCD students marched down to Trinity and Haughey produced a Union Jack which was burned at College Green. A riot developed and the Gardaí had to disperse the crowd with batons.

At university and in the years immediately after his graduation, Haughey established links with some of the most important Fianna

Fáil families in the country. Qualifying as an accountant, he went into business partnership with an old school friend, Harry Boland, son of one of the founding fathers of Fianna Fáil, Gerry Boland, who had been Minister for Justice for twelve years.

Even more important, he married Maureen Lemass, the daughter of de Valera's clearly designated heir, Seán Lemass. Haughey met his future wife while they were both studying in UCD and they were married in 1951.

Haughey was brought into politics by Boland and by George Colley, another school friend from his days at St Joseph's, Marino. Colley, like Boland, was the son of a senior Fianna Fáil figure, Harry Colley, who at that time was a TD for Dublin North East. Haughey's introduction to politics consisted in helping the Boland and Colley election campaigns in 1948. So, by his late twenties he had established connections with the Lemass, Boland and Colley families and was clearly on his way in terms of social advancement and a political career.

Getting elected was initially a big problem. His first outing as a Fianna Fáil election candidate in 1951, the year of his marriage, ended in dismal failure and he also failed on his next Dáil outing in 1954. Though co-opted to Dublin City Council, he suffered the ignominy of losing his council seat the following year. He lost again as a by-election candidate in 1956 but the high profile obtained by that campaign enabled him to make it to the Dáil in 1957, though in the process he knocked out Harry Colley.

The persistence with which he grimly fought his way into the Dáil after this series of electoral setbacks, and his refusal to accept defeat were to characterise his entire political life. Once elected, Haughey quickly established himself as a man with a future. As a backbench TD he set out to hire his own public relations consultant. He first approached Terry O'Sullivan of the *Evening Press*, and when he turned down the job he hired Tony Grey of *The Irish Times*. The strategy paid off and Haughey became the subject of a great deal of media attention, most of it flattering at this stage of his career.

From an early stage he had a media ally in John Healy who wrote the influential backbencher column in *The Irish Times*. Healy regarded the young Haughey as something special and he did a lot to encourage the rising star, praising him in print and denigrating those politicians inside and outside Fianna Fáil who stood in Haughey's way. Not everybody in the media was so star-struck and later in his career Haughey had serious difficulties with the media. In the early days, though, most of the coverage he received was decidedly upbeat.

From the beginning he had a strange charisma. Haughey, though only five feet six inches in height, has always had an uncanny ability to impose his will on others and to inspire fierce loyalty and antipathy. When first elected in 1957 he was in the process of acquiring a fortune for himself. He had qualified as an accountant and set up the firm of Haughey, Boland and Company in 1951 with his old school friend, Harry Boland. He worked hard and by 1960 had acquired a fortune by the standards of the day. It was enough to buy Grangemore, a large Victorian house on forty-five acres in Raheny. During the 1960s, as he climbed the political ladder, he amassed even greater wealth, buying a farm in County Meath, as well as race horses, a chicken hatchery and Inishvickillane, one of the Blasket Islands off the Kerry coast.

In 1969 he bought Abbeyville in Kinsealy, an eighteenth-century mansion which once served as a summer home for the Lords Lieutenant of Ireland. Designed by James Gandon, the house stands on 250 acres of land, and it came over the years to symbolise the Haughey style. The source of Haughey's wealth has always aroused suspicion among political opponents and has been a central question for journalists, but no one has ever been able to get at the facts. Haughey stoutly maintains that his private affairs are nobody else's business and he has dealt brusquely with journalists who have probed him on the issue over the years.

His style has also rubbed people the wrong way. Peter Berry, the long-serving Secretary of the Department of Justice, who was later to be a central figure in the Arms Crisis, recalled in his diaries that Gerry Boland expressed the opinion to him around 1960 that Haughey would one day "drag down the Party in the mire".

Other senior figures in the Fianna Fáil government held the same view of Haughey, according to Berry, but nonetheless he was promoted by his father-in-law, Seán Lemass, in 1960 to the post of Parliamentary Secretary to the Minister for Justice and the following year made a full minister in that department. One story at the time had it that when Lemass offered Haughey his first promotion he said that it was his duty as Taoiseach to offer him the position but his duty as a father-in-law to advise him not to take it.

Haughey grabbed the opportunity with open arms and as a minister he began to make his mark. Important new legislation like the Succession Act, which protected the inheritance rights of wives, and the Extradition Act were introduced and passed by the Dáil. In his first month in office he drew up a ten-point programme that pinpointed the crushing of the IRA as a primary objective. The Special Criminal Court was reactivated and in less than a year the IRA called off their campaign.

"While he was in Justice, Mr Haughey was a dynamic minister. He was a joy to work with and the longer he stayed the better he got," wrote Berry. Mind you, Berry also recalled another aspect of Haughey's personality which manifested itself in arrogant bullying of his officials. At one stage when Berry objected to a blatantly political promotion in the immigration service, Haughey literally flung the departmental file at him and the papers were strewn about the floor of the minister's office.

In his private life too Haughey was breaking new ground. Government ministers in the first forty years of the state's existence had mostly been members of the revolutionary generation whose private lives were conservative and austere. In the early 1960s things began to change. Haughey and other younger Cabinet colleagues, like Donogh O'Malley and Brian Lenihan, flamboyantly enjoyed the good life. Much later in his career, in an interview with John Waters in *Hot Press* magazine, Haughey was to bemoan the fact that he was born too late for the permissive society. "To my dying day I'll regret that I was too late for the free society. We missed out on that. It came too late for my generation," he said in 1984.

Nonetheless, as a rising politician in the late 1950s and early 1960s his lifestyle was certainly liberated by the standards of the time. The stories were legion about the drinking exploits of his set in Groome's

17

Hotel, a haunt for politicians and their hangers on. They also patronised the up-market Russell Hotel on Stephen's Green and Haughey developed a taste for French cuisine and fine wine. In Tim Pat Coogan's phrase, he was at this stage "the epitome of the men in the mohair suits".

Conor Cruise O'Brien, who was to be a fierce political opponent of Haughey's for the best part of a decade and an unremitting critic of the Kinsealy man for the rest of his political life, wrote of his style at this time:

"Mr Haughey's general style of living was remote from the traditional Republican and de Valera austerities. He had made a great deal of money, and he obviously enjoyed spending it, in a dashing eighteenth-century style, of which horses were conspicuous symbols. He was a small man and, when dismounted, he strutted rather. His admirers thought he resembled the Emperor Napoleon, some of whose better known mannerisms he cultivated. He patronised, and that is the right word, the arts. He was an aristocrat in the proper sense of the word: not a nobleman or even a gentleman, but one who believed in the right of the best people to rule, and that he himself was the best of the best people. He was an any rate better, or at least more intelligent and interesting, than most of his colleagues. He was considered a competent Minister, and spoke in parliament with bored but conclusive authority. There were enough rumours about him to form a legend of sorts."

A different perspective on these rumours is given by Haughey's friend, the writer Anthony Cronin, who pondered on his truly extraordinary myth-making powers. "Now I must confess I don't know why legend should attach itself to Charlie Haughey in quite this way. I know of course that he is a remarkable man; and that he has had in many ways a remarkable career; but the mere facts do not account for the phenomenon, so that one must assume some singling out process, to do with the wishes and fears of our society."

Cronin, who has known Haughey since they were students together in UCD, defended his friend against his wilder critics in 1982.

"What makes the caricature version so annoying is that it is in any case so totally unlike the real man. There is a man, with lights and shadows, a complex of human qualities, hard to define but as far from the caricature [hooded eyes etc.] as it would be possible to get.

"In part it is a degree of sensitivity to other people's moods and difficulties which is totally at variance with the image of the ruthless, self centred go-getter. In part it is humour, a never-failing resource. In part it is sheer warmth, a capacity to convey affection which we all should have, but few actually do. And in part it is what I can only call chivalry."

Whatever the reason, and it surely has something to do with his great wealth, the public view of Haughey has always been fuelled by rumours. Back in the 1960s as the economy opened up there was a lot of money around. Fianna Fáil as the party of power attracted the builders and speculators who were making money out of the new economy and Haughey moved in their circle. At this stage he also became a wealthy man and in defiance of Fianna Fáil tradition he flaunted the trappings of a high lifestyle. Riding to hounds like a country gentleman was a long way from his upbringing in Donneycarney and a long way from the concerns of his electorate, but he embraced the new lifestyle as if to the manor born.

This was held against him by the traditionalists in Fianna Fáil and that had an impact when Lemass suddenly retired in November 1966. The media immediately dubbed the succession a two-horse race between Haughey and George Colley. Though the men had been friendly in early life they had by now grown apart. The relationship was strained when Haughey ousted Harry Colley from the Dáil in 1957, but it was when George Colley decided to run for the Dáil in the same constituency as Haughey in 1961 that the two became increasingly bitter foes.

Colley, though he entered politics much later than Haughey, rose rapidly to Cabinet rank and was a leadership contender after only five years in the Dáil. He was a very different character to his rival. Colley exuded respectability and a certain middle class stuffiness. He had nothing of Haughey's "whiff of sulphur" style charm but was clearly someone safe and earnest who could be accepted by the party as a reliable bearer of the sacred flame. An impeccable Fianna Fáil pedigree, enhanced by his fluency in the Irish language, ensured that he became the standard bearer for the traditional values of the party and had the support of elders like Seán MacEntee and Frank Aiken.

The choice between Haughey and Colley was a choice not just between two men but between different sets of values and different visions of what politics was about. It was a contest for the soul of Fianna Fáil. In the event the contest threatened to become so divisive that Lemass stepped in and persuaded Jack Lynch from Cork to enter the race. Haughey immediately withdrew but Colley forced the issue to a vote and was defeated by 52 votes to 19.

Among those who strongly backed Colley was a young TD from Galway, Bobby Molloy, who seconded his nomination. Other strong Colley supporters were Jim Gibbons, David Andrews and Pádraig Faulkner.

Lynch rewarded Haughey for stepping aside from the leadership contest by making him Minister for Finance, and the effective number two in the government. It was during those years in Finance in the late 1960s that Haughey really made his reputation. Popular acts like the introduction of free travel and free electricity allowances for pensioners attracted huge positive publicity. His handling of the national finances has since been questioned but at the time he was regarded as a very successful and innovative minister.

However, there were deep divisions in the Cabinet, with a number of powerful figures like Haughey, Neil Blaney and Kevin Boland making it clear that they regarded Lynch as an interim leader. In those circumstances Lynch gradually began to rely more and more on Colley, and after the 1969 general election he promoted protégés of his former rival, like Jim Gibbons and Bobby Molloy. Colley's reference in 1967 to "low standards in high places" was seen as a thinly disguised attack on Haughey and it emphasised the gulf that was opening up between different factions in the party.

The Northern troubles, which began in 1968, put Lynch under a terrible strain and there was a fierce tussle in the Cabinet over government policy on the issue. Blaney and Boland wanted a much more aggressive interventionist policy than Lynch was prepared to adopt and the divisions in government became public with a series of speeches by Blaney clearly challenging Lynch.

The Arms Crisis of May 1970 brought the whole issue to a head and the result was that Lynch was able to rid himself of his unruly senior ministers and take full control of the government for the first time. The real surprise of the Arms Crisis was not that it happened but that Haughey should be so centrally involved. As Minister for Justice less than a decade earlier he had been deeply hostile to the IRA and his whole political and social development would appear to have brought him far from traditional republicanism. Yet here he was, linked with a plot to import arms.

The affair was confused by the fact that Haughey had a mysterious riding accident just days after the attempted arms importation and was absent from the Cabinet and the Dáil at the time of the sacking. When he recovered he turned up along with Neil Blaney in the Dáil to vote confidence in the government which had sacked them and they joined in a unanimous decision of the Fianna Fáil parliamentary party in upholding the right of the Taoiseach to remove them.

Nothing more clearly illustrates the Stalinist discipline of the Fianna Fáil party than these actions of Haughey and Blaney in justifying their own humiliation. "I have fully accepted the Taoiseach's decision, as I believe that the unity of the Fianna Fáil party is of greater importance to the welfare of the nation than my political career," said Haughey's statement. He let his real feelings show only once. Speaking immediately after his acquittal at the Arms trial in October 1970 to a group of raucous supporters whom he referred to as "my fellow patriots", he said: "I was never in any doubt that it was a political trial. I think those who are responsible for this debacle have no alternative but to take the honourable course that is open to them."

Lynch was in the United States at the time but virtually the entire parliamentary party was on hand to greet him on his return and the first one out on the tarmac to shake the Taoiseach's hand was Brian Lenihan.

An opinion poll also showed that 72 percent of the electorate backed Lynch's decision to dismiss Haughey and that Haughey was the preferred choice for Taoiseach of just 1 percent of those who voted for Fianna Fáil in the previous election. He got the message and backed off.

The ability of the Fianna Fáil government to survive the sacking of senior ministers, their arrest and trial on charges of importing arms and their subsequent acquittal was truly astonishing. Dick Walsh wrote of this traumatic period: "The party's survival bewildered its opponents and amazed its friends. Not only did Lynch's beleaguered government hold out for two and a half years after the Arms Crisis it managed to negotiate Irish membership of the EC and to bring Anglo-Irish relations to the point where, albeit nine months after its departure, agreement on a power-sharing executive in the North proved possible."

Instead of challenging Lynch after his acquittal, Haughey set off on a long course of rehabilitation, slogging up and down the country, talking to any unit of the organisation prepared to issue him an invitation. He was accompanied on these trips by a young P.J. Mara, who was to become one of his closest political confidants in the years following. There was just one constituency where Haughey was effectively barred by the sitting TD. That was Limerick West where Gerry Collins ruled the roost, and this was something that rankled with Haughey for the rest of his political career.

Eating chicken and chips at endless *comhairle ceanntair* and *cumainn* functions was a far cry from the French cuisine and fine claret Haughey relished at top Dublin restaurants like Le Coq Hardi. The tour of the country gave Haughey a unique insight into the Fianna Fáil organisation and how it worked and this experience was something he was able to fall back on when he was in the deepest trouble.

The strategy of cultivating the grass roots worked and he gradually rebuilt a base in the party. He was re-elected honorary Vice President at the Ard Fheis of 1972 and in 1975 he was restored to the front bench by Lynch at a time when the party was in opposition and perceived to be performing badly.

After his return to the front bench, following an absence of five years, he was excluded from the inner councils of the party. These were now dominated by Colley, Jack Lynch's economic advisor Martin O'Donoghue, and by the young Minister for Justice, Des O'Malley, who had been brought into the Cabinet by Lynch after Haughey's sacking in 1970. This trio devised the 1977 election manifesto which resulted in a sweeping victory for Fianna Fáil. Back in government Haughey was brought into the Cabinet as Minister for Health, but still excluded from any economic power. Far from doing him any harm this allowed him to indulge in a series of clever public relations exercises while the economic ministers carried the can for the problems that inevitably developed from the '77 Manifesto. As those problems intensified in 1979 Haughey became surer and surer that his hour was at hand.

2 – Leader at Last

Jack Lynch's luck ran out in the autumn of 1979. After winning a record eighty-four seats in 1977 Lynch had decided that he would not lead Fianna Fáil into another election. By the summer of 1979 he had decided to step down in early 1980 after the completion of Ireland's presidency of the European Community. He made no public announcement about this and while Fianna Fáil TDs believed he was likely to retire, no one could be absolutely sure. Haughey, impatient at waiting any longer, decided not to take any chances and he started to put the screws on the party leader. Even in the flush of victory in 1977 Lynch had recognised that the scale of his win would become a problem. The landslide had brought into the Dáil a number of TDs who would have a very difficult time holding their seats if the party's standing took any dip in the polls, and they were bound to become nervous at the first hint of any swing against Fianna Fáil.

That nervousness was fanned into open revolt by Haughey as the tide of public opinion began to flow against the government in the summer of 1979. Discipline in the party had begun to break down after the 1977 election victory and an unheard of open revolt emerged the following year over a proposal by George Colley to impose a 2 percent income levy on farmers to bring in some taxation from that sector. Cork backbencher Tom Meaney publicly challenged the government's policy on the issue and Kildare TD Charlie McCreevy also attacked it.

After defending the levy at the party's Ard Fheis, Colley later engaged in a humiliating climbdown. That failure of nerve led to an immediate loss of authority, the implications of which were not lost on Haughey. The first direct elections to the European Parliament in June of 1979 accelerated the process because it resulted in a slump in the Fianna Fáil vote to just under 35 percent. Alarm bells began to go off in the swollen parliamentary party as TDs began to fear for their seats.

The economic background was also beginning to deteriorate. While the government did have some successes to its credit, notably the reduction of unemployment to below 100,000, its achievement was based on an expansion of the public service. This in turn added substantially to the cost of the public service pay bill. In an attempt to stop the pay bill spiralling out of control, the Cabinet decided to fight a pay claim by postmen and the result was a protracted postal strike. The government also failed to respond adequately to the second oil crisis which struck in 1979 and long queues at petrol stations provoked further hostile public reaction.

It was against this background that the plot to remove Lynch was hatched. Haughey had been preparing the ground very carefully since 1977. Brendan O'Donnell, a civil servant who had been an associate of his since his days in Agriculture, moved to the Department of Health as an advisor. O'Donnell quickly became Haughey's link man with the parliamentary party and he made continuous soundings among Fianna Fáil backbenchers to establish which of them were favourably disposed to Haughey's cause.

O'Donnell was a regular in the Dáil on sitting days where he established contact with a range of TDs on Haughey's behalf. Encouraged by Haughey, a conspiracy to remove Lynch began in the summer of 1979. Vincent Browne was later to trace this plot to the so-called "gang of five", a group composed of Albert Reynolds, Seán Doherty, Mark Killilea, Tom McEllistrim and Jackie Fahey.

In fact the "gang of five" was just one element in the plot and a number of different groups were called into action around the same time, when Haughey judged that the time was ripe for the move. People like Ray MacSharry, who was George Colley's junior minister at the time, Pádraig Flynn, Brendan Daly, Michael Smith, Ber Cowan, Seán Calleary and Charlie McCreevy all played significant parts in the drama. A house in Harold's Cross, occupied during Dáil sessions by MacSharry, Mark Killilea and Senator Bernard McGlinchey, was where much of the plotting took place. The "gang of five" were more widely known to outsiders than some of the other conspirators because they stayed in Jury's Hotel while the Dáil was in session and did a lot of talking and scheming in the Coffee Dock at the hotel.

At this stage public awareness of the problems in Fianna Fáil was confined to Sile de Valera and Bill Loughnane, who made a number of statements which were a clear embarrassment to the leadership.

Of all the conspirators, MacSharry was probably the most important, particularly as he was a junior minister, while the rest were backbenchers. Along with MacSharry the other key conspirators were Reynolds and Doherty and the future careers of all three became inextricably bound up with Haughey's. McCreevy became the unofficial secretary for the group, summoning caucus meetings in Leinster House as the plot thickened.

MacSharry had been in the Dáil since 1969 and was chafing for Cabinet office by this stage. Though Lynch had made him a junior minister after the 1977 election he was impatient for further promotion. He had also suffered severe financial losses in his own haulage business which added to his impatience for a more senior and financially rewarding position. MacSharry's links with Haughey went back to the Arms Crisis through the Sligo TDs membership of the Committee of Public Accounts which investigated the disappearance of the £100,000 tied up with the arms deal. MacSharry was very supportive of Haughey during the public and private sessions of the Committee and an alliance developed between the two.

On a personal level the two men were like chalk and cheese. MacSharry was rigid and austere in his approach to life and to politics. A teetotaller with a blunt straightforward manner, he had none of the subtlety of Haughey, but carried great inner conviction and once he had decided on a course of action was almost impossible to shake. He was certainly a valuable ally for Haughey and a formidable opponent for Colley.

Reynolds and Doherty, from the neighbouring constituencies of Longford and Roscommon, were, like many of the other Haughey supporters, first-time TDs in 1977. They knew that the Lynch era was coming to an end and they were anxious to get it over with as quickly as possible. They were both to achieve very rapid promotion to Cabinet office, with very different results, on the basis of hitching their star to Haughey's.

Albert Reynolds was a successful businessman based in Longford who had made his money in the showband boom of the 1960s. During that decade he became involved in politics, campaigning for the independent TD in Longford-Westmeath, Joe Sheridan. It was the

Arms trial that had first drawn him to Haughey and he attended the Four Courts for each day of the trial. He had pulled off the difficult political feat of replacing sitting Longford Fianna Fáil TD Frank Carter as the party's candidate in the county. He was clearly ambitious and had spent a lot of money on his first election campaign. A popular "hail fellow well met" personality, he had a key role in winning friends for Haughey among the new intake of TDs.

Seán Doherty, who was equally ambitious, had a different background. His father had been a long-time Fianna Fáil councillor in Roscommon, but Seán had entered the Gardaí and become a detective in Sligo before leaving the force and opting for a political career. Early on he acquired the name of being a "cute" politician whose approach was laced with a strong vein of humorous cynicism about the political process.

Another first-term TD who played a pivotal role in getting Haughey elected was Charlie McCreevy. He was the organiser of a number of caucus meetings and he circulated notices of them among deputies thought to be friendly. Like MacSharry, Reynolds and Doherty, McCreevy also played a leading role in the political life of the next decade but in a guise that none of them could possibly have foreseen in 1979. An accountant by profession, he was outspoken in his belief in the need for harsh economic policies but also held strong republican views and shared the same sentiments as Sile de Valera.

The common thread linking the conspirators was the fact that they were all outsiders to one degree or another. The party establishment was firmly behind Lynch and would back Colley in the leadership struggle. Haughey's appeal was to those outside the magic circle of power and influence. Some of these outsiders saw Haughey's election as their route to the inside track while others believed his elevation would change the power structure of the party.

There was a feeling among some of this group that Fianna Fáil had drifted from its roots and no longer reflected the republican vision that had inspired its founders. The removal of Lynch and his replacement by Haughey was regarded by them as a way of changing the underlying philosophy of the government and reverting to the original Fianna Fáil ethos of vibrant nationalism.

Haughey's attraction for party backbenchers was remarkably similar to that of Margaret Thatcher's for British Conservative MPs four years earlier. Her victory had been described as the "peasants' revolt" and Haughey's campaign had an uncanny resemblance to hers. In both cases the outcasts took over power to the total and utter astonishment of those who believed themselves to be the natural ruling elite of their respective parties.

The Haughey campaign began to develop irresistible momentum in September 1979, when Sile de Valera, granddaughter of the party's founder, who was a newly elected MEP as well as a TD, made a speech implicitly criticising government policy on the North. There was a brief lull at the end of September when Pope John Paul II visited Ireland, but a political crisis blew up in the wake of that visit. Wild rumours began to circulate about an alleged relationship between President Hillery and an unnamed Italian woman. The President was so concerned at the rumours that he called the country's political correspondents to Aras an Uachtaráin for a briefing. During that briefing he denied that he was involved in any extra-marital relationship and the denial was carried prominently by all the media. It was claimed later that the President blamed some of the Haughey conspirators for starting the rumours in the hope that he would be forced to resign. That could have given them an excuse for drafting in Lynch as a replacement, thus opening the Taoiseach's office for Haughey. That theory seemed fantastic at the time but in the summer of 1991 Patrick Hillery gave an interview to *The Irish Times* in which he voiced his deep unhappiness at the events of the autumn of 1979 and hinted that he held Haughey responsible for what had happened.

One way or another the pressure was kept on Lynch. After the presidential rumour incident had blown over, Tom McEllistrim questioned why British aircraft were allowed to overfly Irish airspace. Then in November Lynch suffered a severe setback when Fianna Fáil lost two by-elections in his native Cork. He was on an official visit to the United States and heard the bad news about the by-elections just before he met President Carter. Lynch's press secretary, Frank Dunlop, asked his boss during that trip about his future intentions and was given a strong indication that the Taoiseach would resign in January.

That, however, was not good enough for Haughey, and the two men conducted long-range political warfare from Ireland and the United States. An admission by Lynch to the Washington Press Club that he had given permission for British overflights along the Irish border in order to tackle terrorism sparked a huge controversy at home. Bill Loughnane, a colourful fiddle-playing deputy from Clare, responded by accusing the Taoiseach of lying to the Dáil about security cooperation with the British.

Lynch, after consultations with his Foreign Minister, Michael O'Kennedy, who was on the trip, telephoned Colley to devise a strategy in response. They agreed that Colley would go to a meeting of the Fianna Fáil parliamentary party and have the whip withdrawn from Loughnane.

But Colley failed to carry the meeting and Loughnane was merely asked to withdrew the charge. The writing was now on the wall for both Lynch and Colley. There were more caucus meetings and a petition calling for Lynch to step down was circulated. When the Taoiseach returned from the US there was an atmosphere of great tension in Fianna Fáil.

Lynch went to one parliamentary party meeting saying that he had heard stories of caucus meetings and he asked who was involved. Only Pádraig Flynn stood up to admit his role publicly. Lynch was later to say that Flynn was the only one of the conspirators for whom he could have any respect because he at least had the guts to stand up and be counted.

With the pressure mounting, Lynch announced on 5 December that he was stepping down as party leader and Taoiseach and that his successor would be chosen two days later. If Lynch had wanted to make a stand there is little doubt that he could have defeated his critics in a vote of the parliamentary party, but he decided that it was neither in his own interests nor in that of the party to indulge in a public squabble. Lynch felt humiliated by the fact that he was not even allowed to serve out his term as EC President but he felt impelled to step down at this stage to avoid embroiling himself and the party in undignified internal rows and more crucially because Colley and O'Donoghue convinced him that the timing would catch Haughey on the hop.

There was widespread public surprise at Lynch's resignation as the plotting and tensions within Fianna Fáil were not widely known. Former Fine Gael leader Liam Cosgrave, who had been beaten by Lynch in the 1977 general election, in a tribute to his old adversary described Jack Lynch as "the most popular Irish politician since Daniel O'Connell". It was an assessment that reflected the great affection that existed for Lynch everywhere apart from a significant segment of his own parliamentary party.

Haughey was not taken aback in the least by Lynch's sudden decision and believed that a short sharp campaign would suit him best. Dick Walsh in his book *The Party* recalls that only hours after Lynch made the announcement Haughey met Doherty, McEllistrim, Killilea and McCreevy, and after totting up the figures he predicted he would beat Colley by 58 votes to 24.

"Do you know, you're the worst fucking judge of people I ever met," remarked Doherty who had a much more realistic assessment of the situation.

An intense and unscrupulous canvassing campaign developed over the short period before the vote. Some of the Colley supporters were convinced afterwards that their camp had been infiltrated by agents of Haughey anxious to find out what was going on and to establish the strength of their opponents. There were rumours of bribery and intimidation in the heat of the campaign and claims that uncommitted backbenchers were subjected to a great deal of pressure.

There was also talk of votes being traded for promises of office and the atmosphere was described by one political scientist as "sulphurous". The level of support was about even for the two candidates but there was a vital difference in the composition of that support; Colley had virtually the entire Cabinet while Haughey relied on the backbenchers.

Having worked for years to bring this situation about, Haughey was determined to leave nothing to chance. After Doherty's warning about not overestimating his support, Haughey assembled a team of supporters each of whom was given a doubtful TD to "mark". The late Johnny Callinan was given the task of bringing Máire Geoghegan-Quinn into the fold and others had similar individual tasks.

The Haughey campaign was conducted on a number of levels and only the candidate himself held all the threads. Each of the plotters was given a small group of potential supporters on which to concentrate but even key campaigners like MacSharry and Reynolds were not given the full picture.

Colley, meanwhile, deputed Martin O'Donoghue and Des O'Malley to run his campaign. Neither of them knew the backbenchers at all well. O'Malley had been in the Cabinet for almost all his political career while O'Donoghue had never been a backbencher and had only been in the Dáil since 1977. Not until it was too late in the day did the Colley camp realise that they had totally over-estimated their level of support.

Haughey had his own problems in trying to find a big name to propose him for the leadership. Brian Lenihan was asked but refused. This was a bitter if not unexpected blow for Haughey. While they had been cronies in the 1960s, there had been some coolness since Lenihan's wholehearted backing of Lynch during the Arms Crisis and the two had not been close socially for a decade. But his refusal hurt Haughey.

Major Vivion de Valera, a senior backbench figure and son of the party's founder, was then asked to propose Haughey and he also refused. Though his niece was a strong supporter and Major de Valera was presumed to be on Haughey's side, he declined to back him publicly.

Having been refused by a Cabinet minister and a party elder, Haughey then turned to MacSharry as the most senior of his supporters to propose him. The ignorance in the Colley camp about the whole drift of the party over the previous twelve months is illustrated by the fact that there was huge surprise at the position adopted by Mac-Sharry. Totally unaware that his own junior minister was one of the leading members of the campaign against him, Colley was taken aback at the news of MacSharry's decision to propose Haughey.

A much more severe psychological blow was soon to fall on Colley. Shortly before the vote it emerged that Michael O'Kennedy was backing Haughey despite Colley's total confidence that O'Kennedy was on his side. Frank Dunlop recalls receiving a phone call from Lynch the night before the vote. The Taoiseach asked him how he thought it would go. Dunlop replied that it looked as though Haughey would win. "That is not what I am being told. George and Martin tell me they will pull it off," replied Lynch.

The following morning Haughey rang Dunlop. "Michael O'Kennedy is voting for me, spread the word," was his succinct message. When Dunlop arrived at Government Buildings he met Des O'Malley. "Did you see Michael O'Kennedy?" asked the Minister. "If you are looking for him you are wasting your time. He is going to vote for Haughey," Dunlop told a stunned O'Malley. A short time later Colley, O'Malley and O'Donoghue went to see O'Kennedy to ask for an explanation. O'Kennedy demanded to speak to Colley alone and the other two left while Colley got the bad news.

One explanation for O'Kennedy's last-minute switch to Haughey is a rumour that was going the rounds the night before the vote that David Andrews had been promised the Department of Foreign Affairs by O'Malley and O'Donoghue. With the prospect of losing this prestigious Department, O'Kennedy's *volte-face* becomes more comprehensible, especially as Haughey promised him the EC commissionership as the bait. O'Kennedy was the only Cabinet minister to declare openly for Haughey but it was a devastating blow to the Colley camp.

On the other hand Brian Lenihan, who was widely presumed to have voted for his old friend, was actually suspected by Haughey of voting for Colley. Lenihan in his autobiography published in 1991 says that he did actually vote for Haughey but at the time Haughey was far from being certain about this.

When the secret ballot was taken on Friday, 7 December, Haughey won by 44 votes to 38. The vote was closer than Haughey had expected but there was no taking from his triumph and from the shock and bewilderment of the party hierarchy who were convinced up to the end that Colley would win.

The shattered Colley and his supporters didn't know what to do. Such was the depth of distrust of Haughey that over the next few days Colley had long discussions with O'Donoghue and O'Malley to consider whether he would even vote for his rival's nomination for

Taoiseach. When it came to the vote on 11 December he did vote for Haughey but the palpable hostility of the different factions in Fianna Fáil prompted an extraordinary speech from the Fine Gael leader, Garret FitzGerald.

In his autobiography *All in a Life* FitzGerald refers to the fraught atmosphere in Fianna Fáil at the time and says that he heard rumours of intimidation of TDs during the voting process. His awareness of the bitterness in the Fianna Fáil camp coloured the speech he made on Haughey's nomination.

"I must speak not only for the Opposition but for many in Fianna Fáil who may not be free to say what they believe or to express their deep fears for the future of this country under the proposed leadership, people who are not free to reveal what they know and what led them to oppose this man with a commitment far beyond the normal."

FitzGerald went on to refer to Haughey's "flawed pedigree" and said his motives could ultimately only be judged by God.

"But we cannot ignore the fact that he differs from all his predecessors in that those motives have been and are widely impugned, most notably but by no means exclusively, by people within his own party, people close to him who have observed his actions for many years and who have made their human interim judgement on him …

"The feet that will go through that lobby to support his election will include many that will drag; the hearts of many who will climb those stairs before turning left will be heavy. Many of those who may vote for him will be doing so in the belief and hope that they will not have to serve long under a man they do not respect, whom they have fought long and hard, but for the moment in vain, to exclude from the highest office in the land."

Though he was widely criticised in the media for the bitter tone of his speech and though it did not do Fine Gael any good in the short term, FitzGerald reflected accurately the mood of the defeated faction within Fianna Fáil.

3 – Mismanaging the Economy

Haughey was now in the top job in the land, the one he had longed for all his political life and which had slipped from his grasp nearly fourteen years earlier. He had finally been given the chance to fulfil the great promise he had shown as a Cabinet minister in the 1960s and to prove that his sacking in 1970 had been a huge mistake for the country as well as for himself.

Instead, Haughey's first term as Taoiseach was an enormous disappointment, marked by reckless economic mismanagement in an attempt to woo the electorate. This recklessness did not become apparent until some time after his election as Taoiseach on 11 December 1979.

His first job was to select a new Cabinet and Haughey was initially conciliatory to the most powerful of his sworn enemies in the senior ranks of the party, although three of the old ministers – Jim Gibbons, Martin O'Donoghue and Bobby Molloy – were dropped. The feud with Gibbons went back to the Arms trial where either he or Haughey perjured himself in the witness box. They had been bitter enemies ever since.

Molloy, who had voted for Colley in 1966, remained staunchly committed to the Colley camp but there was no particular bitterness between himself and Haughey. At Defence he was the most junior minister in the outgoing Cabinet and was simply pushed aside to make room for one of Haughey's new appointments. An indication of the bitterness in the party is that Molloy was not accorded the normal courtesy of being contacted by the Taoiseach to be informed that he was being dropped from Cabinet. Having heard nothing, he presumed he was being dropped and seated himself on the Fianna Fáil back-benches to await the arrival of the new Cabinet. Molloy, who never forgot the incident, was to return the discourtesy six years later in the manner of his own departure from Fianna Fáil.

The sacking of O'Donoghue came as no surprise. An economist at Trinity College who had put himself through university after leaving school at fourteen, he had come into politics in 1970 through his role as an advisor to Jack Lynch. O'Donoghue had no Fianna Fáil background and had actually voted Labour in 1969. His close association with Lynch had predisposed him against the new leader and in a newspaper interview in 1977 he said he would never serve under Haughey.

The new Taoiseach took him at his word and not only was O'Donoghue dropped but his Department of Economic Planning and Development was abolished. Lynch later went to Haughey to ask that O'Donoghue be appointed as a European Commissioner but Haughey replied that the job had already been promised to Michael O'Kennedy.

Haughey's chief supporters – Ray MacSharry and Albert Reynolds – were rewarded with Cabinet office in Haughey's first government. MacSharry took over at Agriculture while Reynolds got Posts and Telegraphs after only two years in the Dail. Another new face in the Cabinet was Máire Geoghegan-Quinn, the only other junior minister, apart from MacSharry, to back Haughey. She got Gaeltacht and became the first women Cabinet minister in the history of the state since Markievicz was made Minister for Labour in the first Dáil. Paddy Power from Kildare took over at Fisheries and Forestry.

The key portfolio of Finance went to Michael O'Kennedy in clear recognition of his important role in declaring for Haughey at the last minute. After a year in government he was appointed to the EC commissionership in fulfilment of the bargain he had made with Haughey. Michael Woods was a surprise promotion to Health and Social Welfare in view of the fact that he had voted for Colley.

There was no room in the Cabinet for key conspirators in the coup against Lynch, like Seán Doherty and Pádraig Flynn, but both were appointed junior ministers as were Tom McEllistrim and Jackie Fahey. With MacSharry, Reynolds, Geoghegan Quinn and Power in the Cabinet, this meant that most of the conspirators were rewarded by Haughey for their role in his advancement to the Taoiseach's office, even if there was some grumbling at the limited nature of the changes at Cabinet level. There was no room at all for Charlie McCreevy who had played such a key role in Haughey's campaign.

The overall approach by Haughey to choosing his Cabinet was quite conservative. He dropped only three of the outgoing government and though the rest, apart from O'Kennedy, had voted against him they retained high office. Haughey often remarked that you don't have to like people to work with them and he clearly adopted this philosophy in forming his first government. This was a severe disappointment to those who had voted for Haughey in the expectation of wholesale change but it reflected the cautious approach he would bring to government appointments through all his terms as Taoiseach.

The conservative approach to appointments was dictated by cau-'ion and the desire to unify the party, but there is a large extent to which the new Taoiseach felt he had no choice. The key to the composition of that Cabinet is a crucial meeting with Colley on Monday, 10 December, the day before the Dáil elected him Taoiseach. That meeting came after the series of gatherings over the weekend involving Colley, O'Malley, O'Donoghue and Gibbons among others. They discussed seriously the possibility of refusing to vote for Haughey's nomination as Taoiseach. While that was generally regarded as beyond the bounds of practical politics, the group did discuss on what terms they would agree to serve in a Haughey Cabinet.

That same day, Colley told Haughey of the minimum conditions which would be acceptable if he was to serve in the government. As there were only twenty-four hours to the vote on his nomination for Taoiseach, Haughey did not consider himself in a very strong position to argue and he agreed to the Colley terms. These were that Colley would remain as Tánaiste, that he would have a veto over the appointments to Justice and Defence and that he would have to be satisfied with the overall structure of the government.

As well as agreeing to these terms Haughey offered Colley the Department of Foreign Affairs, but his rival, wishing to retain a domestic portfolio, refused and was given Energy. Having accepted the Colley veto on the security departments, and by implication that he himself was a security risk, the Taoiseach appointed Gerry Collins, for whom he had very little time at that stage, to Justice, and Pádraig Faulkner, a Colley loyalist since 1966, took over at Defence. Despite Haughey's annoyance at him for not backing his leadership bid, Brian Lenihan was made Minister for Foreign Affairs when this was refused by Colley.

One other critical feature of Colley's conversation with Haughey on 10 December 1979, related to comments the new Fianna Fáil leader had made in the euphoria following his election. Haughey had claimed that Colley had pledged loyalty and support, but his defeated rival made it clear that he had never used such words and that he intended to put the record straight on the matter.

This Colley did less than a month later, alerting the public to the qualified nature of his support for the new Taoiseach. On 21 December, at a Fianna Fáil function in Baldoyle, he said Haughey had been mistaken to attribute the sentiments of loyalty and support to him. He also described as "wrong and reprehensible" the attitude of a number of TDs and senators to Lynch.

"A majority of the parliamentary party has, it seems to me – at least for the life of the present parliamentary party – changed the traditional Fianna Fáil rule and legitimised the withholding of loyalty to, and support for, the elected leader. I very much regret this but I am a realist and I accept it," said Colley. The statement was issued to the national media hours before the Fianna Fáil function and marked the beginning of a major public split in Fianna Fáil.

Haughey was furious and considered sacking Colley. He called in a number of Cabinet ministers and strong supporters in the party to seek their advice. All his own supporters urged Haughey to fire Colley immediately. The Taoiseach's new personal advisor, Pádraig O hAnnracháin, and Government Press Secretary Frank Dunlop also urged him to fire the Tánaiste, but having weighed the matter very carefully Haughey's innate caution and his desire to keep unity in the party took over. He held a well publicised meeting with Colley after which the Tánaiste qualified his remarks somewhat but certainly did not retract them.

The gulf between the two men was so great that less than a year later Colley is said to have put a proposition to Fine Gael leader Garret FitzGerald, which would have involved a Dáil defeat for Haughey and a split in Fianna Fáil. In his autobiography *All in a Life* FitzGerald recalls that following the publication by *Magill* magazine of a series of articles on the Arms Crisis, Fine Gael put down a Dáil motion on the issue in November 1980. FitzGerald states that he was approached by Colley with the suggestion that if the wording of the Fine Gael motion were changed to refer to the conflict of evidence at the Arms trial between Haughey and Gibbons, then Colley and up to twenty other Fianna Fáil TDs would vote against their own government.

FitzGerald toyed with the idea but when Colley declined to actually draft the proposed Fine Gael motion the plan was dropped. It does, however, give an indication of how deeply the resentment continued to run in the anti Haughey camp within Fianna Fáil.

In the early weeks as Haughey settled into the Taoiseach's office, he made a number of important changes to the structure of his Department. Noel Whelan, the secretary of the now defunct Department for Economic Planning and Development, was moved into the Taoiseach's office along with some of his senior economic planning officials, including one Padraig O hUiginn. The Department, which up to then had only a small secretariat to service the government as well as the Government Information Service, expanded rapidly with divisions to handle foreign affairs, economic and social policy, cultural and legal affairs.

This involvement in the decision-making processes of other government departments necessarily led to a major expansion of the Taoiseach's own Department. The centralisation of power in the Department resulted in a trebling of the staff by the time Haughey finished his first stint as Taoiseach in 1981.

The most significant appointment made by Haughey was the promotion of Pádraig O hAnnracháin. A senior career civil servant of assistant secretary status, just four years older than Haughey, O hAnnracháin was steeped in Fianna Fáil tradition. He had been private secretary to Eamon de Valera through the 1950s and was appointed head of the Government Information Service in 1957. He held this post for eleven years under de Valera, Lemass and for the beginning of Jack Lynch's term of office and during this period he also travelled abroad with President de Valera to handle his press relations.

In 1968 Lynch moved O hAnnracháin out of the GIS to make way for a Corkman, Eoin Neeson. Though O hAnnracháin continued to hold a senior position in the Taoiseach's Department he was very unhappy at being moved. Briefly restored before Fianna Fáil lost office in 1973 he spent most of the decade in a peripheral role under the Fianna Fáil and coalition governments, waiting for a recall to the centre of things.

Haughey and O hAnnracháin spent the same years in the wilderness, and a bond developed between to two men. Between 1977 and 1979 O hAnnracháin kept in close touch with Haughey and despite his status as a civil servant he was regarded as an important member of the Haughey camp. Immediately on Haughey's election he was promoted to the post of Deputy Secretary and became the key official in the Department and the closest advisor to Haughey.

Haughey relied almost totally on him in his first stint as Taoiseach and took his advice on all important issues. It was O hAnnracháin who saw the Taoiseach first every morning to brief him on the day's events and discuss government strategy.

In theory the Secretary to the Government was the most senior official in the Department, but the incumbent, Dan O'Sullivan, was very close to retiring and never had time to develop a relationship with Haughey. When he retired a few months after Haughey took over, the Taoiseach divided his functions and appointed two people to replace him.

Dermot Nally, who was next in line, was appointed Cabinet Secretary while Noel Whelan was made Secretary of the Taoiseach's Department. Nally, a bright and hard-working public servant, never developed a close rapport with Haughey and did not get a chance to demonstrate the full range of his abilities until Garret FitzGerald became Taoiseach. Whelan, though he was promoted by Haughey to stymie Nally as much as anything else, also had an uneasy relationship with the Taoiseach and never established himself in the role. O hAnnracháin, who in theory was junior to both Nally and Whelan, became the real power in the Department and it was on him that Haughey relied.

Frank Dunlop, who had been Government Press Secretary to Lynch, and who had kept aloof from the leadership contest, was retained in his post but never established a satisfactory working relationship with the new Taoiseach. Haughey regarded him with suspicion and Dunlop could never get used to the cavalier way in which the new Taoiseach treated even his most senior staff.

The Haughey style was utterly different to what had gone before. An abrasive and domineering boss, Haughey didn't mince his words in dealings with his officials and some of them never got used to his sudden bursts of violent temper and his regular use of bad language. What made this all the more disconcerting was that these moods alternated with periods when he was extremely affable and charming and very understanding of personal problems involving any of his staff.

"The tension was incredible," recalls one of his officials from that period. "People were literally intimidated. He was so domineering that ministers were scared of him and stultified into inaction as a result."

He also expected people to dance attention on him and this job in his first government fell mainly to Brendan O'Donnell, the career civil servant who had been his henchman since his days in Agriculture and who had played an important role winning support among back-benchers. Typical of Haughey's attitude was that he never wore a watch or carried anything apart from cash in his pockets. If he needed to know the time or wanted anything, he asked a minion who was expected to respond promptly.

The new Taoiseach also dominated his government. At Cabinet meetings he treated his ministers with courtesy and was regarded by most of them as a excellent chairman, but he took a keen interest in what was going on in every department and interfered to a much greater extent than either Lynch or Cosgrave before him.

"He was an excellent chairman and Cabinet meetings were about making decisions. His fault in this period was that he got too involved in other ministers' business and ended up trying to run all government departments," says one minister who served in that first government.

He treated most of his ministers as subordinates, to put it mildly. Haughey involved himself in all the key decisions in relation to Finance and this process became even more obvious when Gene Fitzgerald took over the position after Michael O'Kennedy went to Brussels. The same was true in relation to foreign policy, particularly Northern Ireland, where it was Haughey rather than Lenihan who made all the running. With Colley and O'Malley, he had a distant and uneasy relationship but he didn't try to interfere in their departments to the extent that he did with other ministers.

Normally in government, discussions on important issues are held by Cabinet sub committees and referred to the full Cabinet for approval. Economic decisions in particular are made by a committee which has at its core the Taoiseach, the Minister for Finance and the Minister for Industry and Commerce. Other ministers such as Labour, Environment or Energy are also regularly involved. Haughey never believed in formal Cabinet sub committees. He always talked to the relevant minister or held informal discussions with a group of ministers. On economic issues he dealt directly with the Minister for Finance and on security issues with the Minister for Justice.

Relations with O'Malley were very poor and there was no proper discussion of important issues. Haughey himself made all the key decisions in relation of financial matters, paying very little heed to his ministers. And as he had not built up a relationship of trust with his senior civil servants, he was operating virtually alone.

With his background as an accountant and at the Department of Finance, Haughey was widely regarded as the ideal person to sort out the burgeoning debt problem which was beginning to strangle the economy. His well known reservations about Fianna Fáil's giveaway manifesto in 1977 encouraged the belief that he would provide capable leadership on economic issues and this was reinforced when he made a special television broadcast in January 1980 to spell out to the nation just how serious the problem of the national debt had become.

"The figures which are just now becoming available to us show one thing very clearly. As a community we are living away beyond our means," Mr Haughey told the nation. "We have been borrowing enormous amounts of money, borrowing at a rate which just cannot continue." He added: "We will just have to reorganise government spending so that we can only undertake those things we can afford."

The diagnosis was correct, but having identified the problem Haughey proceeded to do precisely the opposite. Plans in his first budget to introduce a resource tax on farmers and to spread the tax burden more evenly, were dropped in the face of political pressure as was a proposal to restrict the free bus service for rural school children.

It was in the area of public pay, however, that the most disastrous decisions were made. Between special awards and national pay agreements, public pay rose by 34 percent in 1980 alone. One startling example of Haughey's inexplicably profligate approach was on a teachers' pay award in 1980.

A special arbitration board recommended a pay rise for teachers. The scale of the pay rise was initially rejected by the government and conciliation talks began in the Labour Court. As these talks dragged on, with the teachers taking a firm line, Haughey suddenly instructed his Minister for Education, John Wilson, to concede a pay rise larger than the initial arbitration award. The teachers were as stunned as everybody else by their good fortune and the arbitration board resigned in protest at being made a mockery of by the government.

The failure to curb existing government expenditure and the concession of massive pay increases to the public service undermined the policy announced in January 1980. In line with Haughey's address to the nation, the budget for the year had targeted a reduction in the Exchequer Borrowing Requirement (EBR) from £1,009 million the previous year to £896 million. Instead it rose to £1,217 million, more than £300 million off target.

Things got worse in 1981. Notional cuts were made in the spending estimates for a whole range of government departments but were not followed through in practice. Instead government spending spiralled out of control in the first six months of the year. In the January budget, Finance Minister Gene Fitzgerald set an EBR of £1,296 million or 13 percent of GNP. By the end of June spending was running so far ahead of plan that if it had continued for the full year the EBR would have ended up at £1,973, or 20 percent of GNP, a profligate £700 million over target. That did not happen because Haughey lost office in mid-year and a savage emergency budget was introduced in July by John Bruton. Despite the corrective measures, the EBR was still a massive £300 million over target and exchequer borrowing reached a level never exceeded before or since as a proportion of GNP.

Haughey's spending spree led to massive increases in taxation and borrowing to foot the bill. The total tax take as a percentage of GNP rose from 33 percent in 1979 to 42 percent in 1982. This was a devastating jump in taxation on the population and the stranglehold of extra tax had very damaging effects on the wellbeing of the nation in the years ahead. As if this were not bad enough, borrowing, which had risen steeply under Lynch, continued to rise, from 9.2 percent of GNP in 1977 to nearly 16 percent of GNP in 1981 and 1982.

The Taoiseach justified his policies by using the international recession as an argument for not cutting spending, on the basis that such cuts would lead to unemployment and hardship. Rejecting calls to cut public spending as other governments in Europe were doing in response to the recession, he told the Dáil that such policies "may be called courageous or responsible but in our economic and social circumstances we find them unrealistic and unacceptable." So instead of cuts Haughey increased both taxation and borrowing and by doing so helped to crippled the national economy for the next decade.

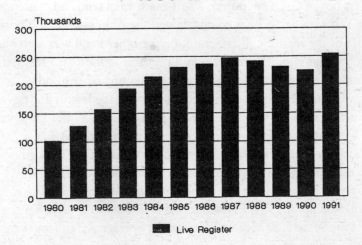

Unemployment
1980 to 1991

Live Register

4 – Rivals

Garret FitzGerald's "flawed pedigree" speech on Charles Haughey's nomination for Taoiseach in December 1979 set the tone for the relationship between the two men for the best part of a decade. There was a feeling of enmity between them which is not normal in Irish politics. Each deeply distrusted the actions of the other and believed the country's fortunes would be imperilled by the election of the other as Taoiseach.

Their rivalry was unique because, whatever the public perception, politicians of different parties do not generally dislike each other. In fact, they get along quite well, away from the rough and tumble of debate. Politicians have more in common with each other than they have with outsiders who do not understand the precarious nature of their life and they generally enjoy each other's company.

Haughey and FitzGerald, though, behaved as if they came from different worlds. Despite the fact that they were educated together in UCD and knew each other slightly from that time, they had virtually nothing in common. Haughey was a Dublin northsider, a Christian Brothers boy, a GAA supporter, a self-made man who had contempt for the self-satisfied elite who dominated the professional and business life of the republic. FitzGerald, on the other hand was a classic product of that elite. His father was a minister in the first Free State government and he was brought up in the comfortable middle class surroundings of Dublin's southside, educated by the Jesuits and never set foot in Croke Park until he became Taoiseach. While he never made a fortune like Haughey, FitzGerald's biography *All in a Life* illustrates the web of connections open to people of his background which eased his passage to a comfortable professional life.

Garret, as he quickly became known to the electorate, had an easy political ride up to 1981. Elected to the Dáil only in 1969, after four years in the Seanad, he became Minister for Foreign Affairs four years later and leader of Fine Gael after another four-year interval. He enjoyed a charmed political existence until his election as party leader, but then the real challenge emerged. He managed to broaden Fine Gael's appeal and win over wider middle class support by modernising his party, bringing in a range of new Dáil candidates, many of them young and a substantial proportion of them women.

The contrast between the backgrounds of the two men heightened their distrust of one another and contributed to a mutual lack of comprehension of the other's motives. The gulf also accentuated the intensity of Haughey's appeal to working class and poorer rural voters and FitzGerald's attraction for the middle classes.

"Politics won't be right until both of them are gone," one senior Fine Gael politician remarked in the early 1980s. This sentiment was echoed by former EC Commissioner and Fine Gael minister Dick Burke in a review of FitzGerald's autobiography in the *Irish Press* in October 1991. In that review Burke attributed the scale of Ireland's economic problems in the 1980s to the rivalry between Haughey and FitzGerald which prevented either of them from facing up to reality while the other was still around.

One of the essential planks in the FitzGerald bid for national leadership was the identification of what became known as "the Haughey factor". Following the internal upheaval in Fianna Fáil and the defeat of that party's establishment, the Fine Gael strategy team, headed by party General Secretary Peter Prendergast, targeted Haughey as an electoral liability among middle class voters and they played this card to the hilt during the three election campaigns of the early eighties.

Anthony Cronin, Haughey's friend and advisor on the arts for over a decade, wrote in 1982 about this campaign: "For what it is worth I have known both Garret FitzGerald and Charlie Haughey for a good while now, one better and more intimately than the other, but both to a degree. Without passing any judgement on their respective politics, or on any politics come to that, I believe we are exceptionally lucky in both, at least in their qualities as human beings.

"There is something wrong, though, when the qualities of one are bruited from the housetops, while those of the other are caricatured, concealed and distorted to a degree unprecedented in our public life."

The gulf between Haughey and FitzGerald was nowhere more obvious than in their attitudes to Northern Ireland. Haughey had always regarded the national issue as the one which was the key to his place in history. He reportedly told Mrs Thatcher during their first meeting in 1980 that a political leader would not be remembered for reducing the balance of payments or for adjusting the scale of government borrowing, but whoever came up with a solution to the problem of the North would go down in the history books.

Given his role in the Arms Crisis of 1970 and his nationalist rhetoric, Haughey, during his early years as leader, was regarded within Fianna Fáil as being sound on the national question. Attending his first Ard Fheis as leader in February 1980 he received an ecstatic welcome from the five thousand-plus delegates. He was piped into the RDS by the ITGWU brass band to the strains of "A Nation Once Again" and his speech reflected traditional Fianna Fáil attitudes to the North. He coined the phrase that Northern Ireland was a failed political entity and he called on the British Government to declare its interest in encouraging the unity of Ireland.

"We look forward to some new free and open arrangements in which Irish men and women, on their own, without a British presence but with active British goodwill, will manage the affairs of the whole of Ireland in a constructive partnership within [the] European Community," he declaimed to wild applause. That first Ard Fheis set the tone for the reaction of the party organisation to him in his early years as leader. In the front row of the audience people erected little shrines to Haughey and their devotion had a religious intensity.

Haughey's emphasis on the traditional goal of a united Ireland contrasted sharply with FitzGerald's support for a devolved power-sharing arrangement in Northern Ireland itself as the first step towards any solution. From the beginning of his first term as Taoiseach, Haughey maintained that decisions could only be taken by the two governments over the heads of the squabbling parties in the North.

One of his first actions as Taoiseach was to embroil himself in a needless wrangle with the Department of Foreign Affairs which soured relations between him and Iveagh House for nearly a decade and contributed to growing middle class distrust of his approach to the issue. It didn't help that Garret FitzGerald was virtually adored in Foreign Affairs, having served as a very successful minister in the Department from 1973 to 1977, and that most of the bright young officials had been promoted during Garret's reign.

The row related to a decision to transfer the Ambassador to the United States, Seán Donlon, to the United Nations. Donlon had taken a very active stance in opposing Noraid and other IRA support groups in the US and had driven a big wedge between such militants and the Irish American political leaders like Tip O'Neill and Ted Kennedy.

One of the people who actively encouraged Haughey to move Donlon was Independent Fianna Fáil TD Neil Blaney. The Taoiseach was persuaded that Donlon was splitting what could be a powerful Irish American lobby group and that a new ambassador was necessary. However, when news of the move leaked, O'Neill and Kennedy reacted furiously and made representations to Haughey who was forced into a humiliating climbdown. The Taoiseach was livid at having been out-manoeuvred by one of his own ambassadors but he had drawn the controversy on himself by taking foolish advice.

On the wider front of Anglo-Irish relations, however, Haughey astounded his critics, particularly FitzGerald, by making a good stab at fulfilling his dream of launching a major political initiative. After six months in office he met the British Prime Minister, Margaret Thatcher, herself in her first year in government, for an Anglo-Irish summit meeting in London. He brought her an antique Irish silver teapot as a present and despite the jokes and the ridicule that followed about "teapot diplomacy" the two leaders got off to a good start.

The really significant follow-up summit took place in December 1980 in Dublin Castle. To emphasise the importance she attached to it, Thatcher brought with her the Foreign Secretary, Lord Carrington, who had just negotiated the Rhodesian settlement. The Chancellor of the Exchequer, Geoffrey Howe, and the Northern Secretary, Humphrey Atkins, made up the high-powered British team. Haughey was accompanied by Brian Lenihan and Michael O'Kennedy for most of the discussions, though the two prime ministers had a private meeting which lasted more than an hour.

The joint communiqué issued after the meeting described the talks as "extremely constructive and significant" and went on to say that the "totality of relationships" between the two islands would be considered in a number of joint studies. These would cover a range of topics such as new institutional structures for the island, security matters, citizenship rights and economic cooperation.

This was a very important breakthrough in relations between the two countries and it paved the way for the Anglo-Irish Agreement signed by Garret FitzGerald in 1985. In 1980, however, FitzGerald as Opposition leader attacked the outcome of the Dublin summit and, sticking to his position that the solution to the problem lay between the two communities in the North, he attacked the new Anglo-Irish initiative. The summit outcome was also denounced by Unionists as the first phase of a British sell-out and Ian Paisley organised a number of protests throughout the North in opposition to the process begun by the joint studies.

Haughey had the makings of a very important initiative after the Dublin summit but he proceeded to dissipate this achievement by insisting that the whole constitutional position of Northern Ireland as part of the United Kingdom was now in the melting pot.

Lenihan went even further and said that the partition question was on the verge of being solved and a united Ireland could become a reality in the next decade. Thatcher was extremely angry at the over-hyping of the summit and denied point blank that the British Government had any intention of altering the constitutional position of Northern Ireland.

When the two leaders next met, at the Maastricht summit in the spring of 1981, Thatcher told Haughey in no uncertain terms what she thought of him. They met on the margins of the EC summit for half an hour. Haughey barely had time to utter "Good morning, Prime Minister" before Thatcher started to lecture him about what she regarded as a breach of good faith over the Dublin summit. She continued to berate him for the rest of the meeting and he hardly had time to get a word in edgeways before she stalked from the room.

Many of Haughey's actions at this time were directed towards winning an overall majority for himself in his first general election as Fianna Fáil leader. A by-election in Donegal South West in November 1980 provided the first opportunity to test his popularity and the result was a triumph for Haughey and a grievous disappointment for Fitz-Gerald. "Fianna Fáil Homage to King Charlie" was the headline in the *Irish Independent*, while Michael Mills of the *Irish Press* predicted that Haughey would call an election in the summer of 1981.

In fact by early 1981 Haughey had decided to call a general election in the spring of that year, while he was still riding the crest of the popular wave, but his plans on that score were thwarted by tragedy, not once but twice.

The initial plan was to call the election shortly after the party's Ard Fheis in February 1981, but on the opening night of the conference, St Valentine's night, a fire in the Stardust nightclub in the Taoiseach's own constituency killed forty-eight young people. The main part of the Ard Fheis, including the Taoiseach's address, was postponed until April as were his election plans. By April, though, the major H Block hunger strike had got underway and the leader of the IRA protest, Bobby Sands, had been elected to the House of Commons.

With all his options closing down and the spending targets of the 1981 budget running out of control, Haughey dissolved the Dáil on 21 May with the general election to be held on 11 June. It was to be the first of five elections during the 1980s.

The Fianna Fáil headquarters team had been changed in advance of the election. Haughey couldn't stand the party General Secretary, Séamus Brennan, and the feeling was mutual. Brennan left the post to build a political base for himself in Dublin South and he was replaced by Frank Wall. Another important internal change at this time was that Senator Des Hanafin, who was in charge of Fianna Fáil fund-raising from the business community, was gradually eased out of his post. Hanafin, who had wide contacts in the business world, had a permanent office in the Burlington Hotel. He was a Jack Lynch supporter and had proved a very effective fund-raiser for the party. But Haughey put an end to Hanafin's operation so that by the time of the 1981 election Haughey himself was in full control of the party organisation and Fianna Fáil's fund-raising activities.

During the election campaign Fianna Fáil continued to promise the electorate more spending programmes to rival the attractive, if equally unrealistic, tax cutting plans being put forward by Fine Gael. One senior Fianna Fáil figure contesting a marginal constituency recalls being contacted by the Taoiseach's Department in the early days of the campaign and being told to announce spending programmes of up to £3 million in his constituency. When he queried the request he was ordered to come up with a list of projects and to make announcements pledging government funding. Similar tactics were adopted in other constituencies.

Haughey and FitzGerald ran presidential-style campaigns and dominated the media coverage. "Charlie's Song", a version of an old folk song about Bonny Prince Charlie, became the Fianna Fáil campaign anthem and it was played at all the party rallies during the campaign encouraging voters to "rise and follow Charlie". Fianna Fáil spirits soared in the early days of the campaign when an IMS opinion poll put the party on 52 percent of the vote. Haughey looked all set for a smashing victory but in a pattern which was to repeat itself again and again under his leadership the party slipped back consistently for the rest of the campaign.

Fine Gael's tax-cutting promises and the swell of sympathy for H Block hunger strike candidates all played their part in cutting Haughey's early lead. T. Ryle Dwyer in his book *Charlie* maintains that Haughey had to deal with a hostile media during the campaign and that reporters covering his tour of the country developed an antipathy to him reminiscent of "the boys on the bus" with Richard Nixon.

Whatever the reason, the Fianna Fáil vote slipped from the opinion poll high of 52 percent at the start of the campaign to 45.3 percent on the day of the vote. The crucial factor in Haughey's failure to win an overall majority was the emergence of the H Block candidates who contested nine constituencies and won two Dáil seats on an abstentionist ticket. The election took place in the middle of the H Block hunger strike campaign, and after the death of Bobby Sands Fianna Fáil were deprived of crucial votes in a string of border constituencies. It was Fianna Fáil's poorest showing in twenty years. The party won only 78 seats in the 166 member Dáil and were replaced in government by a Fine Gael-Labour coalition. That government had just 80 seats and depended on smaller parties and independent TDs to retain power.

The new government had to face up to the immediate problem

created by Haughey's overspending. Garret FitzGerald and John Bruton, his Finance Minister, were presented with a Department of Finance memorandum on their first day in office which detailed the shambles in the public finances.

The Dáil reassembled on 21 July for a supplementary budget necessitated by the state of the nation's finances. Bruton pointed out that by the end of June the deficit on day-to-day spending was £457 million, yet in the budget the planned deficit for the whole year was just £515million. In other words 88 percent of the borrowing for current spending for the year had been used up in the first six months. In the absence of corrective action the deficit would have run to almost £950 million by the end of the year.

Haughey had clearly gambled on winning the election in the middle of June before the full scale of the overspending became apparent and he would have had no choice but to take corrective action himself if he had won.

He refused, however, to be embarrassed at his own record of economic mismanagement and instead denounced the new government's corrective measures. Opposing the supplementary budget, he outlined an economic philosophy which was to guide his public attitudes for most of the decade. It was a philosophy which flew in the face of almost all accepted economic wisdom and one which was being rejected by governments of all political hues across Europe at this time. The opposition of most of the country's economists merely irritated Haughey at this stage and he refused to be influenced by them.

"At no time in the circumstances of any nation will you ever get a professional economist who will not prophecy disaster and demand deflationary measures being introduced ... Economics is a dismal science," he told the Dáil during that debate. Haughey's basic strategy was to attack the government's attempts to get to grips with the national debt as deflationary and monetarist and he rejected what he called the "gloom and doom" being preached by the coalition.

This flight from reality by Haughey deepened the distrust in which he was held by some of the senior figures in Fianna Fáil since he had defeated Colley for the leadership in 1979. A more surprising critic was Kildare TD Charlie McCreevy, who had been an important figure in the campaign to oust Lynch and put Haughey in his place. Now he became increasingly disillusioned with Haughey's attitude to the economy and made his views known in an interview with Geraldine Kennedy in the *Sunday Tribune*. For his pains, McCreevy lost the Fianna Fáil whip in the Dáil and for a time became an independent TD.

Haughey refused to be deflected by McCreevy or other doubters in his own party and he kept up a sustained criticism of the government's performance, buoyed up by the belief, a correct one as it turned out, that the government would not last long.

FitzGerald's first government, which was reckoned by most commentators to be a better and more imaginative one that his second, faced the central economic issues by hiking up taxes to try and reduce the spiralling national debt. This involved Fine Gael jettisoning most of its tax-cutting election promises in the face of economic reality.

That government collapsed unexpectedly on the night of 27 January 1982, when John Bruton's budget was defeated. A series of events took place that night which were to return to haunt Haughey almost a decade later. At the time they passed unnoticed in the welter of excitement generated by the unexpected general election.

What happened was that after the minority Fine Gael-Labour government was defeated the Fianna Fáil front bench met and a statement was issued calling on President Hillery not to grant a dissolution of the Dáil but to look to Fianna Fáil to form a government. After that statement was released, phone calls were made from the Fianna Fáil rooms in Leinster House to Aras an Uachtaráin.

It is still not clear who made those phone calls. Brian Lenihan claimed in May 1990 in an interview with a post graduate student, Jim Duffy, that the calls were made by himself, Haughey and Sylvester Barrett. Lenihan subsequently denied this. His medical condition at the time he gave the interview to Duffy was precarious, following his liver transplant operation of the previous year, and he was on heavy medication. He was adamant during the presidential election campaign in October 1990 and in a subsequent book on the issue *For the Record* that he had not phoned the Aras.

Garret FitzGerald, who spoke to President Hillery that night, says in his autobiography that seven phone calls were made to the President that night but he doesn't say by whom. It has also been alleged that the army duty officer that night, Captain Barbour, was threatened in one of the phone calls for refusing to put the call through to the President. The *Irish Independent* security correspondent, Tom Brady, who broke that story, suggested that the threatening phone call came from Haughey, but Haughey subsequently denied that in the Dáil.

All we know for certain is that calls were made, and that while the President refused to speak to any of the callers, he was extremely angry at what he regarded as improper pressure on him in the exercise of his constitutional duties.

5 – GUBU

The early days of the election campaign which followed the collapse of the Bruton budget in January 1982 gave the first hint that Haughey's leadership of Fianna Fáil was under threat. In the first flush of excitement after the collapse of FitzGerald's government Haughey rejected the central features of that Fine Gael-Labour budget. He was quickly forced to back down, however, when Colley, O'Malley and O'Donoghue threatened to publicly disown him. He reluctantly accepted the outgoing government's deficit targets in a speech drafted by O'Donoghue, but tried to maintain during the election campaign that spending cuts on the scale of the coalition's would not be necessary.

During the election campaign O'Donoghue, who had been brought back in from the cold and was now Fianna Fáil's Finance spokesman, repeatedly refused to answer questions about whether he believed Haughey was a fit person to be Taoiseach. The "Haughey factor" became one of the central issues in the campaign and it was to prove a real liability for Fianna Fáil who should have romped home following the budget collapse of the coalition. The Fianna Fáil director of elections, Albert Reynolds, accused Fine Gael of a smear campaign against Haughey, but it was the incipient divisions within Fianna Fáil itself which really gave the Haughey factor its full impetus.

When the votes were counted on 19 February it transpired that Haughey had again failed to win an overall majority for Fianna Fáil. Though the party had pushed its share of the national vote up to 47.3 percent, and had come tantalisingly close to winning extra seats in a number of constituencies, it ended up with 81, three seats short of an overall majority. It was a bitter disappointment, given the ideal circumstances of the election.

The result triggered off the first of the leadership moves against Haughey. Even as the election results were coming in on the night of 19 February the conspirators were sending signals to each other on television. The fact that known anti Haughey candidates like Jim Gibbons in Kilkenny and Joe Walsh in Cork made comebacks to the Dáil was widely commented on and Gibbons, in an appearance on the television election special, made it clear that he believed the leadership issue would be discussed by the parliamentary party before the resumption of the Dáil.

Haughey was in a difficult corner. With eighty-one seats, Fianna Fáil was easily the largest party in the Dáil and would be in a strong position to form a government if it could do a deal with independent TDs like Tony Gregory and Neil Blaney and possibly even the Workers' Party. However, before concluding deals with any of these parties, Haughey had first to confront the threat to his leadership.

Moving quickly to get a grip on the situation he brought forward the meeting of the parliamentary party to 25 February to ratify his nomination as the Fianna Fáil candidate for Taoiseach. The anti Haughey faction were forced to act more quickly than they expected. The two leading anti Haughey figures in Fianna Fáil, George Colley and Des O'Malley, met to consider their strategy and somewhat reluctantly Colley agreed to drop his own claims to the succession and to throw his support behind the Limerick TD.

O'Malley, who had been elected to the Dáil in 1968 on the death of his uncle Donogh, had from the beginning of his political career found himself in the anti Haughey camp. His incisiveness and courage immediately impressed Lynch, who promoted him to Minister for Justice after the Arms trial and made no secret of the fact that he saw in him a future leader of the party and a future Taoiseach. Those early years in Justice were a traumatic time for O'Malley, whose wife and young family had to share the burden of pressure that was placed on him.

His role in Justice was to affect his political style for many years, turning him into an introverted minister deeply suspicious of the media, who, in his view, had done so much to orchestrate public reaction against his security measures like the establishment of the Special Criminal Court. His family had to receive a level of security protection previously unknown in the Irish republic. The minister's children received a Special Branch escort to school every day and his wife, Pat, was even accompanied to the supermarket by an armed detective. Even though that experience was well behind him by 1982, O'Malley had not changed his political style and reporters found him as difficult to deal with as Haughey.

The chief organisers of the O'Malley campaign were Séamus Brennan, the former party General Secretary who had got himself elected as a TD for Dublin South, and Martin O'Donoghue, who had forced Haughey to accept his budgetary strategy during the campaign.

As 25 February drew nearer, the anti Haughey camp became confident of victory following soundings carried out among a wide range of party TDs. Confidence grew to such an extent that the media began to forecast an O'Malley victory. *Magill* magazine published a list of thirty TDs who would vote against Haughey and claimed that only seventeen were definitely in favour of him, while Bruce Arnold went one better in the *Irish Independent* the day before the vote by listing the names of forty-six TDs whom he said would vote against the party leader.

With just twenty-four hours to the vote, Haughey was now under real pressure, though it was by no means as great as the media had been led to believe. A number of the TDs in the anti Haughey camp were actually on an information-gathering mission for their leader. Others ran scared after they were named because of pressure from the Haughey camp and their local party organisations.

Nonetheless, Haughey was still highly nervous at this stage as I myself found out in no uncertain manner. Working at that time as a general news reporter for the Irish Press group, I was instructed by *Evening Press* news editor Dermot McIntyre to go up to Leinster House, seek out Haughey and ask him if he was going to resign the leadership that day. Apparently the news editor had received information from a good source indicating that such an event was likely to happen.

Along with photographer Pat Cashman, I went to Leinster House with no expectation of getting near Haughey. However, Cashman's ingenuity got us up to Haughey's office. Out on the plinth of Leinster House we had met Ned Brennan, the popular postman, who had just been elected as a Fianna Fáil TD for Dublin North East.

"I would like to get a picture of yourself and the Boss," Cashman told Brennan and without further ado the new TD brought us straight up to Haughey's office.

Ray Burke, Fianna Fáil chief whip at the time, was in the room but left immediately when we entered. Cashman took a few pictures and Haughey stood up to leave. Sensing that I had better move quickly or Haughey would be gone, I approached him and asked bluntly if he was going to resign that day. The reaction was one of instantaneous and overwhelming anger.

"Would you fuck off," he shouted, making a run at me.

I backed against the wall with Haughey shouting in my face. "That's F.U.C.K O.F.F." he roared, spelling out each letter.

Speechless with surprise I made no response but Pat Cashman interposed himself between us and calmed Haughey down saying that we had been sent by our office to ask a question and were only doing our job. Haughey simmered down immediately. "What was your question again?" he asked.

I repeated it carefully this time, saying our newsdesk had been informed he would resign that day and asking him if that was the case.

"That's complete nonsense. I have no intention of resigning," he said calmly and walked away.

That experience of Haughey's volcanic temper was an eye-opener. The pressure he was under and the fact that I materialised in his office out of nowhere probably help to explain his aggressive reaction. I should add that later, as a political reporter and political correspondent, I met Haughey on a number of occasions and he always acted with courtesy and generally with good humour.

Shortly after that encounter I met Albert Reynolds who told me that Haughey would easily win the leadership vote. "Who else will be able to do a deal with Gregory and the Workers' Party?" he said.

Reynolds's calm in contrast to Haughey's temper left me unsure of what was happening and the general media view was still that Haughey was in danger of being forced out.

Ray MacSharry, who was another key figure in the Haughey camp gave a radio interview at lunchtime that day during which he said darkly that the Fianna Fáil organisation would never forgive any TD who voted against the leader. That evening as I left Leinster House I met Ray Burke and I asked him if Haughey was on the way out.

"You must be joking. He's going to walk it if it comes to a vote," remarked Burke and of course he was proved right.

When the parliamentary party met the following morning no vote was needed, as Burke clearly suspected. For openers a number of speakers, including the highly respected Pádraig Faulkner, called on O'Malley not to go through with the challenge. The killer blow came when Martin O'Donoghue stood up and, to the astonishment of his fellow plotters, called on O'Malley to withdraw from the contest in the interests of party unity. O'Malley was furious but felt there was little he could do except back down.

In the days after the abortive heave, stories emerged of threatening phone calls to anti Haughey TDs and of more general intimidation. At the time not much attention was paid to the claims which sounded like sour grapes by the losers in the leadership battle but the atmosphere in the Fianna Fáil party was soured even though O'Malley and O'Donoghue were appointed to the Cabinet. Deep suspicion developed between them for a time.

With his authority restored Haughey was now able to concentrate on doing a deal with independent socialist TD for Dublin Central, Tony Gregory, to ensure his vote for the Taoiseach's post. "As the Mafia say, it is a pleasure to do business with you," remarked Haughey, shaking hands on the deal with Gregory. He did another deal with the Workers' Party to ensure the support of their three TDs.

The details of the Gregory deal fuelled suspicions about Haughey's capacity for economic profligacy. Haughey committed himself to the nationalisation of a twenty-seven-acre site in Dublin port as well as the nationalisation of Clondalkin Paper Mills. £4 million would be allocated to employ five hundred extra people in the inner city and 3,746 jobs would be created in the same area over three years. State funding would be provided to build 440 new houses in the constituency and another 1,600 in the rest of Dublin.

These were the main aspects of the deal and while it was aimed at helping a socially disadvantaged part of Dublin, the fact that Haughey was prepared to commit so much taxpayers' money to ensure the vote of an individual Dáil deputy raised serious questions about his judgement and capacity to run the country's affairs.

He was stuck with the coalition's budget targets for 1982 but the new Minister for Finance, Ray MacSharry, hardly encouraged optimism about the course of economic events when he forecast, on taking office, that "gloom and doom" would be replaced by "boom and bloom".

In fact it didn't take MacSharry long to wake up to the economic realities once he had been thoroughly briefed by the officials in Finance. However, the political pressure of the Dublin West by-election in June 1982 meant that the Haughey government reverted to its old form. There was a climbdown on the budget arithmetic and concessions to those paying higher PRSI rates; the building societies were given special concessions to head off a mortgage rate increase and the budget projections generally began to go off the rails again.

In the middle of that by-election the Haughey government took an initiative which soured the already strained relations between Haughey and the British Prime Minister, Mrs Thatcher. The Falklands crisis was at its height and while Ireland had reluctantly gone along with its European Community partners in supporting sanctions against Argentina during the diplomatic phase of the conflict, Haughey grew steadily cooler on the policy as military action became inevitable.

On 2 May 1982 the government, after some internal conflict on the matter, issued a statement calling for further diplomatic efforts to avoid a military escalation. The statement reaffirmed Ireland's traditional role of neutrality in relation to armed conflicts. That evening a British submarine sank the Argentine cruiser *General Belgrano* and a total of 368 Argentine sailors were killed.

Fianna Fáil supporters were delighted that the government had distanced itself from the British position before the conflict had escalated, but the next day Minister for Defence Paddy Power went one further. Speaking at a Fianna Fáil meeting in Edenderry, County Offaly, he accused Britain of being the aggressor in the Falklands and said that Ireland would immediately take up a neutral stance. He got a standing ovation for his anti British comments and the following day the government duly announced that it would seek the withdrawal of EC sanctions against Argentina and would ask the United Nations Security Council to demand a cessation of hostilities.

The British were furious and the row marked the end of Thatcher's relationship with Haughey. She refused ever again to meet him for an Anglo-Irish summit and even when he became Taoiseach during the last years of the decade she only agreed to meet him on the margins of EC summits, and most of these meetings were frosty in the extreme.

At home, Garret FitzGerald attacked Haughey, accusing him of seeking temporary popularity with the electorate at the expense of Ireland's international reputation and of Anglo-Irish relations. Whatever the public feeling about Haughey's stance on the Falklands, it didn't help Haughey to win the Dublin West by-election which turned out to be another miscalculation.

The offer to Fine Gael TD Dick Burke of the vacant EC commissionership was designed to create an extra Fianna Fáil seat through a by-election in Dublin West but it was a political stroke that misfired. Not only did Fianna Fáil lose the by-election but Fine Gael's victory buoyed up Garret FitzGerald and gave him renewed optimism that Haughey's government could be taken out.

After that debacle the government finally began to come to grips with economic reality at the behest of MacSharry. Spending plans were cut in the summer and public service pay rises deferred. While they backed down again on the pay issue, by the autumn of 1982 the Cabinet began to look realistically at the nation's finances for the first time and started to develop a strategy, published in October as "The Way Forward".

This belated admission of reality was completely overshadowed by the GUBU chain of events which overwhelmed the government in the autumn of 1982. The term GUBU was a joint invention of Haughey himself and his fiercest critic Conor Cruise O'Brien. When a notorious murder suspect, Malcolm McArthur, was arrested in the flat of the Attorney General, Patrick Connolly, in the summer of 1982 Haughey described the situation as "grotesque, unbelievable, bizarre and unprecedented". Cruise O'Brien coined the acronym GUBU from the phrase and it came to signify the whole Haughey style of government in 1982.

The GUBU chain of events encouraged Haughey's long-standing internal critics to think once more of removing him as leader. Those who had fought might and main to prevent him becoming Fianna Fáil leader in the first place were now being joined by other discontented TDs, including Charlie McCreevy who had helped plot Haughey's accession to power but had been openly critical of Haughey's economic policies.

The second heave was launched by McCreevy on Friday, 1 October 1982, without O'Malley even being aware of it. He was away on holidays in Spain when McCreevy put down a motion of no confidence in the leader for the party meeting arranged for the following Wednesday. O'Malley had to rush home, resign his seat in the Cabinet, along with O'Donoghue, and join in a campaign which he had not instigated.

As in February the central figures in the Haughey campaign were MacSharry, Reynolds, Flynn and Doherty, all now key members of the Cabinet, with Doherty in the sensitive Justice portfolio. Just as in the earlier heave the media overestimated the support for the anti Haughey faction while the Fianna Fáil organisation rallied to the support of the party leader and intense pressure was applied to any TD believed to be wavering against the leadership. Dissident TDs again had stories about intimidating phone calls and threats from Haughey supporters in their local organisations.

Going into the meeting on Wednesday, 6 October, the anti Haughey camp were determined to push the issue to a vote this time. They had high hopes it would be by secret ballot as respected TDs like Pádraig Faulkner and Michael O'Kennedy had publicly called for such a secret vote. However, a roll-call vote was taken on the issue and TDs voted by 53 to 27 against having a secret ballot. After a meeting which went on all day and late into the evening, Haughey eventually won the open vote on his leadership by 58 votes to 22. The scale of his victory was very impressive in the circumstances.

When the result of the vote was announced in Leinster House the place went wild. Haughey supporters who had been piling into the House all evening were ecstatic and some of them were drunk. As the TDs came down into the main hall there was a tremendous crush as reporters and Fianna Fáil supporters struggled to get near the participants.

When Haughey's most implacable opponent, Jim Gibbons, appeared and tried to make his way towards the door he was surrounded by a crowd of angry Haughey supporters. One of them struck Gibbons and a group of Dáil ushers had to swoop in to protect him and escort him to his car.

The unruly crowd spilled out into the car park and other anti Haughey TDs, quickly dubbed the "Club of 22" got rough treatment. McCreevy was jostled and called a "bastard and a "blueshirt". The Gardaí helped him to get into his car but the crowd surrounded it, banging on the roof and shouting insults as he drove away.

Haughey had seen off his internal critics for the second time in less than a year but he did not get much time to rest on his laurels. His minority government's position became precarious with the death of Bill Loughnane later in October 1982, followed a day later by the hospitalisation of Jim Gibbons after a severe heart attack. When the government published its economic programme "The Way Forward", Tony Gregory and the Workers' Party withdrew their support and Fine Gael tabled a motion of no confidence. When the vote was taken on 4 November the government was defeated by 82 votes to 80 and an election fixed for 24 November.

Fianna Fáil were catapulted back into Opposition, winning 75 seats and 45.2 percent of the vote. Fine Gael and Labour had a comfortable majority between them and were able to form a coalition government under Garret FitzGerald which lasted until 1987. For Haughey the loss of the election was quickly followed by another crisis which again threatened to destroy his leadership.

Throughout the final months of 1982 there had been rumours and newspaper stories which raised a number of questions about the operation of the Gardaí under Seán Doherty. There was the Dowra affair, which involved a witness from Northern Ireland being held by the RUC so that he was unable to give evidence against a brother-in-law of the minister. There was the Tully affair in Roscommon where Sergeant Tom Tully of Boyle had successfully resisted an attempt, in which Doherty was involved, to have him transferred. The operation of the Gardaí was one of the issues which prompted Fine Gael's motion of no confidence and it also figured in the election campaign.

Now with Fianna Fáil out of power the new Minister for Justice, Michael Noonan, investigated the situation and his findings were sensational. He confirmed publicly on 20 January 1983 that the phones of political journalists Geraldine Kennedy and Bruce Arnold had been tapped on the instructions of Seán Doherty and that normal procedures had not been followed. There had been rumours all through the previous autumn that phone taps had been instituted as part of the internal Fianna Fáil wrangle, and following the defeat of the Haughey government those rumours began to surface in the newspapers. It now emerged that two journalists with very good contacts among the Fianna Fáil dissidents had had their phones tapped on the orders of Doherty in an effort to find out how they were getting Cabinet leaks. Geraldine Kennedy and Bruce Arnold later sued the state for infringing their constitutional rights and were awarded £20,000 each by the High Court in 1987. Noonan revealed the equally sensational information that Ray MacSharry had borrowed Garda equipment to record secretly a conversation with Martin O'Donoghue back in October 1982.

The following day Haughey accepted responsibility in a general sense, but denied any knowledge of the phone tapping. "Any head of Government must take responsibility for anything that happens during his administration. But I want to make it crystal clear that the Government as such and I, as Taoiseach, knew absolutely nothing about any activities of this sort and would not countenance any such abuse."

Doherty and MacSharry resigned from the front bench and a four-person committee was set up by Haughey to investigate the affair. The committee was headed by the chairman of the parliamentary party, Jim Tunney, who maintained from the beginning that "all the evidence shows that Mr Haughey knew absolutely nothing about it". The Tunney committee ultimately cleared Haughey of any involvement in the tapes controversy. Doherty had to take full responsibility and he lost the party whip for his actions. Haughey himself called for a judicial inquiry but the new Fine Gael-Labour government never took him up on the demand.

Fianna Fáil was immediately plunged into another crisis and this time few gave Haughey a chance of surviving. A special party meeting was held on Sunday, 23 January to discuss the implications of the revelations. When the Dáil resumed the following Wednesday there was widespread speculation that Haughey would resign. A number of TDs were reported to have gone to ask him to step down. That night on RTE and in all the newspapers the following morning it was reported that he was on the way out. "Haughey on Brink of Resignation" was the banner headline in the *Irish Press* which even carried on its inside pages a detailed account of the Fianna Fáil leader's career, which was instantly dubbed Haughey's political obituary.

When TDs gathered in the Dáil on the morning of 27 January the general view was that at the Fianna Fáil parliamentary party meeting later that day Haughey would announce his resignation. Nothing, however, was further from his mind.

Upstairs in his office at around 10 a.m. Haughey held a meeting with close supporters, including two senators, his nephew Seán O'Connor and his long-time friend P.J. Mara. They waited in silence while he finished reading the morning papers, then looking up at them Haughey said: "I think we'll fight the cunts."

He then called in the political heavyweights to devise a strategy for a counter offensive. At the party meeting which began over a hour later Ben Briscoe told Haughey it was time to go. Briscoe recalled that a year earlier Haughey had said he would resign the leadership if he felt that it was in the party's best interests that he do so. He added that the time had now come. Succumbing to the intense emotion that gripped the meeting, he went on to praise Haughey for all his achievements and ended up exclaiming: "I love you, Charlie."

"I love you too, Ben," replied Haughey.

"I hope the papers don't hear about this," groaned David Andrews at the back of the room, but the remarks were published in the following day's *Irish Press*.

One of the crucial contributions at this meeting was made by Ray Burke who said that Haughey should be allowed to go in his own time and should not be humiliated by being asked to step down immediately. Haughey himself told the meeting the media would not hound him from office and said he would make his own decision in his own time. Most of the TDs present took Haughey's statement to mean that he would resign in the near future. The Fianna Fáil Ard Fheis was due to be held in a few weeks and there was widespread expectation that he would step down after that. For Haughey, though, it was the breathing space he needed to stage a comeback.

The race to succeed now began, with Des O'Malley being joined by Gerry Collins and Michael O'Kennedy and later by Brian Lenihan and John Wilson. With this confused leadership contest already in progress while the leader was still in office, another meeting of the parliamentary party the following week was adjourned by the chairman, Jim Tunney, because of the death in a road accident of Donegal TD Clem Coughlan.

The anti Haughey faction were outraged at the adjourning of the meeting and a petition calling for another meeting to discuss the leadership issue was circulated and attracted forty-one signatures. This was a clear majority of the party TDs and it looked again as if the game was up for Haughey at a special meeting agreed for 7 February. Briscoe placed a motion before the meeting requesting Haughey to resign.

Crowds gathered on Kildare Street throughout Monday, 7 February as Fianna Fáil TDs debated the issue from 11 a.m. until midnight. Much time at the meeting was spent attacking the media, and Charlie McCreevy who had given a detailed interview to the *Sunday Press* the day before was the butt of much criticism. This time there was a secret ballot but while the vote was closer than in the previous October it still gave the same result as the open vote. Haughey won by 40 votes to 33.

Journalists were corralled in the main hall of Leinster House and the first news of the vote was brought to them by Senator Donie Cassidy who came rushing down from the party rooms to shout that Haughey had won. Pandemonium ensued as Haughey emerged triumphant at the door. Surrounded by reporters and photographers he made his way slowly down the steps of Leinster House towards the main gate.

The crowd of supporters on the street outside went mad. As

snowflakes began to fall, Haughey went to the perimeter of the grounds and shook hands, through the railings, with people in the street. He seemed to be in some ecstatic state, and so well he might, having confounded his critics once again.

6 – Parting of the Ways

With the vast majority of TDs now having no stomach for further fighting, O'Malley was soon isolated. Some of his strongest allies were no longer around to help; George Colley died suddenly in 1983, while Martin O'Donoghue and Jim Gibbons lost their Dáil seats in November 1982. Others had tired of the struggle against Haughey and decided to keep their heads down. The final breach began with the New Ireland Forum designed to established a unified position for all constitutional nationalist parties on the island.

The Forum was set up on the initiative of Garret FitzGerald and while most of his Cabinet were originally unenthusiastic about the move, as was Haughey, it finally got off the ground in May 1983. There was considerable tension in the Forum between Fianna Fáil and the other parties over how the traditional aspiration towards a united Ireland would be presented in the final report and at times this led to frayed nerves.

Garret FitzGerald in his autobiography recalls one dramatic episode which occurred just before Christmas 1983. Annoyed at leaks of the Forum's secret deliberations FitzGerald complained about the stream of disclosures to the press. Haughey then spoke in similar terms, but Dick Spring tackled the Fianna Fáil leader and accused him of being the source of the leaks. Haughey was furious and demanded that Spring withdraw the allegations, but the Labour leader refused.

FitzGerald writes: "At this Haughey, now looking more hurt than angry, appealed to Forum members to realise that he had been entrusted by me with confidences in relation to matters of state, which he had never betrayed, and that it was despicable to suggest that he would be the source of leaks from the Forum. 'No one has suffered more than I have from journalists,' he said – and at that broke down. Because I was sitting on the same side of the table as Haughey I could not see clearly what was happening, and my first impression was that he might be acting a part. I realised almost immediately, however, that this was not the case, for, in an undoubtedly emotional state, he had to be helped from the room by Ray MacSharry. It now became clear that he had arrived at the meeting in a very upset condition because of the recent publication of a book, *The Boss*, written about him and in particular about the GUBU events of the previous year."

This was one of the rare occasions on which Haughey let his private emotions break through into the public arena. Normally in political debate he wore a mask that effectively concealed his personal feelings. He was able to wax eloquent or indignant as the occasion demanded and could divorce his inner feelings from his public persona as political necessity dictated.

As for the Forum itself the debate between the parties about models for a united Ireland continued. Fianna Fáil stressed their attachment to the concept of a unitary state while the other parties pressed for other options to be kept open, particularly those which involved either a federal state or joint authority for the North. After a great deal of haggling, Haughey eventually agreed to a form of words in the Forum Report which acknowledged the unitary state as "the particular structure of political unity which the Forum would wish to see established" but which also referred to the federal solution and joint authority as other options to be considered.

Though the three models were accepted by Haughey for inclusion in the Forum Report, immediately on its publication in May 1984, he dismissed federalism or joint authority and argued strongly that only a unitary state would bring peace to the North. FitzGerald, Spring and SDLP leader John Hume were horrified by Haughey's reaction which almost upstaged the Forum Report itself and which was in direct opposition to the negotiating position FitzGerald was hoping to adopt in his dealings with the British.

There was some disquiet in Fianna Fáil at the manner in which Haughey had effectively decided party policy without a full debate. Senator Eoin Ryan demanded a meeting of the parliamentary party to discuss the issue, but when it was held after some delay there was overwhelming support for the Haughey line. Following the three-hour meeting Des O'Malley publicly criticised what he termed the stifling of debate within the party. Haughey reacted immediately and demanded that the whip be withdrawn from O'Malley. On a roll-call vote the motion to withdraw the whip was passed by 56 votes to 16. Dissent within the party was now effectively crushed. Party Press

Officer P.J. Mara, briefing political correspondents, summed up the new mood in the party with the old Italian fascist party slogan *Uno Duce, una voce*. "There'll be no more nibbling at my leader's bum," he added by way of explanation.

Mara, who took over the position as Fianna Fáil Press Officer in 1984, was a larger-than-life character who quickly established himself as one of the features of Leinster House and did incalculable work for Haughey in mending fences with the media. Born in 1941, Mara was a northsider from Drumcondra who as an ordinary member of Fianna Fáil supported Haughey during the Arms Crisis. He later travelled with him on the "rubber chicken" circuit during the early 1970s, often acting as Haughey's driver.

He was appointed as one of the Taoiseach's eleven to the Seanad in 1982 and Haughey made him party Press Officer in 1984 after the job had been turned down by Frank Dunlop and Seán Duignan, among others. At the time Mara was at something of a loose end after the failure of his carpet distribution business but he took to his new post like a duck to water. An excellent raconteur, he was a fund of witty and politically observant stories of life in Fianna Fáil. He kept the political journalists entertained with anecdotes and impersonations of the leading lights in the party, including his boss. His indiscretions soon became legendary but they were often so scabrous or libelous that they were unprintable. While they didn't do any harm to his boss they conveyed the impression that Mara was telling all there was to know. As a result journalists believed they were getting the inside track on what was happening in government but at the same time they never got much usable information.

In an affectionate piece in *The Irish Times* during the fourth move against Haughey in 1991, John Waters described Mara thus: "P.J. Mara doesn't so much do a job as weave a spell. His social skills are described in terms approaching awe by even those journalists who know that his job is to pull the wool over their eyes. His modus operandi is inseparable from his personality. He creates a web of bonhomie and laddishness around himself which is difficult to resist. He is an apparently bottomless source of witty remarks, epigrams and he is a brilliant mimic."

While Mara made it his business to charm political journalists, he didn't always take the time to impress general reporters who only crossed his path from time to time. "The Boss rarely ventures forth without P.J. at his side. Renowned for colourful language and denials, he manages to keep reporters on side by wit, impudence and telling them to fuck off, something they love," wrote Liam Collins of the *Sunday Independent*.

Another side to Mara was that underneath the jokes and funny impersonations lurked an intelligent and well read man. RTE's Seán Duignan, during one of the periodic controversies surrounding Haughey, likened Mara to Putzi Hanfstaengl, a legendary press officer for the German government in the 1930s who rationalised Hitler's policies to the foreign press. Mara took grievous umbrage at the comparison and was very angry at Duignan. What was surprising was not his anger but the fact that he knew the reference. Apart from Duignan none of the other media people present had ever heard of Hanfstaengl.

Sometimes, though, Mara's relaxed style got him into trouble. His facetious *Uno Duce, una voce* comment was quoted by Geraldine Kennedy in the *Sunday Press* and this got him into extremely hot water with Haughey. "You go into that room where they all hate me, and you give them this," screamed his leader at him the day after the quote was published; but relations were soon mended. It didn't take Mara long to bounce back and he was soon referring to his boss as the *Caudillo* rather than the *Duce*. Mara's irresistible charm ensured that he was quickly on good terms with most political journalists. This was critically important because one of the main functions of a press secretary is to provide a daily briefing for political correspondents, who are known in Leinster House as the Lobby. Mara had the ability to remain on good terms with the Lobby, regardless of whether individual correspondents had used his briefings in a friendly or a hostile fashion, and through all the storms that inevitably beset any government he almost invariably retained his composure and good humour.

As well as getting on well with the political correspondents Mara also won over potentially hostile Fianna Fáil TDs and Opposition politicians. As a former senator he had access to the members' bar in Leinster House and this became another forum for his funny routines and comical stories. All this enabled him to perform the crucial function of acting as Haughey's eyes and ears around Leinster House. Very little happened without Mara being aware of it and this was a vital source of intelligence for Haughey. He was also useful in that he acted as a sounding board and could tell Haughey how the media or the Fianna Fáil parliamentary party would react to any particular development.

P.J., as he was known around Leinster House though Haughey always called him Mara, had a meeting with his boss first thing on arriving at the office each morning, whether in Opposition or in government. They discussed the newspapers and the radio and television coverage of the major political happenings and planned out how to handle that day's news. Even on Sundays, Haughey generally rang Mara for a quick run over the papers. For a man who always publicly dismissed the media and newspaper headlines, Haughey always paid very close attention to what was being said about him.

Mara was joined in the Fianna Fáil press office by two women, Fionnuala O'Kelly and Niamh O'Connor who was a daughter of Haughey's close personal friend and election agent Pat O'Connor. Both women also established good relations with journalists so that the Fianna Fáil press office team became a very useful asset to Haughey and provided a counter to his well known dislike and distrust of the media.

Another member of the Haughey kitchen Cabinet was his advisor on Northern Ireland, Martin Mansergh. A son of a famous Anglo-Irish historian, Nicholas Mansergh, and educated at Kings School, Canterbury, and Oxford, Mansergh was a somewhat incongruous figure in Fianna Fáil. He had been a diplomat in Foreign Affairs and had acted as an advisor to Haughey in government on Anglo-Irish issues. When Haughey went into Opposition, Mansergh resigned from the diplomatic service and took up a post with Fianna Fáil as advisor to the party leader. Despite his Protestant Anglo-Irish background, Mansergh took a hard nationalist line on the North and on a number of occasions managed to irritate the government, particularly Garret

FitzGerald – he annoyed FitzGerald in a manner reminiscent of the way in which Erskine Childers infuriated Arthur Griffith.

Now totally in control of Fianna Fáil, Haughey felt secure enough to bring Seán Doherty back into the fold. Doherty had resigned the whip to save the party embarrassment during the dramatic days of early 1983 and had been agitating for some time to get back into the fold. His return at the end of 1984 showed just how strong Haughey's grip was in Fianna Fáil at that stage.

Meanwhile, Des O'Malley was isolated as an independent deputy without the party whip and the final parting of the ways with an increasingly confident Haughey became inevitable. The breach arose out of O'Malley's refusal to vote with parliamentary colleagues against a bill to liberalise the family planning laws in February 1985. It was not just his refusal to toe the line in the vote which left his fellow party TDs squirming but the fact that he delivered an electrifying speech to the Dáil which severely damaged their case. Defending the concept of a pluralist state, O'Malley stressed the effect a defeat for the Bill would have on opinion in Northern Ireland and he denounced the partitionist mentality of those who opposed the government's legislation.

"The politics of this would be very easy. The politics would be, to be one of the lads, the safest way in Ireland. But I do not believe that the interests of this State, of our Constitution and of this Republic would be served by putting politics before conscience in regard to this. There is a choice of a kind that can only be answered by saying that I stand by the Republic and accordingly, I will not oppose this Bill," said O'Malley.

His use of the old civil war catchphrase "I stand by the Republic" rubbed salt into the wounds of many of his Fianna Fáil colleagues, but the speech was hailed by TDs of all parties as one of the best heard in the Dáil chamber for many years. The Minister for Health, Barry Desmond, said it was the finest he had heard there for thirteen years.

O'Malley, who was now just an ordinary member having lost the party whip, attempted to balance the impact of his speech by abstaining on the vote rather than supporting the government Bill outright. Even still he was hoping that he could have a future in Fianna Fáil, but Haughey thought otherwise. O'Malley was summoned to Mount Street to face a motion calling for his expulsion on the night of 26 February.

O'Malley's wife, Pat, and a crowd of supporters from Limerick waited outside Fianna Fáil headquarters in Dublin's Mount Street on the cold night as O'Malley was hauled before the party's national executive for "conduct unbecoming" a party member. Party leader Charles Haughey, who had seen off three attempts by O'Malley to remove him from the Fianna Fáil leadership, came to that meeting determined to get rid of his old adversary once and for all. "It's him or me," Haughey told a number of people who tried to intercede for O'Malley. Eighty-two people crammed into the meeting room for the final showdown.

O'Malley, who was allowed to address the gathering, asked for a secret ballot on the expulsion motion but Haughey demanded a unanimous public decision. On three different occasions during the meeting he interceded to say: "I want it to be unanimous for the good of the party and the organisation." When a few speakers made it clear that a unanimous vote was out of the question Haughey demanded an open roll-call vote. This was a flagrant violation of the party's own rules which stipulated that all votes should be secret, but nobody protested. Yet another roll call vote was taken and the motion to expel O'Malley was passed by 73 votes to 9.

When the Limerick TD came out into the glare of the television lights on the street outside after the vote there were scenes which recalled the GUBU days of three years earlier. As O'Malley supporters, journalists and members of the party's national executive jostled around on the street, Haughey left the building to a few scattered boos and a chant of *Sieg Heil, Sieg Heil* from one protestor, Kevin Loughney, the owner of nearby Kitty O'Shea's pub; he also reminded P.J. Mara loudly of his memorable *Uno Duce, una voce* remark. O'Malley himself was one of the calmest people present and as he kissed his wife in front of the cameras he remarked: "I hope that is not conduct unbecoming."

The jocularity, however, could not disguise the seriousness of the situation for O'Malley and it appeared to many that night that a brilliant political career had come to an end. At forty-six years of age he had served as a cabinet minister or a frontbench member for fourteen years and had been tipped by many people, including former Taoiseach Jack Lynch, as a future Taoiseach.

While his Limerick supporters stoutly maintained that O'Malley would be back, the omens were not good. Fianna Fáil ministers had resigned or been expelled before only to vanish into the wilderness. A striking example was Neil Blaney who was expelled from Fianna Fáil in 1971 on exactly the same grounds as O'Malley. Blaney, like O'Malley, had been at the top in Fianna Fáil for a decade and a half but once he was expelled he never came in from the political wilderness. There was some irony in the fact that the two men would now for a while sit together on the independent benches in the Dáil because they represented the divergent strands of opinion that had dragged Fianna Fáil in opposite directions for twenty years. Yet the party, which emphasised unity and discipline above all other virtues, had expelled them both.

The expulsion of O'Malley in February 1985 left Haughey in total control of the party. His supporters were delighted with the move and claimed that Fianna Fáil were now a unified and cohesive political party for the first time since Haughey became leader in December 1979. "There is a unity of purpose now that hasn't been there since Charlie took over. We have a united party again," said Albert Reynolds a few weeks after O'Malley's expulsion.

O'Malley's departure marked the final step in Haughey's takeover of Fianna Fáil. With leading opponents of 1979 either dead, expelled or cowed, Haughey had the power to do with the party as he willed. The few remaining deputies with doubts about his leadership – like David Andrews – were simply too weary of the struggle to carry on.

The outsiders of 1979 had now become the party establishment and they looked forward to government when the increasingly unpopular Fine Gael-Labour coalition had run its term. Doherty was now back in the party, MacSharry had won election to the European Parliament and was immediately installed as leader of the Fianna Fáil group in Strasbourg, though he still retained his seat in the Dáil. Albert Reynolds and Pádraig Flynn were leading members of the Opposition front bench. It seemed only a matter of time before Fianna Fáil under Haughey would win a comfortable overall majority and take over the reins of power without any strings attached.

7 – A New Party

On the night Des O'Malley was expelled from Fianna Fáil a leading Fine Gael activist, Michael McDowell, was at home looking at television. Watching the event unfold on the news McDowell commented to his wife that if the former minister started a new political party he was sure to get a fair degree of support because the time was right for it. McDowell's wife, Niamh, said that if her husband felt that way he should make his views known to O'Malley. So he sat down and wrote a letter encouraging O'Malley to form a new political party and offering whatever help he could give.

Michael McDowell was an up-and-coming young barrister who at this stage was growing increasingly disillusioned with Fine Gael's role in government. He had served three years as chairman of the party's organisation in Garret FitzGerald's constituency of Dublin South East and had made no secret of his view that the coalition with Labour was a disaster.

To the deep irritation of FitzGerald, McDowell had used the occasion of his last speech as chairman, at the constituency annual general meeting a year before, to make clear his view that the party was going nowhere and he told his surprised fellow party members that he had decided never to vote for Fine Gael again if what they were offering to the electorate was a coalition with the Labour Party. In the Law Library he regularly discussed politics with Michael O'Leary, the former Labour leader who was now a Fine Gael TD. O'Leary had performed the remarkable feat of getting elected as a Fine Gael TD only weeks after quitting as Labour leader because of a humiliating rejection of his policies at Labour's annual conference. It did not take long, however, for disillusionment with his new party to set in and O'Leary was highly critical of the way the Fine Gael-Labour government operated. In McDowell's house shortly before Christmas 1984 the two men drew up a list of the seats Fine Gael would lose at the next election. They arrived at the grand total of twenty-one (when the election came over two years later it was nineteen) and concluded that there was no way of stopping a Fianna Fáil landslide.

It was not long after that – in February 1985 – that McDowell wrote to Des O'Malley. He got no immediate response, but after Easter he was contacted by Fianna Fáil TD Mary Harney, who had been a close ally of O'Malley in Fianna Fáil and who also knew McDowell through student debates a decade earlier. She asked him if he was serious about joining a new party and he said he was. Subsequently McDowell invited O'Malley around to his house for dinner and the two men met for the first time.

In the meantime Fianna Fáil friends of O'Malley were also considering the option of a new political party. Séamus Brennan, the former Fianna Fáil General Secretary who had been an anti Haughey TD since 1981, Mary Harney and David Andrews were chief among them. An opinion poll was organised by Brennan and financed by Barra O Tuama, the Cork hotel owner and concert promoter, and published on 18 April. The poll showed that 39 percent of people asked were in favour of a new political party headed by O'Malley while 35 percent were against it. An interesting feature of the poll which was carried out by Irish Marketing Surveys was that the most positive reaction came from the middle class voters and large farmers. The strongest support was located in Munster, not surprisingly in view of O'Malley's home base and the sympathy for Jack Lynch.

There were mixed opinions at the time on the significance of the poll. Haughey dismissed it as irrelevant, but for those planning the new party it appeared hopeful, particularly as it was published only a few days after another poll which showed a big drop in Fianna Fáil support due to the O'Malley expulsion.

In the following months, though, the steam seemed to go out of the plan. At the beginning of the summer Séamus Brennan began to go lukewarm on the project and appeared more interested in pursuing his political career within Fianna Fáil. O'Malley's supporters in Limerick were also reluctant to get involved, most of them preferring their TD to stay on as a sort of independent Fianna Fáil deputy who might one day be reconciled with the party.

Mary Harney was still a strong advocate of a new party. She went to the United States for the summer and when she returned she found that while planning for the party was still continuing it was beginning to flag. Brennan had dropped out, but another Fianna Fáil TD, Charlie McCreevy, who had been a Haughey supporter in 1979 but had quickly become a die-hard opponent of the Fianna Fáil leader, had become involved. Another to join in McDowell's scheme was Paul McKay, who had been treasurer of the Fianna Fáil organisation in Haughey's constituency but had resigned in protest at the way the accounts were kept. He undertook a feasibility study on the launching of a new organisation. O'Malley, however, still remained very reluctant to commit himself to a new party.

A crucial meeting of the conspirators took place in Michael O'Leary's house in Wellington Road in September. At the meeting, besides O'Leary, were O'Malley, Harney, McDowell, McKay and McCreevy. At this stage O'Malley had gone very cold on the idea and told the others that they should do nothing for the present at least. Showing his impatience at the delay and indecision, McCreevy told the others that if the new party did not go ahead that night he was out and would have nothing more to do with it. O'Malley was a bit wary of McCreevy because of the way he had put down the motion of no confidence in Haughey in October 1982 without consulting anybody, and he was unwilling to respond to such an ultimatum from him.

A crucial factor in the indecision was the way in which the three attempts to remove Haughey had been botched.

"I think there was a lack of trust among some of us about the reliability of the others because of the way the heaves against Haughey had gone. At this stage each regarded the other as wimps because of what had happened before," said one of the plotters later. Some strongly anti Haughey TDs in Fianna Fáil, like Bobby Molloy and Pearse Wyse, had had a stomachfull of conspiracies and were not involved in any way at this stage. A serious car crash in November, which could have killed O'Malley, gave him a severe shock and that put back discussion yet again.

While they waited to see if a new party would get off the ground McDowell and O'Leary drafted a divorce Bill. O'Leary introduced the Bill in the Dáil but only five TDs supported it. However, it added to the pressure on the Fine Gael-Labour coalition which was theoretically committed to holding a referendum on divorce. Shortly afterwards the Anglo-Irish Agreement, signed by Garret FitzGerald and Margaret Thatcher on 15 November 1985, was denounced in the strongest terms by Haughey. The Fianna Fáil leader had earlier dispatched Brian Lenihan to the United States to lobby leading politicians against the planned Agreement. This attempt to sabotage an Anglo-Irish accord infuriated Irish-American politicians, particularly the Speaker of the House of Representatives, Tip O'Neill, and did nothing to enhance Haughey's reputation.

When the Agreement was announced the old divisions in Fianna Fáil were exposed once again. The Agreement was welcomed by O'Malley and former Taoiseach Jack Lynch and on 20 November Mary Harney issued a statement in favour, saying she would vote for it. She followed this up by going through the government lobby along with O'Malley. Expelled from the party a week later she now joined O'Malley as an independent and continued to encourage him to form a new party. Harney's strong advocacy of a new party and Fianna Fáil's utterly negative attitude towards the Anglo-Irish Agreement rekindled O'Malley's enthusiasm and he now committed himself fully to the project.

At a meeting in Paul McKay's house in late November the decision was finally taken to launch the party. McKay and McDowell leased premises at South Frederick Street. A discussion paper was prepared on the aims of the new party, to be called the Progressive Democrats. RTE reporter and former young Fianna Fáil star Pat Cox had joined the planning at this stage and his advice counted for a lot with O'Malley. Rumours began to circulate in political circles by mid-December that something was up and the newspapers carried speculation that O'Malley was about to establish a new party.

The Progressive Democrats were finally launched on 21 December 1985. To begin with the party had just two TDs, O'Malley and Harney. In acknowledgement of his work in establishing the party McDowell was appointed chairman, which emphasised that the PDs were not simply a Fianna Fáil dissident rump. Michael O'Leary had been willing to join but O'Malley thought this might give the impression that the PDs were simply a refuge for people who couldn't find a home elsewhere. So despite the fact that he had been in on the planning of the new party there was no room for him in it. It was a decision that the founders of the PDs were later to regret, not just on a personal level but because O'Leary, whatever his political inconsistencies, was a marvellous vote-getter and a potential seat was thrown away.

Gemma Hussey records in her Cabinet diaries how the involvement of McDowell came as a blow to Fine Gael. "Dessie O'Malley's new party, the Progressive Democrats, was announced today. Michael McDowell is the chairman. Will it hurt Fianna Fáil more than us? It is depressing that Michael did this; it must be hurtful to Garret."

Four days before Christmas seemed an odd time to launch a political party but the timing actually worked to great advantage. The PDs dominated the headlines and news bulletins and O'Malley sounded very confident as he went on radio asking for donations of £150,000 a year to make the PDs a viable prospect. In the early days of the new year the party took off. Advertisements were placed in the papers on 2 January seeking money and supporters, and the party headquarters were inundated with people wanting to get involved. By 6 January over four thousand people had enrolled as members and £25,000 was contributed by public subscription. Over a thousand people attended the first party constituency meeting in the Marine Hotel in Sutton and the major parties began to sit up and take notice.

Haughey went on radio a few days later and expressed the view that the PDs were not acting in the national interest, but the crowds continued to flock to their public meetings. At these early meetings O'Malley hammered home the core message of the party – that the state was strangling the economy through an involvement matched only by the communist countries of Eastern Europe. He committed the PDs to cutting taxes as the essential first step in putting the economy right. To an electorate crippled with personal taxation, disillusioned with a stagnant economy and rising unemployment, the new party's message sounded attractive. O'Malley's imposing presence and Mary Harney's abilities as a speaker contributed to the air of excitement generated at those meetings.

It was a very unsettling time for Fianna Fáil. A significant number of activists in constituencies like Dun Laoghaire, Dublin South and the Cork City constituencies began to desert to the PDs. The question was whether the deputies for those areas, some of whom had been close to O'Malley, would follow suit. There was a wide expectation in both Fianna Fáil and the PDs that Dun Laoghaire TD David Andrews would switch parties and there were rumours about Seamus Brennan from the neighbouring constituency. Brennan, however, set his face completely against joining and in fact spent a lot of time trying to persuade wavering Fianna Fáil deputies to stay in the party. In the middle of January when rumours developed that Cork TD Pearse Wyse was on the verge of leaving to join the PDs, Brennan and Bobby Molloy were dispatched by Haughey to try and get him to stay on.

Despite the attempt to persuade him to stay, Wyse turned up to the first major PD rally in Cork on 20 January and announced that he was joining the new party. The Cork meeting, which overflowed the Metropole Hotel onto the street outside, confirmed the revivalist air which now attended PD rallies. But if the Cork meeting was emotional the first Galway rally three days later was sensational. Bobby Molloy, who just a week earlier had assisted Séamus Brennan in trying to persuade Pearse Wyse not to leave Fianna Fáil, jumped ship on the day of the PD rally in the Leisureland complex in Salthill. The move stunned Fianna Fáil. Molloy had given no inkling of his departure to anybody in the party leadership. On the day of the PD rally in Galway, 23 January, he set off from Dublin in the early afternoon and rang his secretary later from a phone booth along the road. He told her to open his filing cabinet, get out a letter he had left there and take it to Haughey. The letter contained his resignation from the Fianna Fáil party which he had served as a TD for twenty years.

The Dáil was sitting that day and the shock among Fianna Fáil TDs was palpable. Labour TD Frank McLoughlin remarked that the party front bench looked like "a crowd of cut calves" and it was hardly much of an exaggeration.

Over the following days Fianna Fáil TDs wondered who would be the next to go. David Andrews and Joe Walsh seemed the most likely as they were friends of O'Malley. Others like Noel Davern from Tipperary, Charlie McCreevy and many more were mentioned as possible defectors, but when, after another few weeks of uncertainty, none of them had left, the mood in Fianna Fáil settled down and confidence gradually flowed back. The trauma of Molloy's defection actually marked the end rather than the beginning of the drift from Fianna Fáil to the PDs.

Over the next few months the opinion polls confirmed the impact of the PDs on the public imagination. The first major poll published in *The Irish Times* gave the new party 25 percent, putting the PDs ahead of Fine Gael on 23 percent while Fianna Fáil had come down to 42 percent and Labour were just 4 percent. Fianna Fáil treated the PDs with deep-seated suspicion and hostility but Fine Gael could not make up its mind. The party leader, Garret FitzGerald, seemed to welcome the newcomers as a means of preventing Fianna Fáil gaining an overall majority at the next election and also as a possible coalition partner in place of Labour. Ordinary Fine Gael TDs, though, regarded the PDs as potential rivals who threatened their seats. A number of Fine Gael TDs – like Maurice Manning, Monica Barnes, Hugh Coveney, Ivan Yates, Michael O'Leary and Michael Keating – were rumoured to be considering moving to the PDs, but nothing immediate happened.

While Fine Gael TDs were slow to join the new party it did have two surprising recruits – Labour senators Helena McAuliffe and Timmy Conway who were very much on the moderate wing of the party though neither was regarded as a senior Labour figure.

The PDs appointed two well-known journalists to run the party organisation. Pat Cox, a reporter with the prestigious RTE current affairs programme "Today Tonight" was appointed general secretary with responsibility for developing the organisation. Cox, a former member of young Fianna Fáil, had in fact been in on the founding of the party and was one of O'Malley's closest confidants, but he continued to work in RTE until the party was already a few months old. One of the reasons he did this was because he was working on a programme which aimed at exposing the links between the Workers' Party and the Official IRA and their protection rackets in Belfast.

The other journalist appointed to the party backroom staff was Stephen O'Byrnes. He was news analysis editor with the *Irish Independent* having worked previously on the political staff of the *Irish*

Press. Ironically he had just completed a book, not yet published at that stage, on the development of Fine Gael under Garret FitzGerald. Unlike Cox, O'Byrnes had no involvement in the foundation of the party and did not know Des O'Malley particularly well. Both Cox and O'Byrnes were from Limerick, giving rise to comments about a Limerick mafia running the new party.

Despite its immediate impact with the public, the PDs were still in the spring of 1986 a party of four former Fianna Fáil TDs. Though they had discussions with a number of Fine Gael TDs they had failed to get a positive commitment from any of them to join and the party was open to the jibe that it was merely an anti Haughey Fianna Fáil splinter group. Finally on 9 April, Fine Gael TD for Dublin Central Michael Keating publicly announced that he was joining the new party. He spoiled the move somewhat by issuing denials to the media on the morning of his defection that he was in fact moving. The PDs, however, were very glad to have a Fine Gael TD on board and in recognition of the significance of the move Keating was appointed deputy leader, a position many felt should have gone to the co-founder of the party, Mary Harney.

In the days after the Keating move there was again widespread speculation about other Fine Gael TDs but none was ultimately to join. Michael O'Leary had already been turned down by the party and the maverick TD Liam Skelly was also spurned. Former EC Commissioner and Fine Gael minister Dick Burke was another who made overtures but was not welcomed. Lord Henry Mountcharles received the same treatment. O'Malley held the strong view that the PDs should not be seen as a safe haven for disgruntled politicians who were out of favour with their own parties as that could do enormous damage to their credibility.

In the event, Michael Keating was the only Fine Gael TD to jump and some of the leading PDs regretted later that they had not responded more positively to approaches from the likes of Michael O'Leary and Charlie McCreevy. However, the party did attract a number of big political names. Anne Colley, daughter of George, joined in Dublin South and was quickly selected as a prospective candidate. A number of the Gibbons clan in Kilkenny joined with

Martin, a son of Jim, emerging as the likely Dáil contender. The prominent names in the PDs – O'Malley, Molloy, Colley, Gibbons and Wyse – now read like a litany of the defeated faction in Fianna Fáil. Deep antipathy to Haughey was a strong motivating force among this group and Mary Harney articulated the feelings of many in the new party at this time when she remarked: "I will never vote for Haughey for Taoiseach and will leave the PDs if they ever do."

The main focus of political attention switched in April from the PDs to the divorce referendum instigated by Garret FitzGerald. The PDs supported the pro divorce campaign and campaigned for it around the country. They didn't, however, commit very much money or resources to it, preferring to concentrate their efforts on the general election whenever that would come. The defeat of the divorce proposal further demoralised the coalition government and made it a virtual certainty that they would be defeated at the next election.

After their initial high-flying performance in the polls the PDs now settled back to respectable ratings of around 15 percent though there was still widespread scepticism about the ability of the party to achieve anything like that figure in a general election. The party held its first annual conference in May and the turnout, the general level of debate and the keynote speech by O'Malley were all impressive. In that speech he identified lower taxation as the central thrust of party policy and while party policy was still at the discussion stage he said: "The Progressive Democrats are determined to bring forward policies that will give this country a standard tax rate of 25 percent." The policy discussion document also committed the party to the same figure as well as a 15 percent VAT rate, sizeable cuts in public spending, a property tax and a programme of privatisation. In relation to the North the discussion document supported the Anglo-Irish Agreement, called for changes in Articles 2 and 3 of the Constitution and for closer security operations. These aspirations were to form the unchanging basis of PD policy in the years ahead.

In October of 1986 that policy was fleshed out in detail with discussion papers giving way to actual policies and the central feature remained the commitment to lower personal taxation.

8 – Election '87

By the beginning of 1987 as the country moved towards a general election, Haughey was convinced that his hour was finally at hand. Fianna Fáil attacked every aspect of the coalition's record, particularly the harsh economic policies aimed at controlling the debt. Government spending cuts were singled out for attack and the main slogan of the Fianna Fáil campaign was: "Health cuts hurt the old, the poor and the handicapped."

This message was plastered up on billboards all over the country for months before the election campaign even began. While the party did accept the basic arithmetic of the outgoing government's budget, the populist nature of the appeal during the campaign did not seem to indicate that Haughey was about to address the problem in a serious fashion. Haughey's record of fighting the government tooth and nail on every single public spending cut for the previous four years implied that the situation would be very different under Fianna Fáil. He had maintained again and again that spending cuts were unnecessary and he lambasted the government for its policies. As almost all professional economists were also preaching the need for control of public spending, Haughey attacked them as well.

In June 1984 he maintained: "The failure of this government has been significantly contributed to by the invasion of the corridors of government by a coterie of professional economists, preaching defeatist, monetarist doctrines and peddling unrealistic and unacceptable policies. No previous government has given so much patronage and influence to a whole troupe of economists who seem determined to re-establish economics as a dismal science."

He said that by contrast Fianna Fáil policy was to make every effort to prevent factory closures and job losses. "We adopted a deliberate policy of intervening and providing state aid to keep firms going. We were constantly pilloried for doing so and accused of extravagance and mismanagement."

In a typical speech in 1986 he charged: "The obsession with budgetary arithmetic to the exclusion of everything else is preventing positive thinking. It is an intellectual strait-jacket. The pluses and minuses of the budget arithmetic have become the reality, not the economy. We must break out of this strait-jacket. In fact it is not civil war politics that this country needs to get away from but Victorian economics and financial precepts."

Whether he realised it or not, Haughey's continuous and sustained criticism of the Fine Gael-Labour coalition's policies was not merely misplaced, it was based on a misreading of the economic situation. The government's failure lay not in its desire to cut public spending but in the fact that it was not cutting that spending by nearly enough.

It was not just through Dáil speeches that Haughey, during his period as Opposition leader, hampered the government's ability to convince the electorate of the need for cutbacks. He also offered open support to any and every interest group which engaged in confrontation with the government. Fianna Fáil supported pay demands by the country's teachers and encouraged the teaching unions to take industrial action in pursuit of those demands. There was hardly an interest group in the country which didn't get support from Fianna Fáil in the battle against public spending cuts. They supported the Irish Shipping workers protesting at the closure of the state company because of a disastrous financial performance. The main Opposition party also backed the farmers in their battle to avoid paying a land tax and they openly attacked the deposit interest retention tax and joined the campaign against it.

Towards the end of its term of office the coalition had come up with two dramatic revenue raising schemes which, if they had been begun earlier in the government's life, would have made their job a lot easier. One was the National Lottery and the other was the deposit interest retention tax, quickly labelled DIRT, which was levied directly on the interest accrued by deposits in banks and building societies. Fianna Fáil attacked DIRT on its introduction and Haughey pledged to abolish it when he returned to office. (Of course he did nothing of the kind because DIRT was a massive income earner for the Exchequer and enabled him to cut borrowing quite dramatically. The lottery money was also to play a big part in helping Fianna Fáil cope with the national finances.)

Haughey's opponents believed that his sustained criticism of the coalition's policies was based on either a total misreading of the economic situation or a cynical and opportunistic approach to politics. As far as Haughey himself was concerned he believed he had every right to behave in the traditional adversarial manner of an Opposition leader and oppose the government as strongly as he could on every issue. On top of that, his own self-belief and his desire for power had convinced him that only he could sort out the nation's problems and he felt fully justified in doing everything he could to discredit Garret FitzGerald's government.

The Fine Gael-Labour coalition had been coming apart since the autumn of 1986 and by Christmas of that year it was becoming obvious that the parties in power would not be able to agree on a budget. While they haggled away through January 1987, the inevitable break came on 20 January when the four Labour ministers left the government because they could not agree to Fine Gael's terms for a budget.

There was speculation that Fine Gael might seek to introduce a budget of its own to the Dáil. It was a course of action favoured by some Fine Gael ministers and with hindsight such a strategy might have exposed Fianna Fáil's lack of policy. Instead FitzGerald asked President Hillery to dissolve the Dáil and an election was set from 17 February. Fine Gael then went ahead and published its budget proposals and then got down to the long election campaign to try and explain them to the electorate. FitzGerald had purposely gone for an unusually long four-week campaign in the hope that it would give him time to bring the electorate around.

Fianna Fáil refused to play ball and didn't launch their campaign manifesto for a week to try and get around FitzGerald's strategy. When Haughey did get going he was difficult to pin down on anything. The Fianna Fáil strategy involved an outright refusal to make any commitments while at the same time trying to convince each segment of the electorate that things would be better under a Fianna Fáil government. When Fine Gael and the PDs announced they were in favour of selling off shares in semi state companies Haughey immediately sent a letter of reassurance to the Irish Congress of Trade Unions pledging that a Fianna Fáil government would never countenance the privatisation of state enterprises. Nothing was said by Fianna Fáil during the campaign that would alienate any interest group in the country but no firm commitments were made either.

There were some straws in the wind, however, which indicated that Fianna Fáil was beginning to come to terms with economic reality. In the middle of the campaign the party's finance spokesman, Michael O'Kennedy, told the financial editor of the *Sunday Press*, Des Crowley, that a Fianna Fáil government would probably have to implement most of the provisions of the Fine Gael budget. The paper carried the report but Haughey adamantly declared that no such decision had been made.

The first opinion poll of the campaign confirmed the widespread belief that Fianna Fáil were on course for a resounding victory. The MRBI poll in *The Irish Times* gave the party 52 percent with Fine Gael away back on 23 percent, Labour on just 5 percent and the PDs with a very impressive 15 percent. As the long campaign wore on, however, Fianna Fáil's commanding lead in the opinion polls began to slip just as FitzGerald had hoped, but the benefits did not go to Fine Gael as FitzGerald had planned.

The novelty factor in the election was that it was not a contest between Fianna Fáil on the one side and a Fine Gael-Labour combination on the other. For a start Labour had decided not to go into another coalition, but more importantly there was the new party on the scene whose impact was very difficult to anticipate.

By January 1987 the Progressive Democrats were a force to be reckoned with but even they underestimated the impact they were likely to have on the election. Despite the fact that they were still showing up in the polls at between 12 percent and 15 percent, few gave the new party much chance of getting more than ten seats. During the campaign they managed to attract a lot of attention. A surprise candidate, Geraldine Kennedy, political correspondent of the *Sunday Press*, joined well known names like Michael McDowell, Anne Colley, Martin Gibbons and Pat O'Malley on the PD ticket, all as first-time candidates.

The PDs were initially attacked by both Fianna Fáil and Fine Gael but as the campaign wore on it was clear that the new party was going to make a significant impact. The strength of the PD campaign was a surprise as well as something of a double-edged sword for Fine Gael. The party was staffed mainly by former Fianna Fáil activists but it was poaching Fine Gael votes. On the other hand it represented the only chance of stopping Fianna Fáil getting an overall majority.

This led to a botched attempt by Fine Gael to organise a pre-election pact with the new party. Detailed discussions took place between Fine Gael director of elections, David Molony, and his PD counterpart and party General Secretary Pat Cox about a transfer pact. Both men were acting on the instructions of their respective party leaders. By the last weekend of the campaign Fine Gael understood that a pact was on, but despite an initial acceptance of it by Des O'Malley senior ex-Fianna Fáil figures in the party, particularly Bobby Molloy, were adamant that it would lead to an electoral disaster.

Because of this the PDs pulled back, but FitzGerald went ahead and made a speech calling on Fine Gael voters to give their second preferences to the PDs. O'Malley spurned the offer and studiously avoided any reciprocal gesture, leading to the development of a great deal of bitterness and lack of trust in the relations between the two parties. This was compounded by the election result because the PDs mopped up Fine Gael seats, astonishing themselves as much as everyone else with the performance. Leading figures in the party were later to bemoan the fact that had they realised they were doing so well they could with a little extra effort have gained another three or four seats on top of the fourteen they actually won.

Fine Gael concentrated heavily on Haughey's record on the North, particularly his attitude to the Anglo-Irish Agreement. Haughey had denounced it a number of times since it was signed in November 1985, and had pledged to renegotiate it if elected. At the start of the campaign he changed tack and pledged to continue working the Agreement though he maintained he still could not accept the constitutional implications of recognising partition.

In the debate between the two leaders in the final days of the campaign FitzGerald homed in on this issue and rattled Haughey by forcing him to deny a statement he had made only days earlier. The debate accelerated the slide in Fianna Fáil's fortunes though it didn't do much for Fine Gael.

When the votes were counted on 18 February the result was bitter disappointment for Fianna Fáil who were left with just 81 seats, three short of an overall majority. Fine Gael won 51 seats, the PDs 14, Labour 12, the Workers' Party 4 and others 4. Fianna Fáil supporters couldn't come to terms with the result. The party had confidently expected to sweep into power with an overall majority and from grassroots members up they were shattered at their failure to achieve that objective. It was the fourth time in a row that Haughey had failed to deliver an overall majority and some senior figures now began to despair of him ever being able to do so.

For Fine Gael the result was also a bitter blow but it was not unexpected. The party had managed to rally some support in the final days but not nearly as much as it had hoped. Weary from the trials and tribulations of four difficult years in office there was almost a sense of relief among some ministers that somebody else would have to wrestle with the huge problems they had contended with.

The big winners appeared to be the PDs. They had taken fourteen seats and managed to achieve one of their major objectives – they prevented Charles Haughey winning an overall majority – but they failed in the second strategic objective of holding the balance of power. Many in the PDs harboured the ambition of holding the balance of power so that they could force Fianna Fáil to ditch Haughey as the price of their support. They narrowly failed to put themselves into that position.

Though Haughey was deeply disappointed he did not show it. Instead he acted as if he had won an overall majority and as if there was no question but that he would succeed FitzGerald as Taoiseach. As three of the four independent TDs elected to the twenty-fifth Dáil had voted for his nomination as Taoiseach back in 1982, he had some grounds for optimism on that score, but his prospects if he achieved office looked decidedly gloomy.

However, he took the initiative and correctly read the mood of the electorate by announcing that he was not going to do deals with anyone. This gave him some room for manoeuvre. For a start Fianna

Fáil could hold on to its voting block of eighty-one TDs as the Ceann Comhairle would not have to come from the party's ranks. Former Labour TD Seán Treacy, who had been Ceann Comhairle for the 1973-77, period let it be known that he was available.

Before opting for Treacy, Haughey offered the job to the Fine Gael incumbent Tom Fitzpatrick as that would make him even more secure in Dáil divisions. A number of leading Fine Gael figures, frightened at the prospect of political and economic instability à la 1981-82, thought Fitzpatrick should be allowed to accept, but the idea was knocked on the head by the Fine Gael parliamentary party at the behest of the outgoing Taoiseach, Garret FitzGerald. This meant that there was still no certainty about what would happen when the Dáil resumed on 10 March.

As the day drew near Haughey's prospects of becoming Taoiseach grew more uncertain. Fine Gael, the PDs, Labour, the Workers' Party and Jim Kemmy were all committed to voting against him. That meant there were 82 certain votes against Haughey as opposed to 81 Fianna Fáil votes. His fate, therefore, was in the hands of two independents, Neil Blaney and Tony Gregory. As Haughey was sticking by his pledge not to do any deals and was known to have turned down Blaney's demands to end the Anglo-Irish Agreement and scrap extradition, the situation was very volatile.

So uncertain was the situation that Garret FitzGerald sought the advice of President Hillery about what he should do if the Dáil was unable to elect a Taoiseach. It was clear that he himself would not get enough support but if Haughey could not muster a majority either then a constitutional crisis about who should govern would arise for the first time in the history of the state. The advice he received was that he would have to continue on as a caretaker until the Dáil elected a successor. Going into the Dáil on 10 March, FitzGerald prepared two speeches. One of them was the speech he would make if Haughey was elected, the other outlined his intention to carry on on the advice of the President until a successor was chosen.

In this uncertain atmosphere there were some murmurings about Haughey's position as Fianna Fáil leader. It was clear that any other Fianna Fáil nominee for the Taoiseach's post would easily be elected because the PDs for one would not have any difficulty in supporting someone other than Haughey. With this potential threat to his leadership emerging, Haughey moved to quash any such move before it got off the ground.

Ray Burke went on radio to put the position clearly just two days before the vote: "Let nobody outside Fianna Fáil have any feelings that since they've left the party they can influence our leadership. They tried that when they were on the inside and they're not going to do it from the outside. He will remain leader, and let there be no misunderstanding for any member of the Dáil, the only alternative to Mr Haughey being leader and being Taoiseach is a general election."

On the day of the crucial Dáil vote Haughey repeated the same message to his front bench. Convinced that Tony Gregory would vote against him the Fianna Fáil leader called his front bench together and told them to prepare for an immediate election. He did this to ensure that there would be no attempt to put forward another Fianna Fáil nominee for Taoiseach, but even if the worst had happened he would not in any case have been in a position to call an election.

That was the prerogative of FitzGerald who would have continued as acting Taoiseach and who certainly had no intention of asking the President for an immediate dissolution. In the circumstances the President also had the right to refuse a dissolution to FitzGerald because he no longer commanded a majority in the House. The country lurched towards a constitutional crisis, but Haughey was determined, whatever the outcome, not to relinquish his leadership of Fianna Fáil and the chance of being Taoiseach again.

When the critical moment came Seán Treacy was elected Ceann Comhairle unopposed and Haughey scraped through by the bare minimum. Blaney voted for him and Gregory abstained, leaving the vote tied 82-82. Treacy then gave his casting vote in favour of Haughey and he was Taoiseach again.

Now in office for the third time, Haughey had promised good government with no deals, but going on his record there was a great deal of scepticism about this pledge. During the election campaign he had refrained from rash promises and he had accepted the outgoing government's budget targets. But of course he had done the same in the election of 1982, so there was still a widespread feeling that he might launch another spending spree which would send the economy spiralling out of control. Twice before he had demonstrated a total inability to run the national finances – could he possibly do it third time round?

The opportunity he needed was created for Haughey by his long-term political adversary, Garret FitzGerald. Coming to the end of the election campaign, FitzGerald had come up with the interesting idea of creating an all-party economic forum along the lines of the New Ireland Forum in order to devise an economic strategy outside party politics which could get the country out of its economic mess. At that late stage in the campaign, when Haughey still believed that outright victory was within his grasp, he brusquely dismissed the idea saying it was the government's job to govern and to make economic decisions.

On the night of the election count when the indecisive nature of the result began to emerge, FitzGerald said on television that Fine Gael would support a Fianna Fáil government if it adopted the correct approach to the economy. This signal to Haughey that he would be supported by the main Opposition party if he adopted sensible economic policies was followed up the next day by Social Welfare Minister Gemma Hussey, who said that Fianna Fáil had "terrible problems but we have to make sure we do the right thing for the country".

So as the final results were coming in on Saturday, 21 February, the shape of a political consensus was emerging on economic policy. Haughey, however, gave no indication that he was paying attention to the signals. Instead of responding to Fine Gael overtures he announced a few days later that he was directing senior members of his party – Albert Reynolds, Bertie Ahern and Séamus Brennan – to hold urgent talks with the country's employers, trade unions and financial institutions, to establish the broadest possible consensus on the needs of the economy and to create the basis for his government's budget.

One of the few people who read the political situation correctly from the very beginning was former Labour leader Frank Cluskey.

Joining a group of journalists and politicians of all parties in the Dáil bar on the day after the final election result had been declared, Cluskey listened to the speculation that a new minority Haughey government would collapse in a matter of months. "Lads, you have got it all wrong. All Charlie has to do is to be twice as tough as Fine Gael and the PDs and they won't be able to touch him. If he keeps his nerve he can govern as long as he likes."

The logic of the Cluskey argument was impressive but his listeners were sceptical. In the realm of practical politics it was nearly impossible to believe that Haughey, having denounced spending cuts for the previous four years, could turn around and adopt more stringent financial policies than Fine Gael. On the other hand, out-Fine Gaeling Fine Gael might be his best chance of holding on to office and for the great survivor of Irish politics could anything be more important?

Election results 1981-1989

	Fianna Fail seats	%	Fine Gael seats	%	Labour Party seats	%	PDs seats	%	Workers Party seats	%	Others seats	%
1981	78	45.3%	65	36.5%	15	9.9%	–	–	1	1.7%	7	6.6%
1982	81	47.3%	63	37.3%	15	9.1%			3	2.3%	4	4%
1982	75	45.2%	70	39.2%	16	9.4%			2	3.3%	3	3%
1987	81	44.1%	51	27.1%	12	6.4%	14	11.8%	4	3.8%	4	6.7%
1989	77	44.1%	55	29.3%	15	9.5%	6	5.5%	7	5%	6	6.6%

9 – "Realising His Potential"

Charles Haughey was keenly aware in March 1987 that he had been given another chance to deliver on the political promise which had for so long remained unfulfilled. He took over as Taoiseach for the third time in the face of enormous economic and political problems but he regained the sure touch that had eluded him since the 1960s and it appeared as if the dark days of GUBU had been banished for ever.

Haughey now confounded his critics and began for the first time in almost twenty years to bask in the glow of media approval. Immediately after the election he gave an interview to the *Sunday Press* in which he promised there would be no deals with any of the fringe groups in order to get power. He also pledged that once elected Taoiseach he would move so fast to deal with the country's problems that nobody would be able to keep up with him.

Despite all his denunciations of public spending cuts, he had no difficulty in adjusting to the political reality that such policies could not be avoided for both economic and political reasons.

Since he depended on support from other parties in the Dáil, there was a clear logic in adopting Fine Gael and PD policies because that was the obvious way to stay in power. After all, how could they bring Haughey down if he implemented the policies they had been preaching for so long? Garret FitzGerald recognised this on the night of his election defeat by promising not to bring Haughey down if he adopted responsible i.e. Fine Gael policies.

There was more to it on Haughey's part, however, than a cynical manoeuvre to stay in power. What the voters didn't know, because Haughey was afraid to risk telling them, was that he had undergone a fundamental change of opinion on economic issues in the middle of 1986. Despite his public condemnation of the coalition as being heartless and monetarist, Haughey had already travelled the road to Damascus as regards economic policy. Even though he still complained about economists and dismissed them as practitioners of the "dismal science", he consulted the leading lights of the profession in the summer of 1986. Joe Durkan and Colm McCarthy were among the top economists who were asked to give Haughey their frank advice. In his round of meetings with economists and financiers the Taoiseach had lunch with the leading lights of National City Brokers. Over lunch the Fianna Fáil leader struck up a rapport with the company's boss Dermot Desmond and so began a friendship which in the long term was to have serious consequences for Haughey but in the short term helped him develop the confidence to face up to economic realities.

Colm McCarthy was contacted on Haughey's behalf by an old school friend of his P.J. Mara, and invited to meet the Fianna Fáil leader in his Kinsealy home. Haughey asked McCarthy what he should do and the economist jokingly told him to make sure he did not win the next election because the country was beyond redemption. After a few meetings with McCarthy and other economists, each of whom wrote a short paper for him on the national finances, Haughey came to the conclusion that he would have to introduce much tougher policies than those being pursued by the FitzGerald government. He realised the public finances were in a mess and that the first move towards putting the economy back on the road would involve getting to grips with the enormous national debt.

The Fianna Fáil party and the public were not let in on this insight, though there were some pointers that he was in the process of changing direction. In September 1986 at the Fianna Fáil selection convention for the Kildare constituency Haughey told journalists that he would not be making any promises in the next election campaign. He said that Fianna Fáil would simply be offering "good government" to the people and would hope to get elected on that basis.

The appointment of Ray MacSharry as Minister for Finance was a clear signal that tough decisions were about to be made on the economy and this was noted at the time. "The fact that Charles Haughey appointed MacSharry to the Department of Finance in the first place was itself a sure indication that he meant business this time," said an editorial in the *Sunday Tribune* after the government's first budget.

MacSharry, who had opted out of Irish politics to a large extent, preferring to concentrate on the European Parliament, came back as

The wedding of Charles Haughey and Maureen Lemass 1951

Above: Budget day 1969

Left: The Haughey style – riding to hounds 1970

Above: Haughey with friend and election agent Pat O'Connor
during the Arms trial

Below: Arms trial 1970. Haughey outside the Bridewell

Above: Abbeyville, Kinsealy. The eighteenth-century Gandon mansion which has been the Haughey home since 1969

Below: The front bench – outside Leinster House mid-1970s

Charles Haughey, the day he became party leader
Front row: Ben Briscoe and Michael Woods.
Back Row: Séamus Brennan, Vincent Brady, Joe Dowling
Seán Doherty, Sile de Valera, Eileen Lemass

Above: First Cabinet. *Back row, left to right*: Paddy Power, Albert Reynolds, Gene Fitzgerald, Michael Woods, Ray MacSharry, Sylvie Barrett, Michael O'Kennedy, John Wilson. *Front row*: Des O'Malley, Brian Lenihan, George Colley, Charles Haughey, Máire Geoghegan-Quinn, Pádraig Faulkner, Gerry Collins

Above: Thanks for your support! Campaigning in Cavan with John Wilson in 1981

Opposite below: The Haugheys at the All-Ireland Final

Above: With Michael Smurfit, then chairman of Telecom Eireann

Opposite above: At the helm of his boat in Kerry

Opposite below: With Miss Ireland, Siobhan McClafferty

Above: Proud father. Taoiseach with Lord Mayor Seán Haughey 1990

Opposite above: Return of straying eagle "Iolar" to his American homeland

Opposite below: Rise and follow Charlie. With Brian Lenihan at the Ard Fheis in the spring of 1989

Above: With German Chancellor Helmut Kohl during Ireland's
EC presidency 1990

Opposite above: Speaking to the party faithful at the 1991 Ard Fheis

Opposite below: Rome 1990. Acknowledging the Irish supporters
after the World Cup quarter-final with Italy

Above: With Albert Reynolds at the launch of the Fianna Fáil-Progressive
Democrats Programme for Government, October 1991
Below: O'Malley and Haughey, partners in coalition

November 1991 Cabinet. *Back row, left to right*: Harry Whelehan,
Brendan Daly, Séamus Brennan, Ray Burke, Mary O'Rourke,
Michael Woods, Rory O'Hanlon, Vincent Brady, Noel Davern
Front row: Bertie Ahern, Michael O'Kennedy, John Wilson,
C.J.Haughey, Gerry Collins, Des O'Malley, Bobby Molloy

Responding to Seán Doherty's phone-tapping allegations. Press conference of 22 January 1992

Minister for Finance, the portfolio he had held in 1982. That experience in government had been an unfortunate one for him as it ended with the controversy over his taping of a conversation with Martin O'Donoghue, but it educated him as to the realities of the country's economic situation. MacSharry learned fast. Coming into office now he first declared that "boom and bloom" would replace "doom and gloom" but he quickly changed his tune.

Once he was properly briefed by departmental officials he tried to get to grips with the financial crisis. Though he engendered controversy by deferring public pay awards, he was on the right track. The publication of *The Way Forward* as the programme for government marked out the correct approach for the years ahead but the government fell almost immediately and in Opposition Haughey reversed engines and took the diametrically opposite approach. MacSharry's decision to run for Europe and limit his involvement in local politics was in some respects due to his unwillingness to get involved in this *volte face*.

His recall by Haughey to the Finance portfolio was to have a very significant political effect. It clearly indicated to the social partners and the Opposition parties where the government was headed. MacSharry's own personality, his dourness and doggedness, also played a crucial role in what was to happen. As a politician he had never displayed the affable, easygoing approach that is part of the stock-in-trade of most TDs. If anything he was defensive and suspicious and never tried to court popularity in the usual political manner.

"Dour, dark and brooding Ray" was how one ministerial colleague described him, but it was his very dourness and his refusal to be worried by criticism from any quarter which was to prove essential for the task he had been given. Another feature of his personality was that, unlike most members of the Cabinet, he was not intimidated by Haughey. In fact Haughey was more than a little wary of him.

"There was something odd in the relationship between MacSharry and Haughey. The Taoiseach often appeared fearful that he might lose face by refusing to accept some of the more drastic measures suggested by Ray and I think he sometimes only agreed to things for that reason," says one Cabinet minister. Whatever the chemistry, Haughey and MacSharry complemented each other.

The other key minister in the economic area was Albert Reynolds at Industry and Commerce. With his background in business and an outgoing affable personality, he was the ideal counterpoint to Mac-Sharry.

Both men had been instrumental in helping Haughey to win the leadership in 1979 and had stuck by him through all the heaves. Like the Taoiseach they were acutely conscious of the failures of their two previous terms of office and they were determined to get it right this time. They made up the core of the informal economic sub committee of the Cabinet which decided early on to keep the pressure on the country's financial problems through a whole range of measures like the public service redundancy scheme, privatisation and cutbacks in health and education.

One other individual who played a key role in the formulation of government policy was Padraig O hUiginn, Secretary of the Department of the Taoiseach. His central role in getting the country's trade unions to agree a three-year deal with the government was vital, as it provided the other prong of government policy. When Haughey returned to power in 1987 he began to rely more and more on O hUiginn and the relationship became a very fruitful one to the benefit of the government.

Born in Cork in 1924, O hUiginn was just a year older than Haughey, and at the age of sixty-three had had a very varied and distinguished career behind him when the government changed in March 1987. It had been a very unusual career for an Irish civil servant. After a brilliant university career in UCD and the University of Edinburgh, which he left with a master's degree in economic and social planning, he joined the civil service but did not make his way up the promotions ladder in the normal way. Assigned to the Department of the Environment, or Local Government as it was known in the late 1950s and early 1960s, he worked on the establishment of An Foras Forbartha and then left the Department to become the institute's first chief executive.

Having served as chief executive of An Foras for nine years, he left for a post as economic affairs officer with the Economic Commission for Europe in Geneva. He then moved to Brussels as a director of regional policy with the European Community before going to the United Nations when he was in charge of housing, building and planning at the headquarters in New York.

He came back to the Irish civil service by way of Martin O'Donoghue's ill-fated Department of Economic Planning and Development in the late 1970s. But it was when that department was abolished and amalgamated with the Taoiseach's Department, on Haughey's accession in 1979, that O hUiginn first came to the Taoiseach's attention.

As an assistant secretary in the Taoiseach's Department, O hUiginn's skills as somebody who could get things done quickly won him Haughey's confidence. He was involved at the Taoiseach's request in settling a number of potential public service disputes with teachers, nurses and Gardaí. There was a lot of criticism then and later at the lavish pay rises awarded to settle these disputes, but it was the Talbot deal, also put together by O hUiginn and which guaranteed redundant workers their pay packets for life, that came under sustained criticism from Opposition politicians and economic commentators.

O hUiginn took over as Secretary of the Taoiseach's Department in June 1982 but Haughey's doomed government didn't make it to the end of the year. O hUiginn was the main author of *The Way Forward* which became Fianna Fáil's election manifesto in November 1982. Because of that, and his association with some of Haughey's earlier policies, FitzGerald never trusted him and he was effectively sidelined during the lifetime of the Fine Gael-Labour coalition. The Fine Gael leader relied instead on Dermot Nally, the Cabinet Secretary, as his top civil servant.

O hUiginn did perform one important task during the period of the coalition when he persuaded the social partners to agree through the forum of the National Economic and Social Council on a programme for future economic development. Because of the poor relationship between that government and the trade unions the idea never got off the ground but it was something which Haughey was to capitalise on when he took over.

With Haughey back in office in 1987, O hUiginn came into his own and the two men quickly established a very close partnership. He partly filled the place formerly occupied by Pádraig O hAnnracháin, who had died two years earlier, as Haughey's close political confidant and advisor.

"The key to O hUiginn's influence is that he is psychologically attuned to Charlie's mode of operation. Even though he is a civil servant he has an instinctive grasp of the politics of any given situation and that's why he gets on so well with Haughey," said a senior trade unionist who negotiated with them both at the time. "In the beginning we were astonished at O hUiginn's style of negotiation. We discovered that he didn't give a damn for official Departmental policy, he simply wanted to find solutions to problems and we often found him siding with us against the other civil servants involved in negotiations."

It was this ability to go straight for solutions without any posturing or moralising which led to O hUiginn's reputation as a fixer *par excellence* and won him the admiration of Haughey among others. The partnership with the Taoiseach flourished and ministers quickly came to realise that getting O hUiginn's approval for their plans was the essential prerequisite to getting Haughey's approval.

"Padraig is the single most powerful civil servant in the country and apart from the Taoiseach and the Minister for Finance nobody, including the rest of the Cabinet, has as much influence as he over the course of government policy," commented one senior civil servant in 1989. Despite his powerful position O hUiginn regularly queued for his lunch in the self-service restaurant of Leinster House and chatted amiably with whoever happened to be seated near him at the table. In fact many people who met him were unaware of his position and presumed that he was a junior Dáil official.

O hUiginn was not regarded uncritically by everybody and there was a great deal of suspicion about him in the senior ranks of the civil service, particularly in Finance where some officials believed that his talents as a fixer often took too little account of the state of the national finances. "O hUiginn's longterm view on any issue never extended more than two weeks," said one Finance official dismissively.

Another factor which made Haughey's government of 1987 to

1989 very different from his previous stints in office was his relations with the media. Mutual suspicion is a polite way of describing relations during the 1979 to 1983 period. During Fianna Fáil's term in Opposition the hostility began to die down following P.J. Mara's arrival on the scene, and by the time Haughey returned to office in 1987 there was something resembling a normal relationship in operation.

While Haughey never, ever, came to trust the media, he gradually established a cordial if aloof relationship after his resumption to power. The development of an easy rapport between Mara and the political correspondents was an essential base for the more benign image of Haughey that began to emerge in the media. Mara didn't allow his new status as Government Press Secretary to cramp his style and he continued to entertain the media with his fund of political anecdotes and ready wit. But it took a little time for the civil service to come to terms with Mara and while attending his first EC summit in Brussels he sent the diplomats into a tizzy with an off-the-cuff remark. Giving an impromptu briefing to Irish journalists about the course of the summit in the Brussels press centre, Mara was quickly surrounded by members of the foreign media, desperate for morsels of information about what was going on at the meeting of the Twelve where Margaret Thatcher was, as usual, at loggerheads with the other eleven leaders. "How would you sum it up at this stage?" Mara was asked by a foreign reporter.

"It's Maggie against the Universe," he replied and thought no more about it. Twenty minutes later the Reuters news service put a new lead on its story out of Brussels, quoting an Irish government official as saying "It's Maggie against the universe." Irish diplomats were horrified as they believed the British would take grave offence at such an off-hand reference to their Prime Minister. Mara was advised to go and apologise before the British raised the issue so he sought out Thatcher's press secretary, Bernard Ingham. He told Ingham he was afraid that he had made a gaffe and had come to clear up any misunderstanding. "What did you say then?" asked Ingham, but far from taking offence he laughed when Mara told him. "What's wrong with that?" he asked, not at all unhappy at the image of his battling Prime Minister.

At this, Haughey's first summit since returning to power, Margaret Thatcher made it clear to him that there was no possibility of starting off again on a new footing. At her post-summit press conference she was asked what the atmosphere at her meeting with Haughey was like. "What does it say in the communiqué? I think we worked it up to cordial, didn't we, Bernard?" she asked her press secretary. Haughey made no public reply when told of her dismissive attitude. He was more concerned with retaining his new high standing in domestic politics which wouldn't have been helped by a public row with Thatcher.

While Haughey never lost his deep-rooted suspicion of the media he enjoyed basking in the favourable coverage that began to develop. Early in his new term the Haughey personal style also underwent a change. Instead of snapping like a terrier in public in response to any criticism, he adopted what can only be described as an imperial approach. The Taoiseach appeared to regard himself as above any mere petty squabbling and both in the Dáil and in public adopted the pose of a benign father-of-the-nation figure.

In Cabinet too ministers noticed a big change in style since the 1979 to 1982 period. He no longer tried to meddle in everybody's department but accepted the more traditional role of Taoiseach, allowing ministers to get on with running their own departments. This is not to say that he was not in control of the government – he certainly was. Most of the ministers were still in awe of him and jumped when he made demands. Nonetheless it was a much healthier form of control than that exercised during his first two terms and it produced incomparably better government.

Of course all the best public relations in the world couldn't have boosted Haughey's image on their own. Far more important was that he began to demonstrate that he was serious about tackling the country's economic problems. His first major challenge was the 1987 budget and he got that crucial test right by accepting MacSharry's argument that the government should seize the initiative and make even deeper cuts than those planned by John Bruton. Once that was done the road ahead suddenly became easy.

"Charles Haughey may at last be about to realise the potential that many saw in him when he first became Taoiseach. For the sake of the country let's hope so," wrote the editor of the *Sunday Tribune*, summing up the general mood at that stage.

Announcing that budget to the Dáil on 31 March, MacSharry reflected the public mood. "It is evident that conditions are extremely difficult and that there is no room at all for soft options. On the contrary, it is in all our interests that the government follow a very strict discipline. There can be no concessions to interest groups and all sections of the community will have to bear some of the burden."

What the budget did was to cut spending across a range of areas particularly in the big spending departments of Health, Social Welfare and Education. The enormity of the public service pay bill was tackled by a total embargo on new appointments. MacSharry cut Bruton's target of an exchequer borrowing requirement from 11.7 percent of gross national product to 10.7 percent, or in money terms from £2,028 million to £1,858 million. It was a bold move which took the Opposition's breath away.

"I have great pleasure today in welcoming Fianna Fáil's acceptance of the Fine Gael analysis of the problem and of the targets which we have set down," Fine Gael's Finance spokesman Michael Noonan couldn't resist remarking. He went on: "This is grand larceny of our policy as put before the electorate. The road to Aras an Uachtaráin will now take precedence over the road to Damascus. We had fifteen on the road to Aras an Uachtaráin."

Noonan bemoaned the fact that Fianna Fáil, in the Dáil session preceding the election, had put down thirteen motions, each of which involved irresponsible extra public spending. After a few ritual swipes at the government, Noonan pledged that his party would mark Fianna Fáil to ensure that they stayed on the new-found road of fiscal rectitude though he expressed doubts about whether they would be able to last the pace.

Michael McDowell, the PD Finance spokesman, took a different tack. "I find it remarkable that somebody could be so abusive and scornful when on the Fianna Fáil benches we now see a change of heart of a very substantial kind which has been made in the interests of the country at large. Everyone should have the generosity to accept it. It ill befits people behind him in his party to forget that when people choose to do the right thing, albeit at the eleventh hour, they deserve support for it and not derision."

On the night of the 1987 budget both Fine Gael and the PDs abstained on the vote leaving only the left-wing parties to oppose the financial resolutions which gave it effect. It was the first time in modern Irish politics that a government had been allowed to get its budget through the Dáil without being opposed by the major Opposition parties.

The way Fine Gael and the PDs behaved on that vote testified that a sea change had come over political life and that the country was beginning a new era where, for a time at least, old style adversarial politics would be put to one side.

10 – An Bord Snip

Haughey had startled the Opposition with the boldness of the budget and much to the astonishment of most observers the strategy had put him in a very secure position in the Dáil, despite the government's minority position. As soon as the dust settled he wasted no time in beginning the process of formulating the following year's spending estimates for each Department which would underpin his budgetary strategy for 1988.

His old rival, Garret FitzGerald, took nearly everybody by surprise by announcing his decision to step down as Fine Gael leader on 11 March 1987, the day after Haughey was elected Taoiseach for the third time. FitzGerald's decision came as a shock because he had stoutly maintained in the immediate aftermath of the election that he had no intention of resigning.

One person who didn't appear to be surprised by the move was Alan Dukes. Within an hour of the resignation announcement he was canvassing support from Fine Gael TDs and senators in Leinster House. Ivan Yates, the young Wexford deputy, immediately took over as the Dukes campaign manager and he went to the political correspondents' room in Leinster House that day to tell them his man had it in the bag.

The fact that Dukes was so fast off the mark led to suspicions among his opponents that he had been aware of FitzGerald's intentions. Though the former Taoiseach did not take an active part in the campaign to elect his successor, and spent most of the ten-day interval between his resignation and the vote in the United States, he was widely regarded as giving his backing to Dukes. The other candidates for the leadership were Peter Barry, the deputy leader of the party, who received the support of most of the former Cabinet ministers, and two-time Finance Minister John Bruton, the last to declare.

The main support for Dukes came from the class of 1981 who had entered the Dáil with him after Garret FitzGerald's first campaign. Significantly though, Dukes had virtually no support among his former Cabinet colleagues.

There was some resentment among Dukes's opponents about the

fact that outgoing senators had a vote in the election. The TDs who voted were members of the twenty-fifth Dáil, but the senators were members of the parliamentary party by virtue of their election to the twenty-fourth Seanad which had now been dissolved with a new election in progress. A key factor was that the old Seanad had a number of Taoiseach's appointees who would not be in the new Seanad but had a vote in the leadership election. Supporters of Barry and Bruton felt that some of FitzGerald's Seanad appointees, who were clearly in the Dukes camp, had no real right to vote in the election.

As it turned out every single vote counted. In a bizarre decision the party decided that the number of votes received by each candidate would be kept secret and that only the name of the winner would be announced. The votes were counted by Garret FitzGerald and Kieran Crotty, the chairman of the parliamentary party. They are the only people who really know what happened but it is generally accepted that on the first count Dukes came first, Bruton was second and Barry was third.

As Dukes hadn't reached the quota, Barry was eliminated and his second preferences distributed. There is a dispute also about what happened next. Bruton is convinced that on the second count he drew level with Dukes. FitzGerald denies this but Crotty has remained silent and there are a number of people in the party who are convinced that Bruton is right and that the vote was tied on the second count. If that happened then Dukes was declared the winner on the basis that he had more first-preference votes.

One way or another the decision was extremely tight, but Dukes emerged as the winner. It was an extraordinary achievement for a man less than six years in the Dáil at that stage to have taken over the leadership of the second largest political party in the country.

It was even more extraordinary considering that Dukes was such an enigmatic figure. He was often described in the media as cold and bureaucratic but that doesn't really capture the nature of the man. The impression he created on associates was not simply one of coldness, but that he appeared to lack an emotional dimension. Most of his frontbench colleagues were never able to figure him out and could not establish even the semblance of rapport with him.

Very tall, and thin as a bean pole, Dukes was a chain-smoker whose emphasis was on logical argument rather than rhetoric. Born in 1945, he was reared in Drimnagh and Ballymun in Dublin and attended the Irish-speaking Christian Brothers school of Coláiste Mhuire before going to UCD to study economics. His background as an economist with the Irish Farmers Association in Brussels and later with the European Commission prepared him for a career as a top-flight administrator rather than as a politician.

There were uncanny resemblances between Haughey and Dukes on a number of points. Both were reared in Dublin and, while not poor, did not come from the fashionable parts of the city. Both were educated by the Christian Brothers and had gone to UCD and both had carved out powerful positions for themselves without the aid of family connections. Both had taken over their parties against the wishes of the party establishment and they had cultivated the back-benchers as the road to power. There were many in Fine Gael who believed that Dukes modelled his strategy for winning the leadership on Haughey's example and they were soon to complain that he tried to run the party in the same dictatorial fashion that Haughey ran Fianna Fáil. A dislike of the media was another thing he had in common with Haughey.

As Dukes tried to get to grips with the role of party leader, Haughey was revelling in his third term as Taoiseach. Having begun by cutting public spending he was determined to continue the process and in May he circulated a letter to all government departments spelling out in clear language the kind of cutbacks he wanted for 1988. The letter was aimed not just at the ministers, who already knew what he wanted, but at the senior civil servants in each Department who traditionally sought to squeeze extra money out of the Exchequer each year regardless of the overall financial position of the State.

Traditionally ministers had taken on board the concerns of their senior civil servants and at Cabinet adopted a stance of special pleading for their Department rather than focusing on wider concerns. The success or failure of individual ministers had come to be judged on the basis of what they managed to achieve for their own Departments regardless of the consequences for the Exchequer. Haughey sought to break this attitude decisively with the letter he circulated on 13 May 1987. The letter is worth quoting in full because it set down the philosophy underlying his administration between 1987 and 1989.

"It is imperative that we carry further the progress we have made so far this year in getting public expenditure under control. Unless we achieve further significant cuts in expenditure the growth in public sector debt will continue to be a burden on the economy, inhibiting economic growth and employment and making it impossible for us to get development underway.

"We must begin to identify the specific programmes and expenditures for further cuts now if we want to get results for the remainder of 1987 and 1988.

"I am anxious to get this process underway as soon as possible. I therefore ask you to submit to me, and to the Minister for Finance, a paper by Friday, May 22, at the latest, identifying the proposed reductions to expenditure. The proposals must have the effect of achieving a significant reduction on your Department's present level of spending. They may cover capital as well as current expenditure.

"Your paper should state whether legislation, or other important preparatory steps, would be required in order to bring them into effect, and the timetable you would envisage in taking these steps. It should also cost the proposals made, showing the possible long term as well as 1987 and 1988 savings.

"In arriving at your proposals all options should be considered, including the elimination or reduction of particular schemes and programmes, rooting out overlaps and duplications between organisations, the merger of organisations, the closure of institutions which may have outlived their usefulness, the scaling down of the operations of organisations and institutions and the disposal of physical assets which are no longer productively used. A radical approach should be adopted and no expenditure should be regarded as sacrosanct and immune to elimination or reduction. We do not want a series of justifications of the status quo or special pleadings.

"I am depending on you to make it clear to officials that their full cooperation in and commitment to this exercise is required and that the government expect worthwhile results to emerge.

"Following May 22 the Secretary, Department of Finance, will head a team of Finance officials to meet each Accounting Officer to review each group of votes to identify the savings that can be made. The proposals identified will come before government for decision. The timetable I want to hold to is that these decisions be made on a weekly basis from end-May, and that we be in a position to have the full programme of reductions agreed by end August-early September."

The Haughey letter was leaked to the media by the Worker's Party and published in the national newspapers on 22 May, the day when ministers were due to deliver their proposals for cuts to the Taoiseach. The Workers' Party was rumoured to have some senior civil servants in its ranks in one of the secret branches of the party. If they wished to thwart further cuts the plan backfired because Haughey now felt himself publicly committed to the policy outlined in the letter and he was determined to live up to it.

Another pivotal development in getting economic strategy right was the establishment of the Expenditure Review Committee, which became known as An Bord Snip. On the committee were the Secretary of the Department of Finance, Seán Cromien, an assistant secretary of the Department, Bob Curran, and independent economist Colm McCarthy. Among civil servants the committee was likened to a Star Chamber because each Department in turn was called in to justify every item of expenditure proposed for the following year.

This committee put strong pressure on departmental officials to come up with ideas for spending cuts and it also came up with its own range of suggestions for cuts. The committee drafted a number of memorandums which were presented to the Cabinet in the name of the Minister for Finance.

The key factor which gave the committee such influence was not that the range of cuts it suggested was particularly clever or original, but that the political will was now there to implement its proposals.

"The vital thing was that MacSharry was prepared to back the committee to the hilt and insist that his Cabinet colleagues bite the bullet in relation to the suggested cuts," said one senior official who observed the process.

In fact many of the suggestions for spending cuts had been circulating in the Department of Finance for a number of years and had been presented as options year after year only to be turned down by the Cabinet. This menu of cuts had become known among coalition ministers as "The Asgard List" because the scrapping of the sail training vessel *Asgard* was a recurring item on the Finance agenda. Now, though, former Fine Gael and Labour ministers were astonished to see cuts they had rejected as being politically impossible to implement being recycled by Haughey's government. Not alone that but the government was able to get away with them with the minimum of political flak.

In the few months after the MacSharry budget, Dukes adhered to FitzGerald's policy of offering support to the government. It quickly became clear that Fine Gael were prepared to support the government in a much more positive way than the PDs. A variety of measures including the health estimates for the year were passed through the Dáil by huge majorities. Most of the disgruntlement at the cuts came from the Fianna Fáil backbenches whose TDs had not been prepared in advance for the scale of the U-turn. Despite the grumbling the government kept its TDs in line and backed down on issues such as the immediate abolition of housing grants where it seemed that they might run into real political difficulty.

The Supreme Court created one political difficulty when it found the Single European Act, clearing the way for closer integration in the European Community, to be unconstitutional. Fianna Fáil had been severely critical of the Act when it was passed through the Dáil six months earlier but the party now had the embarrassing task of spearheading the referendum campaign in its favour. But another U-turn, in a year of U-turns, did not prove too embarrassing because the government just knuckled down and along with Fine Gael and the PDs urged a vote in favour and the electorate duly obliged.

It was in the Dáil, though, that the transformation of Irish politics was most obvious. On division after division Fine Gael were prepared to troop through the lobbies with Fianna Fáil or at the very least to abstain. The PDs sometimes voted with the government or more often abstained but they were much more critical of government policy than the main Opposition party. Des O'Malley needled Haughey regularly in the Dáil and stuck much more closely to old-style adversarial politics than Dukes, even if the PDs often ended up on the same side in the division lobbies. As a result a great deal of tension in the relationship between Fine Gael and the PDs developed in the early months of the twenty-fifth Dáil. Dukes had declared his intention of targeting the PDs and the smaller party responded in turn by trying to embarrass Fine Gael at every opportunity.

In the Dáil this meant that O'Malley regularly tried and succeeded in upstaging Dukes. His much greater experience gave O'Malley the edge in Dáil exchanges and he found it easier to score points against both the government and Fine Gael. The old needle between Haughey and O'Malley added spice to the exchanges and the Taoiseach did not try to conceal his contempt for the PDs, whom he generally referred to as "that party". With Dick Spring also beginning to find his feet as an Opposition leader, Dukes found himself squeezed as he attempted to carve out a role in the Dáil. Everybody found something strange in the fact that a minority government was regularly able to command majorities of more than a hundred in Dáil divisions. TDs on all sides of the House were puzzled by what was going on. Fianna Fáil backbenchers had not expected to be implementing public spending cuts even more severe than those of the Fine Gael-Labour coalition and the last thing Fine Gael TDs ever expected was to end up supporting a government led by Charles Haughey.

Garret FitzGerald, now a backbencher, summed up the political situation well. "There seemed to be two Fianna Fáil parties. Fianna Fáil in Opposition and Fianna Fáil in government and any resemblance between them has become totally coincidental; in fact not only coincidental but almost unfindable at this stage."

In June 1987, a little over three months after his election as party leader, Alan Dukes responded to internal criticism of his Dáil tactics by attempting a more macho line. With the cuts in the health service proving to be a major liability for the government the Fine Gael front bench decided that in the absence of some Labour TDs who were abroad it could try a little sabre-rattling. The party front bench decided to try and capitalise on public hostility to the scale of the cuts by voting against the government's health estimate. Even though John Bruton argued strongly against the move it was adopted by his colleagues.

Because of poor tactics the decision was announced too early and Haughey threatened Fine Gael with an election. A terrified Fine Gael front bench met and instructed Dukes to find a way out.

On the morning of the crucial vote Dukes met his parliamentary party to get their backing for a climbdown. His TDs were seething with anger and frustration but they didn't want an election, so Dukes was given a mandate to meet the Taoiseach to try and resolve the problem.

Dukes negotiated a climbdown with Haughey but the incident so traumatised Fine Gael that the front bench decided such an event could never be allowed to happen again. Before the Dáil summer recess there were intensive discussions at the top level of the party about formulating a strategy which would enable them to indicate support publicly for the government as long as Fianna Fáil kept to certain broad lines of economic policy.

Meanwhile, having set the mechanisms in place for coming up with ideas for significant public spending cuts, Haughey then opened talks with the Irish Congress of Trade Unions, the employers and the farming bodies for a new national agreement to cover the next three years. The trade unions were the key to the deal as control of public service pay was a vital requirement for the government if it wished to keep inflation down and begin to get borrowing under control.

Any other government would have found it difficult, if not impossible, to proceed with two apparently contradictory policies at the same time. One that involved huge cuts in public spending and the other that involved doing a deal with the trade unions designed effectively to tie them into the process of government. Haughey managed to follow both these roads simultaneously.

His overriding concern in the talks with the unions was to get a national pay deal. He started off with the great advantage that the trade union leaders liked him. They had fought bitterly with the Fine Gael-Labour government because they perceived Labour to be an arm of the union movement rather than a party in government and could never establish a proper working relationship with the coalition.

Haughey, on the other hand, in his first term of office, had been generous, far too generous for the national good, but generous nonetheless in his dealings with the unions. What impressed the union leaders was that the Taoiseach did not treat them condescendingly or lecture them about the morality or lack of it in relation to their demands. He dealt with them on a purely pragmatic basis and tried to find a *modus vivendi*.

The government had a number of things going for it. For a start the unions, having witnessed how Thatcher had destroyed the trade union movement's power and influence in Britain, were desperately looking for a way of avoiding a similar fate in Ireland. The sour relations with the previous government meant that Fine Gael and even Labour were distinctly unsympathetic to the unions' position. The rise of the Progressive Democrats on a platform which emphasised the necessity for tax cuts to go hand-in-hand with public spending cuts had frightened them and they could see a strong anti union drift developing in Irish life. In contrast Haughey offered the union leaders a lifeline, one which would recognise their importance in society and involve them in decision-making at the highest level, if they agreed to accept moderate pay increases for their members.

"Haughey just mesmerises them," said a Labour politician, appalled at the way the unions responded to the Taoiseach. "When we were in office they wouldn't forgive us for not delivering everything they wanted and they just didn't take us seriously. They seem to regard Fianna Fáil as the real party of government and are prepared to deal with them in a way they would never deal with us," he added disconsolately.

While Ray MacSharry and Albert Reynolds were also involved in the talks, the other minister, apart from the Taoiseach, who did most to bring the process to a successful conclusion in the autumn of 1987 was Bertie Ahern, Minister for Labour. Newly promoted to the Cabinet, having served the party well as chief whip during the three leadership heaves, his low-key conciliatory approach was suited to the delicate task and he quickly impressed the union leaders as a man they could do business with.

Padraig O hUiginn, the Secretary of the Department, also came into his own in the negotiations. He had got the social partners to agree to the NESC report on the future of the economy during the coalition's term of office and now he brought all his skills into play to keep talks on a national programme between the social partners going, despite all the publicity surrounding the government's programme of public spending cuts.

Haughey pursued the two prongs of his policy in tandem and had no compunction about reassuring the unions from time to time by uttering public denials that huge cutbacks in public spending were planned. Meanwhile his ministers devised plans for major cutbacks while O hUiginn and Ahern hammered out a deal with the unions.

It was that deal, which become known as the Programme for National Recovery, that was the first to be agreed on 9 October. The programme involved the government agreeing with all the social partners – unions, employers and farmers – on a range of targets for the economy over the following three years. The nub of the programme was an agreement with the unions on a public service pay deal which pinned back wage increases to just 2.5 percent per year for three years and deferred a range of special pay awards which were in the pipeline. The government was delighted with the deal and while the Opposition parties complained, there was broad public consensus in its support.

Having got the deal with the unions out of the way the government was in a position to publish its spending estimates for the following year and this took place five days later. The Book of Estimates for 1988 contained massive spending cuts of £485 million. Far from damaging Haughey, cuts on this scale only underlined his serious intent in dealing with the problem of the national finances and there was a broad welcome for the measures. Part of the package was a public service voluntary redundancy scheme. Such a plan would have met fierce resistance from the unions during the lifetime of the FitzGerald government but they meekly acquiesced in the plan. With the unions tied down on the one hand and a firm economic policy agreed by the government on the other, all Haughey needed was the political stability to implement both programmes and by October 1987 that too had been organised.

11 – The Tallaght Strategy

By the time the huge cuts were announced in October 1987, Charles Haughey was in a stronger position that any Taoiseach in the history of the state. That position stemmed from an initiative by Fine Gael leader Alan Dukes, which became known as the Tallaght Strategy. The strategy was an attempt to formalise the position that had developed in the Dáil since the February 1987 election and gave the Fianna Fáil minority government an assurance of support as long as it pursued "responsible" economic policies.

The Dukes initiative, which was launched on 2 September, marked a fundamental change in Irish politics. Here was the leader of the main Opposition party promising to support the government, rather than trying to hound it out of office as had always been the practice in the past.

Of course there were sound political reasons why Dukes wanted to keep Fianna Fáil in office and avoid a general election in the autumn of 1987, but the formal announcement that he was prepared to support the government caused astonishment all round, not least in his own party.

While he prepared the media for the event, through a series of lunches with newspaper editors during the summer, Dukes did nothing of the kind in relation to his own front bench who had known of his ideas in a very loose way only and were totally unprepared for the launch of a formal plan. To the backbenchers, who had been given no warning of the new approach, it came as a massive shock, and many of them had serious misgivings about the policy.

The announcement also came as a shock to the Progressive Democrats as some of that party's TDs had been toying with the idea of a similar announcement themselves. Younger deputies, like Mary Harney and Geraldine Kennedy, believed they had missed a golden opportunity by not getting in first with their own "Tallaght Strategy" and they felt that they were in danger of being marginalised by Fine Gael's move. After all, the PDs had been established as the party of fiscal rectitude, committed to breaking the mould of Irish politics.

Fianna Fáil deputies were also astounded at the Tallaght Strategy.

It was not politics as they knew it, but the strategy would keep them in government for the foreseeable future, so they had nothing to complain about.

The warm reaction from the media to the new Fine Gael approach, with editorial writers expressing the view that it was a noble policy in the national interest, helped to sell the plan to the reluctant TDs but there was deep-rooted unhappiness all the same. The public reaction, going on the next opinion poll results, was neutral, with little change in support for Fine Gael. The government's support went up in that poll and that was before the successful conclusion of the negotiations with the social partners and the publication of the swingeing cuts in the Book of Estimates.

One way or another the Tallaght Strategy marked a fundamental change in Irish political life. As time went on it became apparent that the strategy was mainly "give" on Fine Gael's part and mostly "take" on Fianna Fáil's, but the change it brought in Irish politics was profound.

The working of the strategy was not tested until the Dáil resumed in October 1987 and it took all the political parties some time to find their balance in the new situation. The day-to-day operation of the strategy fell to the government chief whip, Vincent Brady, and his Fine Gael counterpart, Fergus O'Brien.

The business of the Dáil is arranged by the government of the day through its chief whip who consults with the whips of the other parties about the scheduling of legislation and the timing and duration of debates. As a result of the Tallaght Strategy, Fianna Fáil and Fine Gael consulted each other first to iron out any difficulties. Brady and O'Brien met a few times a week to arrange Dáil business and then presented a united front to the other whips at the official meetings. The PDs and Labour became increasingly angry at what they regarded as collusion between the two big parties to arrange business behind their backs, but there was nothing they could do except kick up a rumpus in the Dáil.

The business of the House was arranged between Brady and O'Brien to minimise the friction between Fianna Fáil and Fine Gael. If Fine Gael had problems with legislation, O'Brien arranged for the party spokesperson to have a meeting with the relevant minister and amendments to various Bills were agreed in this way. Finance Minister Ray MacSharry held many such meetings with his Fine Gael counterpart, Michael Noonan, to head off potential trouble. The Dáil now became a very different institution to what it had been before. Between the two big parties there was now a spirit of close cooperation which led to the smooth operation of the House.

It was not all plain sailing however. While problems between the two parties over legislation could be patched up by a few amendments, there was still the problem of private members' time in the Dáil. This is the slot every week where the Opposition parties are entitled to put down either a motion of their own or to introduce a private members' Bill. In the past this time had always been used by the Opposition to embarrass the government and Fianna Fáil used it unmercifully when Fine Gael were in power with Labour.

After the first few months of the new Dáil, when private members' time rotated equally among Fine Gael, the PDs and Labour, Dukes moved to change the system to reflect the proportionally greater number of Fine Gael TDs than the PDs and Labour put together. By agreement with Fianna Fáil, to the accompaniment of outraged howls from all the smaller parties, the system was changed so that Fine Gael got much more private members' time and the other two parties much less.

Because of the Tallaght Strategy Fine Gael did everything possible to avoid embarrassing the minority government through a Dáil defeat. This took some delicate footwork on private members' time motions because if all the Opposition parties joined forces on a vote, Fianna Fáil faced inevitable defeat. In order to avoid this, Fine Gael tried to devise private members' motions which would be unacceptable to Labour or to the Workers' Party and yet be critical of the government. This was achieved by including references to privatisation or the need to keep public spending in check.

While Fine Gael could control its own Dáil motions it had to face the problem of dealing with the motions put forward by the PDs and Labour. Usually the solution involved putting down amendments which would be unacceptable to the left-wing parties. This regularly ensured a split vote by the Opposition parties and let the government off the hook.

A crisis did arise on a Fine Gael private members' motion at the end of November which called for a rejection of the controversial education cutbacks contained in circular 20/87 issued by the Minister for Education, Mary O'Rourke. The circular aimed at saving money by reducing the number of national teachers in the country and increasing the pupil-teacher ratio. There were street demonstrations by teachers and parents and a very well organised campaign by the Irish National Teachers' Organisation against the plan.

The Fine Gael motion was ambiguous and the other Opposition parties put down their own amendments to make it stronger. It appeared that this would save Fine Gael the embarrassment of defeating the government as all the Opposition groups would go their separate ways. The government blundered, though, by putting down its own amendment supporting the controversial educational policy. As the government amendment would be voted on first, all the Opposition parties, whatever their differences, would be united in rejecting the government's stance.

In the face of this problem and the storm of opposition from teachers, O'Rourke came up with a compromise formula. A Quota Review Committee would be set up to examine the effects of the cuts and ensure that disadvantaged areas did not suffer. The minister annoyed her colleagues by leaking the announcement of this committee before they had formally agreed to it, but after some recriminations at Cabinet it was decided to adopt it as the basis for a deal with Fine Gael on their Dáil motion. The Review Committee effectively involved the withdrawal of the controversial circular 20/87 though O'Rourke did not want to state this overtly. The committee had the power to issue guidelines on class sizes which meant that the government's plans to increase the pupil-teacher ratio had been modified considerably. Negotiations were carried on between Brady and O'Brien to find a formula which would allow Fine Gael to drop their Dáil motion.

Dukes felt himself put into an unnecessary corner by the government's amendment and he demanded a public commitment that the controversial circular would be withdrawn. After three meetings between the whips Haughey authorised Brady to give the commitment and Dukes was told that if he asked O'Rourke across the floor of the House that night if the circular was being withdrawn she would say yes. As far as O'Brien and Brady were concerned they had a deal.

The problem was that the Taoiseach did not spell it out to O'Rourke and he went off to attend a function in the RDS that night when the debate was due to wind up. In that debate Dukes dramatically announced that he was prepared to withdraw his motion on the basis of a commitment he had received that the circular was being withdrawn. He called on the minister to say yes to his assertion that the commitment had been given.

O'Rourke, clearly thrown into confusion, tried to fudge the issue but declined to give a clear yes or no answer to Dukes.

Brady, who was sitting behind her, wrote a note to his minister telling her to say yes to Dukes, but Ray MacSharry, who was sitting beside her, urged her strongly to say no. As Fianna Fáil TDs shifted about uneasily and Labour and PD deputies taunted Dukes with being in cahoots with Fianna Fáil, Dukes asked one last time if the minister would say yes to confirm the agreement. With MacSharry now clearly telling her not to respond she refused to give the commitment and Dukes announced that he would have no choice but to press ahead with his motion.

The result was that Fianna Fáil were defeated for the first time since taking office. While private members' motions are not binding, it has been a tradition in the Dáil that governments do not accept defeat lightly, and any defeat may cause a general election. Haughey was furious when he was informed but there was little he could do as he had created the muddle himself. He hadn't told O'Rourke that he expected her to concede without it appearing that he had backed down, but the strategy backfired.

The episode showed the vulnerability of the Tallaght Strategy. Dukes was almost equally embarrassed by the fact that the deal between the two parties had unravelled in public. The covert cooperation that had been going on between the two traditional enemies was exposed to view and neither of them liked it. From then on Dukes and

Haughey had regular meetings to sort out potential problems which might develop in the Dáil.

One problem that was raging even as the education cuts controversy blew up was the issue of extradition. As on so many other issues Haughey had to confront a problem of his own making because his attitude to extradition in Opposition was the direct opposite of what he was required to do in government. At the end of 1986 Haughey and Fianna Fáil had been instrumental in preventing the Fine Gael-Labour coalition from sorting out the extradition issue once and for all.

While the Supreme Court had already extradited a number of people by disallowing the political defence in certain terrorist cases, FitzGerald had agreed in the negotiations on the Anglo-Irish Agreement to put the system on a legislative basis by incorporating the European Convention on the Suppression of Terrorism into Irish law. The sustained Fianna Fáil objections and the reservations among some Labour TDs about extradition led to a compromise whereby the Extradition Bill was passed into law in December 1986 but with a stay of execution for a year.

This left Haughey in the unenviable position as a Fianna Fáil Taoiseach of having to preside over the introduction of the legislation. A carefully orchestrated campaign developed in the months before the deadline arrived in December 1987 and a number of Fianna Fáil backbenchers came under severe pressure on the issue. It became a much more contentious issue for Fianna Fáil TDs than any of the public spending cutbacks, the exact opposite of the public's perceived priorities.

With the pressure mounting on Fianna Fáil TDs, it appeared that Haughey would not be able to stand over the introduction of extradition. P.J. Mara, on Haughey's behalf, accused the British Ambassador, Nicholas Fenn, of over-zealous interference in local politics because of a briefing he gave to Peter Barry and Des O'Malley about the British position on extradition. It looked as if Haughey was preparing the ground to postpone ratification of the Extradition Bill. But the whole situation was changed utterly in early November.

In the early days of that month two of the most horrific terrorist outrages in the whole litany of violence since the trouble began shocked the nation. Dublin dentist John O'Grady, who had been kidnapped in October, was finally rescued by Gardaí on 5 November and it emerged that two of his fingers had been hacked off by his kidnappers in an effort to force his father-in-law, Austin Darragh, to pay a £1.5 million ransom. The kidnappers had threatened to cut up Dr O'Grady piece by piece until a ransom was paid and under this pressure Haughey agreed to let Darragh organise payment. Luckily the Gardaí captured the gang shortly before the transfer was to take place, but the brutality of the episode horrified the country.

Another horror followed three days later with the IRA bombing of the Remembrance Day ceremony in Enniskillen which left eleven people dead. The moving account of the explosion by Gordon Wilson, whose daughter Marie died in the blast, had a profound impact on the whole country.

As these two events came only days after an IRA arms shipment from Libya was captured on board the *Exund* off the coast of France, and it emerged that over £20 million worth of bombs and guns had got through in earlier consignments, the public attitude towards terrorism had hardened considerably. In Fianna Fáil, however, the mood was still strongly against extradition in any circumstances.

At a meeting of the parliamentary party on 18 November no less than fifty-seven deputies and senators spoke out against extradition. Some were against it in any circumstances while most argued that it should not be introduced unless it was accompanied by very tough safeguards such as an insistence on *prima facie* evidence being provided to Irish courts in all cases. Seven junior ministers joined the chorus of protest, with one of them – Denis Gallagher – telling the meeting he had been told by his local organisation not to come back to Mayo if he agreed to the measure.

One of the TDs most strongly opposed to the introduction of extradition was Noel Dempsey of Meath who had just been elected as a TD. He articulated the views of a number of younger TDs who were unhappy at the way Haughey was reversing virtually every policy he had stood for in Opposition.

In the face of this internal opposition, Haughey came up with a formula which allowed extradition to come into operation alongside certain safeguards which involved the Irish Attorney General vetting all extradition applications. It was much less than most of the Fianna Fáil TDs had demanded but it was accepted with hardly a whimper.

This process would be repeated again and again in the following few years. Fianna Fáil TDs would express outrage, Haughey would express concern at their predicament, follow that by doing precisely the opposite of what they wanted and the process would be completed by his backbenchers mutely accepting that which they had so strenuously objected to in the first place.

Meanwhile, at the end of 1987 Fianna Fáil experienced its second private members' time defeat within weeks over the issue of extra funding for the National Social Services Board (NSSB). While this was not nearly as big a shock as the defeat over education cuts, the Taoiseach was determined that the rot would have to stop and that his government would not have to face any more serious defeats.

As the extradition controversy came to a head Haughey threatened a general election if his proposals to give the Attorney General special powers were defeated in the Dáil, as appeared likely at one stage. When it came to the actual vote there was clear cooperation between Fianna Fáil and Fine Gael, with the government accepting some minor Fine Gael amendments in return for a trouble-free passage of the legislation. Vincent Brady and Fergus O'Brien worked hard to mend the fences after the government's defeats in private members' time and they ensured that there was no possibility of a defeat on an election issue like extradition.

In another extension of the Tallaght Strategy, Fianna Fáil agreed to accept Alan Shatter's private members' Judicial Separation and Family Law Reform Bill which allowed the granting of judicial separations by the courts on more simplified grounds and widened the access to the courts for couples who wanted separations. Fianna Fáil faced a possible defeat if they didn't give way on the issue, but still it was an historic breakthrough that for the first time in over thirty years a private members' Bill had been accepted by the government.

To make sure the Tallaght Strategy would stay on course despite the setbacks for the government on education cuts and the NSSB,

Haughey and Dukes held an important meeting before Christmas 1987 to discuss the overall political situation. The two men had a wide-ranging discussion and they agreed that a general election would not be in either's interest for the first half of 1988 at least. Haughey was reassured by Dukes that he would face no major challenge in the Dáil for the following six months and this effectively guaranteed the government a trouble-free existence until the autumn of 1988.

All-in-all it was a remarkable interlude in Irish politics. Here were the two civil war parties cooperating in the implementation of extremely tough policies designed to bring the country out of the economic crisis in which it had languished for nearly a decade. Fianna Fáil were understandably happy with the deal as they had the spoils of office. While there were some in Fine Gael who could see little point in the exercise, most leading members of the party supported it. They were exhausted after four years of grappling with the country's problems themselves and the last thing they wanted was an early general election. But there was more to it than pure self interest and some leading Fine Gael TDs, like John Bruton, made no secret of the fact that they agreed completely with the view of Alan Dukes that the strategy was in the national interest and should be continued whatever the short-term political cost.

12 – Larry Goodman

Even though the Tallaght Strategy was in full swing throughout 1988 political problems could not be avoided altogether. The closure of Barrington's Hospital in Limerick provoked a mini crisis early in the year. Des O'Malley's support for the campaign to prevent the closure of the hospital ran counter to his party's espousal of public spending cuts, but the pressure of local politics triumphed over party principle and the PD leader lined up with the left-wing parties in fighting the campaign.

Despite behind-the-scenes attempts by Alan Dukes and Michael Noonan of Fine Gael to cobble together a compromise with Health Minister Rory O'Hanlon, the government was defeated on private members' motion about the issue on 17 February 1988. Intense political manoeuvring couldn't prevent all the Opposition parties ending up in the same division lobby and they were joined by Limerick Fianna Fáil TD Willie O'Dea as they defeated the government.

There were threats of an election but the Fine Gael pact with the government kept things on the rails and the political temperature gradually came down again. This process was helped by the fact that Fianna Fáil's standing steadily improved in the opinion polls and Haughey got the kind of approval ratings he had always craved. With the media generally supporting government strategy, Haughey for the first time in twenty years was able to bask in popular adulation. Rows about the controversial rod-angling licence and the staffing levels of the Ombudsman's office did little to change popular perceptions of the government.

The only cloud in the sky was a personal one. Haughey was troubled by painful kidney stones, and this made an official visit to Australia in the summer of 1988 an agonising experience. In October he received treatment in the Mater Private Hospital, but shortly after returning home he suffered a severe respiratory collapse and was rushed back to hospital in the early hours of 14 October. Though P.J. Mara maintained that the Taoiseach's condition was not serious it emerged in the following weeks that he had been near death at one stage.

He was so ill that he missed almost the entire autumn session of the Dáil and when he returned he spoke with a noticeable wheeze and at times had obvious difficulty breathing. Haughey never fully regained his old zest after this setback and while he still retained the ability to rise to the occasion when circumstances demanded, his health problems slowed him down, particularly in the damp winter months. On occasions he was attended by a nurse before fulfilling major public engagements and in the Dáil he used an inhaler from time to time.

Whatever the Taoiseach's health problems, his political health was never better. The budgetary strategy for 1988 exceeded his wildest dreams. It emerged in October that a tax amnesty which had been expected to raise about £30 million had instead realised £500 million. On top of this the National Lottery and the DIRT tax, both of which had been devised by the Fine Gael-Labour coalition now came good and provided almost another £500 million for the exchequer. All of this enabled the government to make huge cuts in borrowing at a time when economic growth was booming because of favourable international trading conditions.

One serious development at the end of 1988 was that the Minister for Finance, Ray MacSharry, was appointed by the government as EC Commissioner in Brussels. MacSharry made no secret of the fact that he wanted the EC job though Haughey was very reluctant to give it to him because of his value to the government as Finance Minister. The Taoiseach simply didn't want to change a winning team but MacSharry was determined to go and Haughey granted him his wish. Albert Reynolds was promoted to Finance from Industry and Junior Minister Michael Smith came into the government.

Throughout 1988 the Fianna Fáil government worked the Anglo-Irish Agreement, despite Haughey's denunciation of it in Opposition. There were regular and friendly meetings between Foreign Minister Brian Lenihan and Northern Secretary Tom King under the auspices of the Anglo-Irish Intergovernmental Conference. Progress was made on issues like fair employment and other matters of concern to nationalists in Northern Ireland.

It was another example of the way Haughey in power reversed

engines and adopted what were in effect Fine Gael policies. Of course the fact that he was in a minority and all the Opposition parties favoured the continued operation of the Agreement made it politically easier to continue good relations with Britain rather than provoke confrontation. On extradition too the government cooperated with the British, though some decisions of the Irish courts and incompetence in the British handling of the issue delayed the smooth operation of the procedure.

The Taoiseach also re-established a good working relationship with the Department of Foreign Affairs despite his previous hostility to that Department and all its works and pomps. He once referred to the diplomats from Iveagh House as "dog handlers" and in Opposition never concealed his dislike of them.

"Can we now hope that all the sophistry, ambivalence and self-deception that has oozed out of Iveagh House for some time now will cease and that the cold harsh reality will be accepted: that Ireland's interests are best defended by Irish men and women and that all the appeasement, the platitudes and honeyed words mean nothing when the chips are down," he had told the Dáil in March 1984 in a debate on the outcome of an EC summit. "At the Brussels summit we have seen the … current favour-currying type of Iveagh House diplomacy exposed for what it is."

He had been equally scathing about the Iveagh House approach to Northern Ireland. "If we are prepared to bundle Irish citizens out of their own country without a care for their rights to a fair trial, if we are prepared to adopt a subservient and apologetic role in the conduct of our foreign affairs, then we cannot expect the world to place great value on what we have to offer politically," he told the last Fianna Fáil Ard Fheis before the 1987 election.

Haughey's attitude in the period 1982-87 was coloured by his poor relationship with the Secretary of the Department, Seán Donlon, whom he had tried and failed to move from the position as Ambassador to the United States in 1980. It was not just Donlon that Haughey saw as a problem in those years but the whole ethos of the Department which he regarded as alien and unsympathetic to his cause. His attitude of suspicion was fuelled by Garret FitzGerald's clear admiration for the officials in Iveagh House and the reciprocal response of the diplomats to the Fine Gael leader.

When he came into government in 1987 there were fears in Iveagh House that Haughey would take vengeance on the Department. However, that did not happen. After an initial attempt to control the flow of media information from the Department and channel it through government Press Secretary P. J. Mara, Haughey let Iveagh House diplomats run their affairs much as before. Brian Lenihan as Minister for Foreign Affairs quickly developed a good working relationship with his civil servants and relied on their advice. Lenihan then acted as a buffer between Haughey and Iveagh House and the expected bloodbath at the Department never materialised.

The departure of the Department Secretary, Seán Donlon, to become a senior executive with the aircraft leasing firm Guinness Peat Aviation helped to smoothen out potential differences, and other senior diplomats like Michael Lillis, who had also been close to FitzGerald, soon left the Department.

In the Dáil Haughey had little difficulty dominating the chamber. He was well able to handle Alan Dukes in debate and anyway the Fine Gael leader was constrained by the Tallaght Strategy. The Labour leader, Dick Spring, was only beginning to find his feet in Opposition but had as his first priority the task of binding his party together after the difficult years in government. It was the PDs who were Haughey's greatest bugbear in the Dáil and he never lost an opportunity to have a go at them. Haughey never referred to the PDs by name but dismissed them as "that party" and sparks regularly flew in his exchanges with O'Malley.

The PDs began to develop problems of their own as they struggled to define a role for themselves in the twenty-fifth Dáil. They scored a serious own goal when they launched their proposals for a new constitution. The document was launched initially on 13 January 1988, and passed without much critical comment. A number of radical reforms were proposed in the draft constitution including the replacement of Articles Two and Three which embody the claim to the North, the dropping of the ban on divorce, more extensive powers for the President and clear separation of church and state.

Apart from some polite editorial comment the PD proposals for a new constitution were largely ignored as the political parties concentrated on the tricky voting situation in the Dáil. However, after the party's annual conference, which was held in Cork at the end of May, the issue of God's role in the Constitution suddenly became a hot political potato after delegates had adopted the draft constitution as party policy. The following morning the *Irish Press* Religious Affairs correspondent, T.P. O'Mahony, wrote a story about the conference, leading off on the fact that God had been dropped from the Constitution. The item was picked up by P.P O'Reilly on RTE radio in the "It Says in the Papers" slot. He pointed to the irony of the fact that the previous day's decision to drop God had been taken by the PDs on Trinity Sunday.

The story suddenly took off and though the PDs protested loudly that God was still referred to in their document they were quickly dubbed as the party that wanted to take God out of the Constitution. Though the publicity was initially something of a laughing matter the public reaction, particularly in rural areas, was no joke. The controversy provoked more phone calls from members to party headquarters than any other issue since its foundation. Fianna Fáil TDs fanned the flames and the PDs found they had a serious embarrassment on their hands. The party's standing in the polls began to decline from then on and it never recovered. There were many reasons for this decline but some people in the party are convinced that the God factor was an important element in turning public opinion against the party.

By the end of 1988 as a result of tough economic policies, the Tallaght Strategy and that most valuable of all commodities, luck, Haughey had never been stronger. The other Opposition parties – the PDs, Labour and the Workers' Party – deeply resented the cosy arrangement between Fianna Fáil and Fine Gael, but throughout 1988 there was little they could do about it. In fact the PDs began to suffer because while the electorate expected the left-wing parties to attack the government, the PDs, as the party of fiscal rectitude, damaged their credibility by continual criticism of the government.

Haughey, despite his illness, was in a very powerful position. The PDs were in decline, Fine Gael were making little headway and neither was the left. Opinion-poll ratings of 50 percent and over indicated that the electorate were more than happy with the way the Fianna Fáil minority government was carrying on the nation's affairs.

The Tallaght Strategy had a serious weakness as far as Fine Gael was concerned because it inhibited the party's TDs from attacking the government on anything. Not alone did the main Opposition support government economic policies, as the strategy demanded, they felt constrained from attacking Fianna Fáil on any issue and as time went on it appeared that Haughey had a blank cheque from Fine Gael in all areas of government policy.

Despite record approval ratings, one of the doubts that continued to surface about Charles Haughey related to his choice of friends. One of those who was regarded as a friend of Haughey was the beef baron, Larry Goodman, whose rags-to-riches story was as remarkable as Haughey's rise to the top of Fianna Fáil.

Within months of Haughey coming to power he and Goodman gave a major press conference on 18 June 1987, to promote a massive development of the beef industry to be undertaken by Goodman's companies. A grandiose scheme for the industry was unveiled which involved a planned investment of £260 million in Goodman's operations. It was the biggest investment programme ever drawn up for the food industry and was to consist of £60 million in assistance from the IDA and the European Community, a £30 million investment by Goodman himself and a package of loans under Section 84 of the Finance Act which would involve a benefit of £170 million.

At the press conference the Minister for Agriculture, Michael O'Kennedy, and his Junior Minister, Joe Walsh, vied with each other for a place on the platform near the Taoiseach, and O'Kennedy was deeply insulted when his place was taken by Walsh. The ambitious plan never got off the ground, however, despite continuous prodding of Goodman by the state agencies involved. No government agency made any direct investment in the abortive plan but the Goodman companies did draw down a considerable portion of the Section 84 loan finance agreed.

One effect of the massive publicity surrounding the project was to associate Charles Haughey and Larry Goodman in the public mind.

This association began to become a political issue in the early months of 1989. Firstly, in February the Oireachtas Committee on State Sponsored Bodies got embroiled in controversy when it emerged that Goodman was interested in buying the state-owned Sugar Company through a company controlled by him called Food Industries. The chairman of the Oireachtas Committee, Liam Lawlor, was also a director of Food Industries, and a potential conflict of interest was raised by PD committee member Pat O'Malley. Lawlor was put under severe pressure and forced to resign as chairman of the committee. Agriculture Minister Michael O'Kennedy also came under attack and faced a series of Dáil questions on the issue.

At this stage the media were pursuing various stories about Goodman but because of fear of libel a number of stories were suppressed and RTE was forced to issue a cringing apology for an item on its "Farm News" programme containing allegations made in New Zealand about Goodman.

On 5 March the *Sunday Press* carried a report about a raid by government officials on a Goodman plant on Dublin's North Wall. The Eirfreeze meat plant was raided by Department of Agriculture inspectors and the *Press* carried the bare facts of the case. The story provoked the usual threats of libel action from Goodman but the allegations about fraud in the company could be held back no longer.

In the Dáil later that week Labour TD Barry Desmond caused a sensation when he made a series of damning allegations about the way the Goodman companies were operating. Speaking under privilege in the House, Desmond spoke about Garda fraud squad investigation into Goodman companies and he said that £20 million in export refunds had been withheld from the company because of its fraudulent practices. Desmond added that these matters had not been reported by the newspapers because "writs were flying all over the place".

Tomás MacGiolla of the Workers' Party followed these allegations by referring to the *Sunday Press* story about Eirfreeze and he wondered why the story had died following its publication the previous Sunday.

Haughey immediately sprang to Goodman's defence. In a reply to the debate he deplored the attacks on Goodman and said they could damage employment and growth. By this stage, however, the allegations had developed into a major national controversy. Goodman challenged Desmond and MacGiolla to repeat their claims outside the privilege of the Dáil chamber and he said he was examining methods of legal action against the two TDs.

"We'll leave no stone unturned. It was an abuse of Dáil privilege and we're not going to stand for it," Goodman told the *Irish Press*. RTE broadcaster Gay Byrne leapt to Goodman's defence and accused Desmond of indulging in malicious publicity-seeking.

Desmond, however, continued to pursue the issue. The following week he told the Dáil that a fine of over £1 million had been imposed on one Goodman company by the Department of Agriculture. The fine had arisen from a number of offenses including over-statement of weights, incorrect declarations in relation to the export refund scheme and the aids to private storage scheme, both of which were funded by the European Community.

When the Labour TD again raised the issue on the order of business in the Dáil on 15 March, challenging the Taoiseach or the Minister for Agriculture to deny that a fine of over £1 million had been imposed on Goodman, Haughey reacted angrily: "I, in turn, accuse Deputy Desmond, with a full sense of responsibility, of trying to sabotage the entire beef industry in this country." Later the Taoiseach added: "I repeat my statement that Deputy Desmond, for his own base political purposes, is trying to destroy one of our most important industries."

That afternoon Michael O'Kennedy issued a statement which defended the Department of Agriculture and its role in regulating the beef industry. Adding that all the requirements of domestic law were being adhered to, the minister also denied that the Department had initiated any court proceedings against Goodman companies. Within weeks, however, O'Kennedy was forced to admit that irregularities amounting to £7.5 million in the beef industry had been notified by his Department to the EC in the previous three years.

In the midst of all these allegations Bobby Molloy of the PDs established the embarrassing fact that Goodman's private jet was being parked at Casement Military aerodrome at Baldonnel. This military facility was not open to private individuals and questions arose about why Goodman was given the facility and what he was paying the state for the privilege. The revelation only fuelled the suspicion that Goodman was getting privileged treatment from the government.

It wasn't long before another controversy arose in relation to Goodman. This time it involved the operation of the export credit insurance scheme and the way Goodman's exports to Iraq were being underpinned by the state insurance scheme.

A series of Dáil questions from Pat O'Malley of the PDs in April 1988 established that the Goodman organisation has been given massive export credit insurance cover for its trade with Iraq. Cover to Iraq had been withdrawn in 1986 by the Fine Gael Minister for Industry and Commerce, Michael Noonan, because of the risks involved in trading with that country.

However, on Fianna Fáil's accession to office in 1987 the cover was restored for trade with Iraq and the vast bulk of it went to Goodman companies. In 1987 export credit insurance for beef exports to Iraq was for £41.2 million and in 1988 it came to £78.5 million. In fact almost one-third of all the available export credit insurance provided by law for all Irish exporters was absorbed in covering Goodman's beef exports to Iraq.

When the figures were examined closely it emerged that the insurance cover provided for the beef trade to Iraq in 1987 and 1988 actually exceeded the total value of beef exports to that country for the two years by £57 million. A major controversy developed over why the cover for Goodman's exports to Iraq was so much greater than the value of the beef itself and questions were also asked about why Fianna Fáil had restored export credit insurance to Iraq in the first place, considering it was such a risky market.

"Members of this present government, from the Taoiseach down, are extremely close personally to the leading figure in the group concerned," PD leader Des O'Malley told the Dáil on 10 May. "The Taoiseach personally announced a £260 million investment programme by this group in June 1987. Almost two years later none of that programme appears to have commenced. As I said then, we can hardly blame the government. They have been generous and helpful to a fault.I instanced on that occasion their willingness to accommodate Mr Goodman's private jet in a state military airbase.

"In addition we can now instance their provision of this extraordinarily generous export credit insurance support to the almost entire exclusion of everybody else in that trade and to the considerable detriment of hundreds of other exporters in other sectors of business. The closeness and helpfulness exhibited by the government to the group concerned in terms of export credit insurance may well be echoed in the non enforcement by the government of the terms of the Mergers, Takeovers and Monopolies (Control) Act, 1978, in respect of a different group, the Master Meats Group."

The Minister for Industry and Commerce, Ray Burke, who had again cancelled export credit insurance to Iraq early in 1989, strongly attacked O'Malley in the Dáil for his allegations and accused him of being out to get the Goodman Group. "Throughout it has been my impression – and it has been confirmed tonight – that many of the questions raised on this matter have been characterised by insinuation, innuendo and hints of abuse regarding the operation of the scheme and they have been stated here tonight."

Of course what neither Burke nor O'Malley could know was that within a matter of two months the PD leader would be Minister for Industry and Commerce and he would then be in a position to carry out an investigation into all the allegations he himself had made. On 10 May when they debated the matter nobody in their wildest dreams would have predicted that O'Malley and Burke would soon be sitting together around the Cabinet as government colleagues.

13 – Unnecessary Election

By May of 1989 the Fianna Fáil minority government had been in power for over two years and Haughey never had it so good. He was still basking in the glow of media approval and was secure in office for the foreseeable future under the terms of the Tallaght Strategy. His government's genuinely remarkable performance on the economy had impressed the public, despite the various cutbacks which that achievement entailed.

Government borrowing, much of it carried out by Haughey himself in his first spell as Taoiseach, had finally been brought under control. Under the FitzGerald coalition borrowing had stabilised at around £2.5 billion a year or just under 13 percent of GNP. In 1987 Fianna Fáil yanked the figure down to 9.9 percent of GNP and in 1988 broke the back of the current problem by bringing it down to a remarkable 3.3 percent of GNP, the lowest for more than twenty years. This achievement was helped by the windfall of the tax amnesty but the key to the solution was the political will to do it and Haughey had provided that.

The dismal scientists, as Haughey used to call economists, were universal in their praise. The business community was equally happy with the achievement because the massive cuts in borrowing were accompanied by sustained economic growth fuelled by the booming economies of Britain and the United States. Apart from occasional private members' time defeats in the Dáil, which did not count as confidence issues, it appeared as if there wasn't a dark cloud on the horizon.

Then out of the blue Haughey chose to make one of the biggest blunders of his political career. He returned from a successful visit to Japan on 27 April to discover that his government was about to lose a Dáil vote on a private members' motion calling for an allocation of £400,000 to help haemophiliacs with AIDS. Though he had instructed Health Minister Rory O'Hanlon, before he went to Japan, to deal with the issue he can hardly have been too surprised at the tight situation in the Dáil.

RTE reporter Charlie Bird met the Taoiseach at the airport to interview him on his return and instead of beginning the interview with the expected questions about the Japanese trip, he asked Haughey for his response to an impending Dáil defeat. The Taoiseach appeared overcome by rage after the interview and having made a quick visit to his Kinsealy home, near the airport, where he consulted a few friends, he headed for Leinster House. He had just completed an arduous sixteen-hour journey from the other end of the earth and there was no need for him to be in the Dáil as he was paired with Fine Gael leader Alan Dukes, but he insisted on going.

On his arrival in government Buildings the Taoiseach summoned the available ministers and subjected them to a tongue-lashing for allowing the situation in the Dáil to develop as it had. The chief whip, Vincent Brady, was instructed to impress on the Opposition just how serious the issue was. He contacted the Opposition whips with dire warnings about the consequences of a government defeat and the situation began to spin out of control.

Fine Gael whip Jim Higgins, PD whip Geraldine Kennedy and Labour whip Brendan Howlin, all told Brady that they would not change their positions at that stage. Higgins had to make frantic attempts to contact his leader, Alan Dukes, who was at a soccer international and it took him some time to get him.

The Taoiseach came into the Dáil chamber very angry that his government was facing its sixth defeat since taking office just over two years before. "He was hopping mad and just fit to be tied," said one Fianna Fáil TD who met him shortly after his arrival and quickly got out of the way.

Haughey then went to a meeting in Brady's office which was attended by Higgins of Fine Gael and a number of Fianna Fáil ministers to see if anything could be patched up. In front of the Opposition whip the Taoiseach heaped abuse on his own ministers and chief whip for having allowed the crisis to develop. Higgins backed out the door in the middle of the tirade while the ministers present were clearly taken aback by the vehemence of Haughey's anger.

At the informal Cabinet meeting which ensued the Taoiseach expressed the view strongly that he would not tolerate a defeat and that he was going to call a general election if the government was beaten. Most of his ministers were shocked to hear Haughey talking about a general election. They saw no need for such an extreme response to what in real terms merely represented a political embarrassment rather than a political crisis.

As news of the threatened election spread, TDs gathered in the Dáil chamber while journalists flocked to the press gallery. The public gallery also filled up with party activists – P.J. Mara, Fianna Fáil General Secretary Frank Wall, and party organiser Seán Sherwin, as well as officials of the other Dáil parties.

The stage looked set for a drama but nobody was sure what would happen. After the critical vote was called, Haughey's humour appeared to have improved considerably as he bowed, Japanese style, to colleagues and chaffed the Opposition. When the votes were counted, however, the government had lost by 72 to 69. Brady told Brendan Howlin at this stage that the game was up and the Dáil would be dissolved.

However, as the TDs waited for the second vote, on the Opposition motion, Albert Reynolds sat down beside Haughey and spoke earnestly to him for ten minutes urging him strongly not to make a hasty decision to call an election but to sleep on the matter. The Taoiseach agreed reluctantly and headed home to bed after the second vote without committing himself to any definite course of action.

The following day Haughey briefed political journalists and he refused to rule out a general election. With European elections already scheduled for 15 June the possibility of holding two elections on the same day began to circulate. Most of the Cabinet was against an election and that view was put most strongly by Reynolds.

Two ministers, Pádraig Flynn and Ray Burke, were strongly for it. Both men were close to Haughey. Flynn had supported him loyally and given him encouragement at times of crisis down the years. He often wandered into the Taoiseach's office for a chat and had an unusually casual and frank relationship with The Boss. Burke had not been an uncritical loyalist like Flynn and had voted against Haughey during the last heave in 1983. Nonetheless he made it back into Haughey's good books and re-established himself with the Taoiseach, whose Kinsealy home was in his constituency of Dublin North.

Urging Haughey to go for an election, both men pointed to Fianna Fáil's privately commissioned opinion polls which gave the party 51 percent. They also pointed to the low standing of the PDs and expressed the view that the time was ripe to wipe out O'Malley's party. Even though Haughey had calmed down in the days after the Dáil defeat he couldn't resist the temptation to go for the overall majority that had eluded him on four previous occasions. He became convinced that his government's strong record and the widespread support he had received, including that of the media, would win him an election.

Throughout May election speculation dominated the media. Haughey could have killed it off with one definitive statement that he wasn't going to go to the country. He pointedly refused to do this leaving only one conclusion, that he was going to dissolve the Dáil. Though he waited for weeks, Haughey moved inevitably towards that decision and he dissolved the Dáil at 7 p.m. on 25 May 1989, setting the election for 15 June, the same day as the European contest.

The weeks of speculation in the lead up to the calling of the election had given the Opposition plenty of time to prepare. Drafts of party policies, advertising strategy and the preparation of election literature and posters had all been completed by the Opposition parties before Haughey dissolved the Dáil and printing houses all over the country were on standby, geared up and ready to go on 25 May.

In fact the Opposition parties seemed far better prepared than Fianna Fáil. It wasn't just a matter of nuts and bolts, the Opposition had a strategy while the government appeared confused and was content to rely on its record. All the Opposition parties, particularly Labour and the Workers' Party, hounded Fianna Fáil on the health cuts which quickly became the dominant issue of the campaign while the economic achievements of the previous two-and-a-quarter years were pushed into the background.

The delay in calling the election also gave Fine Gael and the Progressive Democrats an opportunity to negotiate a pact to put an alternative government before the people. This came as a huge surprise to Fianna Fáil because they believed that the very bad relations between the two parties would stand in the way of an agreement.

There had been some tentative feelers over the previous six months or so. Ivan Yates of Fine Gael had made a speech saying Fine Gael and the PDs should recognise that an alliance of the two parties was the only alternative to Fianna Fáil, while in February 1989 O'Malley had delivered a speech which opened the way to a pact.

Dukes, however, was very reluctant to engage in talks with the PDs. His first priority was the elimination of O'Malley's party and the retrieval of Fine Gael votes which had gone to it in 1987 and he didn't see the point of doing a deal. Former Taoiseach Garret Fitz-Gerald saw things in the same light but most senior members of the front bench took a very different view, Bruton and Mitchell in particular arguing strongly in favour of the need to present the country with an alternative government.

The negotiation began immediately after the government's Dáil defeat on the haemophiliac motion. The day after that vote Dukes asked to meet O'Malley and they set the process in train. Most of the actual negotiation was done by Bruton and Mitchell for Fine Gael and Michael McDowell and Geraldine Kennedy for the PDs. Dukes and O'Malley stayed out of it until most of the details had been sorted out.

The deal was announced two days after the election was called but as things turned out it failed to capture the public imagination in any significant way. It did, however, unsettle Fianna Fáil and it prevented the two Opposition parties attacking each other during the campaign. Instead they joined in a systematic assault on the government along with the left-wing parties.

This assault from all sides began to eat into the government's lead in the opinion polls. As had happened in almost every election since opinion-polling began in 1977, Fianna Fáil lost support as the campaign progressed. The first published poll of the campaign put Fianna Fáil on 51 percent but the poll showed that people believed the election was unnecessary. In subsequent polls Fianna Fáil's share of the vote dropped steadily as the election date got nearer. Despite spending more than all the other parties combined, over £3 million, the government appeared lethargic and unable to wrest the initiative away from the Opposition, all of whom focused in on cuts, particularly the health cuts. In fact Fianna Fáil did not launch its own manifesto until a little over a week before polling, and by that time there was deep anxiety in the government camp, with its own internal polls showing the party down to 41 percent.

In the final days of the campaign Fianna Fáil did manage to get some of the focus away from the health cuts and on to its record of economic achievement. However, an admission by Haughey in a radio phone-in that he was unaware of the impact of the health cuts provided more negative publicity. This was redeemed somewhat by a good performance in the major television debate two days before polling but the overall effect of the Fianna Fáil campaign was unimpressive.

The impact of the Opposition parties was noisy but confused. The Fine Gael-PD pact failed to make any great headway during the campaign and the polls continued to be very gloomy for O'Malley's party. They did appear to show a big surge for the left, with Labour and the Workers' Party making significant gains and there was much talk in the media about the emergence of a left-right divide in Irish politics. This prospect had been spoken about for decades but it appeared that a breakthrough for the left might finally be in store.

One group who were not taken very seriously in anybody's calculations were the Greens, despite the favourable trend towards them in Europe.

On 15 June there was one of the lowest turnouts of any recent general election with just 68.5 percent of voters going to the polls. The results when they came in the following day proved a bitter blow for Fianna Fáil. The party ended up with just 44 percent of the vote and dropped four seats in the process from 81 to 77. There was a feeling of devastation in the party, not just because of the losses but because an election was so unnecessary.

"Of all the mistakes Haughey has made this has to be the biggest," said one minister privately on the night of the count. "We had the best of all possible worlds in office because not only were we being underpinned by Fine Gael but we were getting all the credit for the economic achievements and they were getting none. We could have continued on for at least another two years and if they brought us down at any stage we would have won an election." An added personal disappointment for Haughey was that his son Seán failed for the second time to win election to the Dáil.

As it was, Fine Gael only improved marginally from 27 percent to 29 percent, gaining four seats. The PDs were decimated, dropping from 14 seats to 6. The new party lost some of its brightest stars including McDowell, Kennedy, Anne Colley, Pat O'Malley and Martin Cullen. On the night of the result the party looked headed for oblivion. Ray Burke, smarting from his own party's failure to win a majority said bitterly: "It couldn't happen to a nicer bunch of people."

Both Labour and the Workers' Party gained votes and seats by eating into the working class Fianna Fáil support, but it was hardly the big breakthrough for the left that had been predicted. The total left-wing vote was barely 15 percent, falling a long way short of opening up a left-right divide in Irish politics. The total left vote was still below the Labour total in both the 1965 and 1969 general elections, while as far back as 1943 Labour had won over 15 percent. For the Greens it was a big breakthrough. The party won its first seat in the Dáil and its performance in the number of constituencies it contested on a shoestring budget was quite remarkable.

The most immediate issue when the result became clear was how a government could be put together. Fianna Fáil had 77 seats, Fine Gael 55, Labour 16, the Workers' Party 7, the PDs 6, the Greens 1 and others 4. In a radio interview as the results came in, Labour's Barry Desmond maintained that there was no problem. Fianna Fáil and the PDs had the numbers between them so Des O'Malley should go back to Fianna Fáil from whence he had come and they could form a government. At the time that appeared far too simplistic an analysis.

Haughey went on television the morning after the election result became clear and surprisingly he gave a much more relaxed and confident performance than he had at any time during the campaign. He stated his willingness to form a government and said he was prepared to consult with the other political parties before the Dáil resumed on 29 June. He gave the clear impression that he felt he could form another minority administration and that Fianna Fáil could

156

simply take up where it had left off under the Tallaght Strategy.

The prospects for that looked good the following day when one of the surviving PDs, Mary Harney, said publicly that her party should support Haughey if that was necessary to provide the country with a government. The fact that the six surviving PDs were all ex-members of Fianna Fáil added to the belief that they might step into Fine Gael shoes and support a Haughey minority government.

Haughey quickly began a series of meetings with the other party leaders. On the evening of 20 June he met O'Malley to ask for support for a Fianna Fáil minority government and he promised a very generous accommodation. Harney's intervention had provoked a very hostile reaction among PD supporters and at least three of the party's six deputies were adamantly against voting for Haughey as Taoiseach. A meeting between the Taoiseach and Alan Dukes on the following day, 21 June, brought home to many in Fianna Fáil for the first time that things had changed fundamentally and that the party would have to pay a stiff price for its decision to call an election.

Dukes said he was prepared to help Haughey form a government but only if Fine Gael got seven of the fifteen Cabinet posts and if the office of Taoiseach was revolved between them during the lifetime of the government. The Fine Gael front bench had divided sharply about the hardline proposals. As there was no way Fianna Fáil could accept such an arrangement, some leading members of Fine Gael felt the exercise was a transparent attempt to ensure there could be no compromise with the government.

The deputy party leader, John Bruton, and other former ministers like Jim Mitchell, Michael Noonan and Seán Barrett were in favour of a realistic proposal to Fianna Fáil on power-sharing. They felt that if they demanded four or so Cabinet seats the likelihood was that it would be turned down but that at least it would be seen as a genuine attempt to do business. Dukes though had the strong support of younger frontbenchers like Ivan Yates, Alan Shatter and Gay Mitchell for his hardline demands and he was highly impatient with the experienced ex-ministers who wanted to pitch the demand lower.

"There are a number of people on the front bench who can't wait to get their bums on the seat of a Mercedes again," said one Dukes supporter who couldn't hide his displeasure at those who disagreed with the leader's tactics.

Although the Fine Gael proposals were rejected out-of-hand, as Dukes clearly had anticipated, they did bring home to the government just how difficult forming a new administration was going to be. They also brought the PDs into the picture as the only realistic option for a deal. With just six deputies, the PDs did not appear to be in a position to make the same kind of demands as Fine Gael but there was intense opposition within the PDs to voting for Haughey in any circumstances. Their six deputies may all have been ex-Fianna Fáil but they had left the party precisely because they couldn't accept Haughey's leadership.

As the agonising in the PDs continued, it became clear that the party would not be prepared to vote for Haughey when the twenty-sixth Dáil met for the first time on 29 June, whatever might happen after that. With the left also committed to voting against him, when the Dáil met that day it became obvious that Haughey would be beaten on the vote for Taoiseach though nobody else would have sufficient support either. That is exactly what happened and for the first time in the history of the state the Dáil failed to come up with a majority for any individual as Taoiseach.

As if that wasn't sensational enough, Haughey added to the drama of the day by initially refusing to tender his resignation to the President as the Constitution apparently obliged him to do. The issue was raised by Dick Spring who challenged Haughey about why he was not proposing to go to Aras an Uachtaráin to tender his resignation. Dukes had been advised by Garret FitzGerald to raise that precise point with Haughey but had declined to do so on the basis that he had his own legal advice which suggested Haughey need not resign immediately. Establishing a pattern that was to be repeated again and again in the twenty-sixth Dáil, Spring seized the initiative from Dukes and the Fine Gael leader was then obliged to follow.

When challenged by Spring, Haughey argued that he need not resign immediately but should be allowed time to consider his future course of action. With the other Opposition leaders rowing in behind Spring and refusing to accept Haughey's view of the Constitution, the

Taoiseach was thrown into confusion. The Dáil was adjourned for two hours while the Fianna Fáil leader met his Cabinet and considered the advice of his Attorney General, John Murray, that he need not resign but should have some time to consider his position.

At a stormy Cabinet meeting Haughey initially insisted that he would not resign. A number of his ministers, including Albert Reynolds, lost patience with him and demanded that whatever the legal niceties of the situation he should formally resign. They were extremely worried that an apparent attempt to flout the Constitution would only make forming a minority government more difficult than it already was. That view was confirmed by a remark of O'Malley to Junior Minister Joe Walsh as they left the Dáil chamber. "This won't make it any easier," said the PD leader cryptically.

After a great deal of argument and persuasion at Cabinet, Haughey finally agreed to resign. He went back into the Dáil to announce his decision and then drove to Aras an Uachtaráin where he handed a written note of resignation to President Hillery.

As the Constitution states that an outgoing Taoiseach should remain in place until a successor has been appointed by the Dáil, Haughey and his ministers remained in office although there was considerable debate about the powers of an "acting Taoiseach" and whether he had the authority to get a dissolution of the Dáil to hold another election. The Constitution does not appear to make adequate provision for the situation that arose after 29 June and there is considerable ambiguity about the role of the "acting government".

One way or another Haughey was still in power but it had been brought home to him and his party that they would remain in that position only if they got down to business and made some real compromises with the other parties. The one unmentionable compromise, then and later, was the possibility of Haughey stepping down as leader of Fianna Fáil to let somebody else take over and try and put a government together. Members of the Cabinet and most Fianna Fáil TDs knew that almost any leader other than Haughey would have allowed them to retain office as a minority government but the memory of the bitterness and divisiveness caused by the heaves of the early 1980s meant that nobody in the party dared to broach the subject.

14 – Coalition

The day after that inconclusive first meeting of the twenty-sixth Dáil the first real break in the logjam developed. The PDs, who had voted for Alan Dukes as Taoiseach in fulfilment of their pre-election pledge, now offered to open talks with Fianna Fáil on a nine-point framework for dialogue which had as its core the principle that everything was up for discussion. The key point was number seven: "that prior to any negotiations taking place, all discussion on all matters be open and that nothing be ruled in or ruled out in advance".

Haughey agreed to open talks on the basis of the framework and the two negotiating teams met on the evening of 30 June. The PD negotiators were former Fianna Fáil minister Bobby Molloy and newly elected MEP Pat Cox. The government team was Minister for Finance Albert Reynolds and Labour Minister Bertie Ahern. Any issues that could not be resolved between the negotiators were to be referred to the party leaders.

A number of TDs, particularly Joe Walsh and Charlie McCreevy of Fianna Fáil and Mary Harney of the PDs, also kept up contact during the negotiations and helped to facilitate dialogue when the process ran into trouble.

Bobby Molloy, whose participation in the talks was to be vital to the PDs, was formally asked by O'Malley only on the morning of 30 June to be a part of the negotiating team. The PDs, despite strong objections from Pearse Wyse and Máirín Quill to voting for Haughey in any circumstances, decided that they could do a deal with Fianna Fáil but only on the basis of a formal coalition arrangement.

Entering negotiations, the central tactic of the PDs was not to agree a policy programme until the issue of coalition had first been accepted by Fianna Fáil. "Our main fear was that Fianna Fáil would agree to every policy proposal we put forward but in the last analysis refuse to give us Cabinet posts," said a leading PD later. "They could then have broken off the talks, pointed to the agreed programme and put us in the dock as the party which had wrecked the prospect of stable government out of a naked desire for mercs and perks."

This determination to ensure that the coalition issue was tackled head-on torpedoed the first session of talks. The two negotiation teams met in Dublin's Mansion House. Pat Cox put the PD side, then Bertie Ahern put the Fianna Fáil view including the bottom line that they had no mandate to agree to participation in government with the PDs. Molloy, sticking rigidly to the tactic of getting agreement on coalition before discussing anything else, intervened immediately to say coalition had to be part of any deal.

This effectively scuppered the talks, but the negotiators agreed to meet formally the following morning so that the talks and their breakdown could be publicly announced. Haughey and O'Malley met later in the day at the Mansion House to see if there was any possibility of a breakthrough, but had no success. Both men spoke to the media and their comments indicated that agreement would be extremely difficult.

"Coalition is completely ruled out," Haughey told journalists as he left the Mansion House meeting. He added: "We went before the electorate on the basis that we wouldn't form a coalition. A majority of the people voted for Fianna Fáil government and our position was always, if we hadn't an overall majority we would form a minority government."

That weekend it appeared as if another general election was inevitable. When the Dáil convened on Monday, 3 July there was still no change in the situation. The Fianna Fáil parliamentary party met that morning but there was no indication of any way out, only an endorsement of the efforts being made by the Taoiseach to form a government.

The Dáil adjourned again for three days but speculation was rife about another election. The possibility of agreement appeared so remote that Fine Gael arranged selection conventions for the following weekend in anticipation of an immediate election. Fianna Fáil TDs were openly talking about the same thing though the general view was that the result would be much the same. The realisation also dawned that if there was another Dáil stalemate, following a new election, Fianna Fáil's only option would be to put forward somebody other than Charles Haughey as the party nominee for Taoiseach.

Haughey could see that scenario more clearly than anybody else and on Tuesday, 4 July he made the decisive move. That morning Haughey contacted O'Malley to arrange a meeting with the PD leader in the Berkeley Court Hotel for 5 p.m. and then called a Cabinet meeting at which he broached the subject of coalition with his ministers for the first time. Most of them were stunned by the realisation that the Taoiseach was considering coalition with the PDs.

A clear majority of the Cabinet led by Reynolds were strongly opposed to any coalition arrangement. Pádraig Flynn, Michael O'Kennedy, Rory O'Hanlon, John Wilson, Michael Noonan and Brendan Daly all spoke against a deal. Flynn was the most vehement and shocked everybody by accusing Haughey of opting for coalition out of a personal pursuit of power.

Two key ministers, Gerry Collins and Ray Burke, took the opposite view and in coded language spoke in favour of a deal with O'Malley, even if the price was coalition. Brian Lenihan as ever supported Haughey and said they would be able to sell coalition to the organisation, if that was the ultimate decision. No formal decision on a change of policy was taken by the Cabinet and Flynn went on radio that evening to say that refusal to enter coalitions was a core value with Fianna Fáil.

At about the same time as that interview was broadcast, Haughey met O'Malley in the Berkeley Court and made it clear to the PD leader that he was prepared to concede on coalition. Another meeting was arranged for the following day to formalise the decision. Pat Cox and Bobby Molloy accompanied their leader to this meeting but Haughey didn't bother to invite either of his two negotiators along. At the meeting Molloy challenged Haughey about Flynn's widely publicised remarks of the evening before – that coalition wasn't on – and also about anti-coalition views expressed by Reynolds that morning.

"It's all right. I just haven't told them yet," was Haughey's cryptic response. The supreme audacity of the Taoiseach's reply didn't surprise the PD team who knew his form only too well and if anything they were impressed by the utter confidence and self-belief with which he conducted himself.

Having agreed to coalition in principle Haughey then went back to brief his Cabinet, but he didn't give them the full picture. He hinted that a coalition deal might be on but he didn't spell out the concession he had made to the PDs. Some of his ministers were appalled at the news and Reynolds in particular was deeply indignant at the effrontery of Haughey in making the fundamental concession without letting his negotiators know. Salt was rubbed into the wound when Reynolds and Ahern subsequently learned that the two PD negotiators had met Haughey along with their leader while they were not even aware that a meeting was taking place.

Despite the misgivings of some ministers there was no clear objection to an announcement that evening that the negotiations with the PDs would resume. Haughey told his two negotiators to go back to the discussions about policy, but the actual make-up of the government and hence the question of coalition would be left to the Taoiseach himself. There was little doubt in anybody's mind what that meant in practice, but some ministers tried to avoid facing up to the reality.

When the public announcement of the talks was made around 5 p.m. the media had no doubt about what had happened and that a Fianna Fáil-PD coalition was now on. Some ministers still clung to the belief that any deal would have to come back to the Cabinet for final approval and they comforted themselves that they would have the last word. This never happened of course, but Haughey read his Cabinet correctly in assuming that while they might huff and puff behind his back none of them would do anything about it. Haughey's attitude to his Cabinet was dismissive, to say the least. At one stage while his ministers agonised about coalition, Haughey bumped into a TD who asked how the Cabinet was reacting to events and Haughey airily dismissed their views. "They are only a crowd of gobshites," he said.

The announcement on the evening of 5 July that the principle of coalition had been conceded came as a severe shock to many in Fianna Fáil, particularly ordinary party members. Many TDs had already come to terms with the reality that if they didn't form a coalition another election was the only alternative and such an election would probably reduce the party's strength even further. When the Dáil met the following day, 6 July, another adjournment was agreed to allow

Fianna Fáil and the PDs to negotiate their programme for government. Haughey, who a few days earlier had ruled out coalition in any circumstances, told the Dáil that the "higher national interest" required an arrangement to put a government in place.

With the Dáil adjourned for six days to allow the two parties to conclude an agreement, there was intense pressure on both sides. Having conceded the principle of coalition, Fianna Fáil tried to limit the PD representation at the Cabinet table to just one minister, but again the PDs and particularly Bobby Molloy adopted a very tough negotiating stance, demanding that Haughey concede two Cabinet posts.

The Fianna Fáil parliamentary party met twice to debate the issues involved but on both occasions gave Haughey a free hand without being told how many Cabinet places the PDs were getting. Some deputies were strongly opposed to coalition at any price, among them Junior Minister Máire Geoghegan-Quinn, Dick Roche of Wicklow and Meath TD Noel Dempsey. While the majority didn't like it they were anxious to avoid another election at all costs and were prepared to let Haughey make whatever decisions he thought necessary to avoid an election.

In the Fianna Fáil organisation the mood was very different and there was total and utter astonishment that Haughey had given way to O'Malley of all people. Morale throughout the organisation was in shreds after the news about coalition was announced. Few members of the party cared to face up to the reality that they had not won an overall majority in the election and that they had a duty to the nation to form a coalition with another party.

Meanwhile the talks between the two negotiating teams resumed but they were relegated to the status of a side show. The PDs produced their own policies while Fianna Fáil relied on briefing documents from the Department of Finance. A number of expert advisors were brought in by the PDs, including former Fianna Fáil minister Martin O'Donoghue.

With the principle of coalition conceded, the battle between Fianna Fáil and the PDs now continued over the number of Cabinet seats. Haughey tried a number of manoeuvres to avoid giving two ministerial posts to his junior coalition partner but the PDs, at the insistence of Molloy, held out to the end. Haughey met O'Malley regularly to iron out difficulties. Shane Kenny in his book *Go Dance on Somebody Else's Grave* quotes O'Malley as telling Haughey that one PD seat at the Cabinet table was not a realistic option, whatever the relative strength of the two parties. He said he would not be happy to sit in Cabinet as the only PD and he argued that the government would not be seen as a coalition of two parties.

O'Malley kept the PD negotiating team abreast of what went on at these meetings but Haughey didn't even tell his negotiators that they were taking place, never mind informing them fully of what transpired.

Disillusioned Fianna Fáil TDs and ministers now maintained that the bottom line was one Cabinet post for the PDs and not two as they were demanding. Even moderates like Bertie Ahern and Séamus Brennan, who were willing to go along with the notion of having O'Malley in the Cabinet, maintained that they would draw the line at two ministerial posts for the PDs. Haughey met ministers and TDs individually to sound them out about how they felt. That process threw the ranks of the anti-coalitionists into confusion because no one was sure what the other was saying directly to the Taoiseach.

Junior Minister Máire Geoghegan-Quinn was so adamantly opposed to the prospect of her constituency colleague Bobby Molloy getting a Cabinet post that there were rumours she would resign in protest if that happened. There were also dark hints that Pádraig Flynn might resign from the Cabinet and he certainly had a stormy face-to-face session with Haughey during which he suggested that the Taoiseach should step down as Fianna Fáil leader and let somebody else try to form a government, rather than share power with the PDs.

The Fianna Fáil parliamentary party met the day before the Dáil gathered for its crucial session on 12 July. Haughey told the deputies and senators that the negotiations with the PDs had not concluded and he did not mention the issue of how many posts they were to get at Cabinet. The anti-coalitionists, Noel Dempsey, Máire Geoghegan-Quinn and Noel Treacy from Galway East, spoke against any deal. Geoghegan-Quinn said that she had sold a number of U-turns to the organisation – on extradition, the Anglo-Irish Agreement, the Single European Act and spending cutbacks – but she drew the line at selling this one. She refused to accept that what the Taoiseach was doing was in the national interest.

But the number of open critics at the parliamentary party were few and there was no objection to a decision to hold a further meeting the following morning just before the Dáil convened. As well as mollifying the parliamentary party the Taoiseach also met his party's national executive that night. While a good deal of opposition to coalition with the PDs was expressed, there was no open challenge and Haughey's interpretation of the meeting was that he had been given a free hand.

A number of meetings between the Taoiseach and O'Malley took place during that day and the final shape of the coalition agreement was ironed out. There are different views as to whether the crucial issue of the number of PD Cabinet seats was settled that day but the official version is that the final decision on that did not take place until little over an hour before the Dáil met on the afternoon of 12 July.

On the morning of that fateful day for Fianna Fáil, Haughey demonstrated all the old political skill which had helped him through earlier crises. He first met O'Malley at around 10 a.m. and half an hour later went into a Cabinet meeting to tell his ministerial colleagues that there were still some problems that remained to be cleared up before the coalition arrangement could be finalised.

No one challenged Haughey about the precise nature of the deal and there was no discussion on the number of PD Cabinet seats. Interviews with Reynolds and Ahern had been broadcast on radio that morning and the two ministers said the PDs should only get one Cabinet seat. Ahern had received a dressing down from Haughey before the Cabinet meeting for making the statement, but there was no discussion of the issue at Cabinet. Haughey side-stepped it by saying that the coalition deal was not finalised.

From the Cabinet meeting Haughey went straight to the final meeting of the parliamentary party. He also told his backbenchers that there was no final agreement but he did circulate a document: "Fianna Fáil-Progressive Democrats Programme for Government 1989-

166

1993". The TDs didn't have time to digest the details and anyway the crucial question of Cabinet representation was not mentioned in it.

There were no objections and Haughey left the meeting before lunchtime. He was now completely in the clear; neither the Cabinet, the parliamentary party or the national executive had given him a precise instruction not to concede two Cabinet posts to the PDs. His deftness in avoiding an open confrontation meant that he had a free hand to act as he saw fit, even though he knew the deep-seated hostility in the party to what he was planning.

At 1 p.m. Haughey met O'Malley and the PD negotiating team of Molloy and Cox. As before, the Fianna Fáil negotiating team were not informed of this meeting. Haughey formally agreed to two PD Cabinet positions and to one junior ministry for the party. The four men then shook hands on the deal. "Nobody but myself could have done it," remarked the Taoiseach good humouredly to the PDs and they could only agree.

After they left the Taoiseach's office, Molloy was sent for again to be formally asked would he accept the Cabinet post as Minister for Energy. Between that time at the meeting of the Dáil at 3 p.m. Haughey put the rest of his Cabinet together, making very few changes but dropping old supporters Brendan Daly and Michael Noonan to make way for the PDs.

The joint programme for government was essentially another victory for the PDs. The central commitment on tax reform would be popular with the voters and Fianna Fáil TDs had to be content with pointing to a continued commitment to reducing the national debt. A programme of law reform and reform of the Oireachtas was also part of the deal.

There was one issue on which Haughey drew the line and that was Northern Ireland. The first draft of the joint programme included a commitment to support a devolved government in the province, but Haughey wouldn't have it and the PDs agreed to drop the pledge in the final draft. When the Dáil met that afternoon Haughey was duly elected Taoiseach with the support of the PDs.

In the short debate on the vote for Taoiseach, O'Malley and Haughey publicly buried the animosity which had divided them for so long as they paid fulsome tribute to each other.

"I want to acknowledge the courage and skill exhibited, particularly by Deputy Haughey in recent weeks, courage and skill which I know he possesses in abundance and which has been utilised in the national interest during this time," the PD leader told the Dáil.

After his election Haughey responded: "I want to say about them all, particularly Deputy O'Malley, that I was able to conduct my conversations with them in a way that was always not just courteous but constructive, and I shall always remember that as one of the most important developments in this new Dáil as it went about its arduous and complicated business."

After a visit to President Hillery, Haughey returned to announce his Cabinet to the Dáil. It had taken a full twenty-seven days since the election to put a government together but in the end the logic of political arithmetic ultimately proved irresistible.

There were enormous stresses and strains in Fianna Fáil as the party sought to come to terms with the notion of coalition. Things eventually settled down but one result was a decisive shift in the balance of power within Haughey's Cabinet. Ministers like Reynolds and Flynn, long-time Haughey supporters who made up the old inner circle of the Cabinet, were excluded from favour because of their opposition to coalition. Ahern remained closer to Haughey but the relationship became somewhat ambiguous.

Reynolds and Ahern, who made up Haughey's negotiating team with the PDs, were deeply disillusioned and very angry over the whole process. They feet they had been treated with contempt by Haughey, who had carried out all the important negotiations himself without telling them anything of importance that was going on.

The experience of being treated in this fashion did not come as a total surprise to Reynolds. While he had backed Haughey in three early leadership heaves a coolness had developed between the two men since 1987, particularly as Reynolds began to emerge as a strong runner in the succession stakes.

With his old supporters feeling aggrieved Haughey had to rely for a while on two of the most experienced ministers in the Cabinet, Gerry Collins and Ray Burke. They occupied a position of trust they had not experienced since Haughey became leader of Fianna Fáil in December 1979.

There was something supremely ironic in the fact that Haughey was now closest to the two Fianna Fáil members of his Cabinet who had voted against him in the most recent leadership contest, while he had brought into the government, out of necessity, two others who left the party because of his leadership.

Even more ironic was the fact that as the early months of government progressed the trust that developed between Haughey and O'Malley during the coalition negotiations developed into a strong political bond.

"The central relationship in government is the one between Haughey and O'Malley. They clearly meet and make the key decisions before the Cabinet even gets around to considering them," said one minister in late 1987. Lenihan was even more frank. "I am nominally Tánaiste in this government but the reality of the situation is that O'Malley is the real Tánaiste. He is the actual number two in the government," he said in the autumn of 1989.

A real worry for Haughey, though, was that the coalition decision had destroyed his power-base in the organisation. Party members were shell-shocked and his strongest supporters, at all levels, were the ones most horrified by the decision to form a coalition. The dropping of two staunch supporters like Brendan Daly and Michael Noonan to make way for the PDs in the Cabinet caused a lot of bitterness.

However, there was widespread public support for the coalition government and opinion polls revealed that Fianna Fáil's standing went right back up to its 50 percent-plus level when things settled down.

O'Malley, as Minister for Industry and Commerce, now had responsibility for the operation of the export credit insurance scheme. He immediately set up a departmental inquiry into the discrepancies revealed by PD parliamentary questions back in April which showed that the insurance cover given to Goodman companies for beef exports to Iraq was for a value greater than the total exports in 1987-88. Having got the results of the inquiry O'Malley cancelled export credit insurance policies worth nearly £40 million after it was found that 38 percent of the beef covered had been sourced in Britain and Northern Ireland. Goodman responded by beginning a legal action against the state for £50 million.

O'Malley's action was taken after consultation with Haughey and no obstacles were put in his way by the Taoiseach. Neither were there objections when O'Malley's inspectors concluded that Goodman was the beneficial owner of Classic Meats and the meat baron was ordered to dispose of it. O'Malley's ability to take independent action surprised many people, but it appeared that the parties in government could learn to live together in harmony. This impression was confirmed by the appointment to the Seanad of three PD senators. Again there were murmurings in Fianna Fáil, but they amounted to nothing. The PDs, on the other hand, showed their mettle by refusing to vote for the Fianna Fáil nominee for Cathaoirleach of the Seanad, Seán Doherty, because of his role in the GUBU controversies of 1982.

By the end of 1989 Haughey was back in the driving seat despite his disastrous decision to call a general election in June. Regardless of the rumblings in the party he made it clear he wanted to lead on for some time. "What else would I be doing if I wasn't leading Fianna Fáil? It's my life," he told Shane Kenny in a radio interview a few months after the government was formed.

However, his hold on power now depended on Des O'Malley and the PDs. That was something which rankled with Fianna Fáil members up and down the country, but all they could do was swallow their pride and accept the situation. Fianna Fáil TDs were relieved when 1989 drew to a close because they never wanted to see another traumatic year like it again. It was just as well they didn't have the benefit of being able to see into the future because 1990 held even worse in store.

15 – Presidential Election

Haughey was on top of the world for the first half of 1990. With Ireland holding the presidency of the European Community, the Taoiseach projected himself successfully as President of Europe at a time of historic change in the world. However, another presidency, the Irish one, brought him tumbling down to earth. The presidential election campaign of 1990 turned into one of the most sensational campaigns in the history of the state and it plunged Fianna Fáil and Fine Gael into crisis.

The Fianna Fáil Tánaiste and the leader of Fine Gael both lost their jobs as a consequence and serious questions began to be asked about Haughey's position. For Alan Dukes the whole thing was an unmitigated disaster but Haughey managed, yet again, to survive what can only be described as a calamity for Fianna Fáil.

The countdown to disaster began in January, even as the Taoiseach was beginning to glory in his EC role. Ireland's presidency coincided with a time of momentous change in the world. The communist regimes of Eastern Europe were collapsing, the Berlin wall had just come down and the dream of German unity was suddenly a realistic political option. Haughey facilitated German Chancellor Helmut Kohl's desire to get full EC backing for German unity. A special summit to discuss the issue was held in Dublin on 28 April 1990 as well as the regular one in June. Haughey's handling of the problem was impressive and it added to his stature.

Even in his hour of glory a new problem was building up. In January the leader of the Labour Party, Dick Spring, announced his determination to ensure that there was a presidential contest. There had been no election since 1973 and the office had been filled on three occasions by agreement among the Dáil parties. Spring said that if necessary he would stand for election himself to ensure the people were given a choice.

He didn't have to go that far because he was able to persuade former Labour senator Mary Robinson to accept the party's nomination. There was already a move by left-wingers in the party to run Noel Browne, but Spring staked his authority on Robinson's candidature. Robinson's nomination was not achieved without some division in the Labour Party. Left-wing TDs like Emmet Stagg and Michael D. Higgins still wanted Noel Browne but Spring got his way when the parliamentary party selected Robinson in early April.

"In the early stages we believed that if we managed to appeal to a wider electorate we had a good chance of coming second. To aim at that wider electorate we printed 70,000 posters and 1.6 million pieces of literature not one of which had a Labour logo," said Fergus Finlay, Dick Spring's advisor.

Robinson was not even a member of the party, having resigned five years earlier in protest at the way the Anglo-Irish Agreement was concluded without consultation with the Unionists. This posed some difficulty in seeking the Labour nomination but it was a great help to her for the rest of the campaign as it enabled her to claim that she was independent.

The campaign team that gelled around her represented a much wider spectrum of Irish politics than Labour-Workers' Party activists. Robinson's long-time friend and political ally Bride Rosney was on the campaign committee, as was her husband Nicholas, along with Labour people like Ruairi Quinn, who was director of elections, and party press officer Fergus Finlay. Another person who made a vital contribution was ex-RTE producer and former Workers' Party guru Eoghan Harris. A key member of the WP for over twenty years and the architect of their Stalinist policies, Harris had left the party in the spring of 1990 following a row over a document written by him called "The necessity for Social Democracy". That document advocated the abandonment of socialism by the WP and a move towards the centre. It was rejected by the party at a bitter Ard Fheis in Dublin and this led to the resignation of Eamonn Smullen, the party official who had published it.

When, in early April, Harris heard she was likely to be Labour's candidate, he wrote to Robinson advising her how to fight the campaign. "My view is that you can win the campaign or come so close as to give you a famous political victory by presenting yourself as a democratic rather than liberal candidate and never as a liberal-left candidate." Encouraging her to broaden her appeal he went on: "You have some hard choices to make and one of them is not to listen to every Tom, Dick and Harry – and especially Dublin Four Dicks. On your team you need some who are racy of the soil, who have a feel for Catholic cultural mores, who are at home at a noisy Fine Gael function, who could watch a hurling match with relish and who know who Packie Bonner is.

"Politically you have huge ground to make up. You must secure the entire Fine Gael vote – which you can't do unless you deal with the Distortion issue (Divorce and Abortion). You need to split the Fianna Fáil vote – which you can do by pulling their progressive women voters away by a bravura campaign. You need Labour/Dublin 4/Divorce/Abortion/Rape Crisis/Incest and all that like a hole in the head. You have that."

Harris followed up his letter with a campaign blueprint four days later and one of the key recommendations was that Robinson should travel the length and breadth of the country during the campaign. She did just that, setting out on a trek which took her through every county in the state in a six-month campaign for the presidency – something which was entirely new in Irish politics.

Meanwhile the Dáil was rocked by a controversy over the government's plans for commercial broadcasting. The new national independent radio service, Century, had severe financial problems and Communications Minister Ray Burke began to examine the whole area of broadcasting legislation. In February Burke denied a claim in the Dáil by Jim Mitchell of Fine Gael that he intended to take some of the licence fee money from RTE.

In May Burke produced legislation which proposed to do precisely this, as well as cap RTE's advertising revenue. There was uproar when the plan was announced. It was denounced by RTE as well as all the Opposition parties, who created bedlam in the Dáil. Incredibly, it then emerged from Fianna Fáil sources that Fine Gael leader Alan Dukes had had a secret meeting with Haughey at which he lobbied for action to help Century. Fine Gael were as deeply embarrassed by the affair as Fianna Fáil and the incident fatally undermined Dukes's leadership.

In the face of all the opposition Burke then modified his proposals.

He dropped the plan to take some of the licence fee but he tightened up the plan to cap RTE's advertising revenue. There was a renewed storm of protest with widespread opposition to the plan. Among those opposing it were some of the national newspapers who had put pressure on Burke to limit RTE's advertising in the first place.

Another embarrassment for Fianna Fáil in the early part of the year arose from Seán Doherty's position as Cathaoirleach of the Seanad. Doherty lost his Dáil seat in 1989 and only got his party's nomination for the Cathaoirleach's position when his name was pulled from a hat after he tied with Des Hanafin. In March 1990 he got embroiled in a wrangle with colleagues for failing to disclose a legal opinion arising from a complicated dispute with Senator David Norris. The storm abated as quickly as it blew up but it reminded people about the events of 1982 in which Doherty had been involved.

With the presidential election looming the controversy came at a very bad time for Fianna Fáil. By this stage, after her early forays into the country, Mary Robinson became convinced that she was in with a real chance of winning. At that time nobody took this very seriously, with most Labour people hoping for a good performance and second place, ahead of the Fine Gael candidate, as the likeliest outcome. Robinson, though, was sustained by the belief that she could become the country's first woman president. "The thing that struck me most forcibly about her when I met her first in the early summer was her strong belief that she was going to win," said Eamonn Gilmore, the Workers' Party TD who joined the campaign committee when his party decided to back Robinson.

Throughout the summer she continued the hard slog up and down the country while the major parties waited until autumn to select their candidates. One evening in July, Fergus Finlay was in the Dáil bar when he heard a rumour that Austin Currie was being mooted as the Fine Gael candidate. Convinced that Robinson could beat Currie and probably win on his transfers, Finlay set off the next morning to find a bookmaker and asked for the odds on Mary Robinson. He was the first to inquire and was quoted odds of ten to one so he promptly placed a bet of £100. By the time Fianna Fáil had got around to nominating Brian Lenihan and Fine Gael had come up with Austin

Currie in September, the Robinson campaign had managed to capture the public imagination and the strong response of women had become the central feature.

Before the major parties got around to nominating their candidates, another sensation emerged in the shape of the threatened collapse of the Goodman group. The Dáil was hurriedly recalled on 28 August to pass special legislation so that the company would not go to the wall immediately with devastating knock-on effects for farmers. O'Malley told the Dáil that Goodman International owed a consortium of international banks an incredible £460 million. The company was owed £180 million from meat exports to Iraq, which had just invaded Kuwait and was unlikely to be in a position to pay. Massive losses of £200 million had also been run up by Goodman in an ill-fated foray into the British stock market to buy sugar shares.

Goodman tried to put pressure on the government to come up with a rescue package for his operation. He helicoptered into Kinsealy ten days before the special Dáil sitting to try and persuade Haughey to bale him out, but the scale of the losses was so great that the Taoiseach was in no position to attempt a rescue. All the government could do was to pass the legislation to put an examiner into the company so that the debts to the banks could be rescheduled.

The whole affair was an embarrassment to Haughey, given his close association with Goodman in the past. However, the decisive handling of the issue by O'Malley helped to calm public disquiet – It was an instance of where the participation of the PDs in coalition worked to the advantage of both parties in the government.

With Robinson campaigning away it was now time for the other parties to take the presidential election seriously. Brian Lenihan had been talked about as the likely Fianna Fáil runner for nearly a year, though before that Marine Minister John Wilson had been regarded as the most likely candidate. Lenihan's name began to circulate in late 1989. The subject of his possible candidature was raised at a lunch hosted by the Tánaiste in McKee Barracks for the Government Press Secretary, P.J. Mara, and the Australian Ambassador to Ireland and former Labour Prime Minister of Western Australia, Brian Burke. Mara raised the subject of the presidential election with Lenihan and did not have a great deal of trouble persuading him that he would be the ideal Fianna Fáil candidate. This was somewhat surprising in view of Lenihan's health. For the previous couple of years his condition had declined and it became clear at the beginning of 1989 that he would need a liver transplant to save his life. This operation had been carried out in early summer at the Mayo Clinic in the United States and the Tánaiste missed the general election campaign as a result. However, he topped the poll in Dublin West and he remained in the Cabinet though he was moved from Foreign Affairs to Defence.

The Taoiseach gave a broad hint to the annual Fianna Fáil fundraising dinner a few weeks later in December 1989 that Lenihan would be the candidate and it became accepted as a fact of life by most party TDs and senators. There were worries though that as a man with a liver transplant his health might not stand up to a gruelling campaign and that he might not survive for seven years in the Aras. There was also a great deal of concern at the prospect of Fianna Fáil losing the seat in a Dublin West by-election which would be necessitated by his election. During the first half of 1990 the Taoiseach was rumoured to be worried on both these counts and there was speculation that he would ask Lenihan not to put his name forward.

This did not happen, however, but John Wilson did emerge with a late challenge to the Tánaiste. Wilson only declared himself less than a week before the parliamentary party was due to choose its candidate on 17 September when it was too late. He did manage to win support from some ministers of state like Máire Geoghegan-Quinn and Pat "The Cope" Gallagher but the only Cabinet minister to back him publicly was constituency colleague, Rory O'Hanlon, who acted more out of a sense of duty than commitment to his cause.

Minister for Finance Albert Reynolds caused some worry in the Lenihan camp when it became known that he was considering coming out in open support of Wilson, but Cabinet colleagues Bertie Ahern and Pádraig Flynn persuaded him to back off and stay neutral. Wilson attracted support in particular from party TDs most hostile to the coalition and as the chief opponent of coalition there was a clear temptation to Reynolds to get involved. Intervention by the Finance Minister on Wilson's side could have made a big difference but he was persuaded that it would not be in either the party's interests or his own longterm interests to get involved. Backers like Geoghegan-Quinn and backbench Meath TD Noel Dempsey held strong views on the coalition issue, but despite an intensive phone-lobbying campaign Wilson was defeated by 51 votes to 19.

Fine Gael in the meantime had come up with former SDLP politician Austin Currie, but only after an embarrassing delay and a botched selection process which involved him taking the nomination after it had been turned down by a range of people in the party, including himself at an earlier stage. It wouldn't have been too bad if eminent party figures like Garret FitzGerald and Peter Barry had been the only ones to turn down the nomination, but it was also refused by a cross-section of people in the party from Jim Mitchell to Avril Doyle. Kerry playwright John B. Keane had even been approached by local TD Jimmy Deenihan to see if he was available.

Currie had been approached before the summer and had been encouraged to run by Garret FitzGerald. As a newcomer to southern politics he was reluctant and the approach was not followed up. One of the reasons for that was that research commissioned by Fine Gael headquarters in early summer showed that Currie had a very low recognition rating with the public and that his northern background was a distinct liability. At the beginning of September, though, Dukes knew he had to find a candidate if he was to avert an immediate leadership heave.

He had lost the confidence of a majority of his front bench following the debacle over the Broadcasting Bill and during the summer the rumblings in the party had grown. By the end of August the discontent on the front bench was palpable and there were rumours of a plot against Dukes. Eventually Currie agreed, reluctantly, to let his name go forward and Dukes was able to tell the front bench meeting on 5 September that a candidate had been found.

Finding a candidate enabled Dukes to head off his opponents but it was only to prove a stay of execution. Though Lenihan had not been nominated he had been talked about for months as the Fianna Fáil candidate and meanwhile Robinson was barnstorming her way up and down the country. It was already a two-horse race and there was nothing Currie could do about it. A poll carried out by Lansdowne Market Research in mid-September when the three candidates' names were known gave Lenihan 53 percent, Robinson 32 percent and Currie just 15 percent. An MRBI poll published in *The Irish Times* gave Currie slightly more support but he was still below 20 percent. Meanwhile, Fianna Fáil's daily tracking polls in the first weeks of the campaign showed Currie making no impact but Robinson gradually improving her position and Lenihan dropping.

Jim Mitchell and Michael Noonan were put in charge of the Currie campaign and it was only when they had taken over that they were given the research which showed that he hadn't a chance. The conduct of the campaign did nothing to help, with frequent late night rows at party headquarters involving Dukes, Mitchell and other members of the campaign staff. Towards the end of the campaign there was a blazing row between Dukes and Madeleine Taylor-Quinn, the party's spokeswoman on the marine, which shook her confidence in her leader.

The campaign had now been firmly polarised into a race between Robinson and Lenihan, and by mid-October Lansdowne Market Research found that Robinson had risen to 36 percent and Lenihan had fallen to 45 percent with Currie getting just 19 percent. In fact this poll was very close to the end result with Robinson gaining a bit more by polling day, 7 November, and Lenihan and Currie dropping slightly. In the meantime though, the country was rocked by a controversy which flared directly out of the campaign.

The controversy was instigated by Garret FitzGerald with the encouragement of Jim Mitchell, who was trying desperately to get his candidate into the campaign. FitzGerald was sent on to the television programme "Questions and Answers" specifically to tackle Lenihan about the events of 27 January 1982, when calls had been made to Aras an Uachtaráin by senior Fianna Fáil members in a effort to persuade President Hillery not to grant a request by FitzGerald to dissolve the Dáil but instead to ask them to form a government. FitzGerald had been made aware of the calls when he went to the Aras that night in 1982.

The issue was raised by Currie in a radio debate between the three candidates at the very beginning of the campaign but nobody paid much attention. Now in the campaign's dying days Fine Gael clutched at the issue again. FitzGerald was in Italy when the decision was taken to send him on and he was not briefed about it until he returned the day before the programme. A number of Fine Gael activists who were going on the programme were also briefed by Mitchell, as the format of "Questions and Answers" allows each politician to bring along a group of supporters who are entitled to ask questions and intervene in the discussion.

The issue arose on television when one of the Fine Gael activists had a question accepted asking about the discretionary powers of the president to refuse a dissolution of the Dáil to a Taoiseach who had lost his majority. When Lenihan concluded his answer by saying that this option had never been exercised by an Irish president, FitzGerald intervened to ask: "Why were there phone calls to try and force him to exercise it?"

Lenihan replied: "That is a fiction of Garret's."

"It is not a fiction, excuse me. I was in Aras an Uachtaráin when these phone calls came through and I know how many there were," said FitzGerald, and from there the controversy took flight.

Later in the discussion Fine Gael activist Brian Murphy intervened to ask Lenihan directly if he had made a phone call to Aras an Uachtaráin when Garret FitzGerald was seeking a dissolution of the Dáil.

"No, I didn't at all. Nothing like that ever happened. I want to assure you that it never happened," replied Lenihan.

With this answer a time bomb began ticking under Lenihan's campaign and political career. Brian Murphy, the Fine Gael questioner in the audience, knew something that neither Garret FitzGerald nor any of the other Fine Gael activists present knew at this stage – that a tape existed on which Lenihan spoke freely of how he had phoned Aras an Uachtaráin on the night in question and it detailed a conversation he said he had with the President.

The person who had made that tape was a post-graduate politics student at UCD, Jim Duffy. He was watching "Questions and Answers" that night and looked on in growing disbelief as Lenihan categorically denied on air that he had made any phone call to Aras an Uachtaráin because this flatly contradicted the colourful account the Tánaiste had given to him a few months earlier about a conversation he had with President Hillery that night.

To compound the issue, Duffy had written a series of articles for *The Irish Times* a month earlier about the presidency and had referred on the basis of the taped information to phone calls by Lenihan, Haughey and Sylvester Barrett. Following Lenihan's denial on television Duffy contacted *The Irish Times* the next day, Tuesday, and events began to take an inevitable course. In the meantime Lenihan went on television again on Tuesday night to say that he had had no hand, act or part in phoning Aras an Uachtaráin on the night in question.

By Wednesday morning rumours about the taped interview were flashing around Leinster House in advance of the Dáil's resumption after the long summer break. *The Irish Times* carried a lead story saying they had independent evidence that Lenihan had phoned the President. Lenihan in the meantime assured his director of elections, Bertie Ahern, and other ministers that there was nothing that could do him damage. He told them he had met a post-graduate student before the summer but said there was nothing in the taped conversation that could cause embarrassment.

The Tánaiste came into Leinster House to consult his colleagues in the party but he was not on the government benches when the sitting began. There was immediate uproar and Alan Dukes and Jim Mitchell both referred to the fact that there was a tape which proved that Garret FitzGerald was correct. Throughout the day there were denials from Fianna Fáil ministers that any phone calls had been made to the President. Lenihan in reply to reporters who asked about an academic tape said: "I don't know what you are talking about. I've seen no tapes about anything."

That night in the Dáil Dukes made a comprehensive speech on the role of the presidency in which he outlined the various documentary references to the phone calls made in 1982. In the Dáil on Thursday morning an angry Taoiseach called FitzGerald a liar. Replying to allegations by Dukes about the phone calls to the President, the

Taoiseach said he should "look behind him at Deputy Garret FitzGerald who has been completely exposed as telling lies".

Only hours later the bombshell of the tape finally exploded. On the tape Lenihan referred to a conversation he had with President Hillery on the night of 27 January 1982 and he also said that Haughey and Sylvester Barrett, as well as himself, had rung the Aras. He was quite specific on tape about what he had done that night. Asked if he had got through to the President, Mr Lenihan replied:

"Oh yeah, I mean I got through to him. I remember talking to him and he wanted us to lay off. There was no doubt about it in his mind, in fact looking back on it it was a mistake on our part because Paddy Hillery would be very, what's the word, strict or conventional in that way you know, he wouldn't want to start breaking new ground, he's not that sort of man, very cautious man. The sort of fellow that wouldn't, it didn't break new ground. But of course Charlie was gung ho."

In his book *For the Record* published a few months after the election, Lenihan explained that he was on heavy medication to counteract a complicated condition arising from his liver transplant when he gave the interview to Duffy on 17 May. He cited medical evidence to show that he was in a confused state at the time he gave the interview and he had no recollection of ever giving it. However, when the transcript of a portion of the tape was released the effect was shattering.

Even worse was to follow because at that stage Lenihan did not provide the explanation that was forthcoming in his book. In the Dáil, Fianna Fáil TDs were visibly reeling when they read the transcript of the tape and most of them headed quickly for their constituencies in a deep state of shock. In the meantime Lenihan returned from the campaign trail for a consultation with Haughey. On the advice of Government Press Secretary P.J. Mara he decided to go on television and radio immediately to rebut the clear evidence of the tape. Lenihan was driven to RTE where he appeared on the 6 p.m. news on television, interviewed by Seán Duignan. He tried to convince the bemused electorate that what he had said on tape to Duffy was not true and he stuck by his original story that he had never phoned the

President. Looking directly into camera Lenihan said: "My mature recollection at this stage is that I did not ring President Hillery. I want to put my reputation on the line in that respect. I have sought a meeting with President Hillery tomorrow and I intend to confirm that with him. That is the situation."

When Seán Duignan put it to him that he had either not told the truth to the nation or he had not told the truth to Jim Duffy the Tánaiste responded: "I must have been mistaken in what I said to Duffy on that occasion. It was a casual discussion with a research student and I was obviously mistaken in what I said."

The effect of Lenihan's performance was extraordinary and it knocked the wind right out of his campaign. The combination of what he actually said and how he said it destroyed his credibility at that stage in the campaign. The general reaction was well put by former rugby international Tony Ward, who is actually a member of Fianna Fáil. "The whole thing made me cringe. It was pathetic to see someone continuing with a lie when the truth was there for everyone to hear. I just wanted to say: Stop, stop. Get off the television screen."

A subsequent radio interview with Seán O'Rourke only compounded the damage and another television appearance later that night added to Lenihan's woe. By the end of the evening the Lenihan campaign was in tatters and it looked all over for the Tánaiste. Events then took another extraordinary twist.

16 – The Sacking of a Tánaiste

On the night of Brian Lenihan's humiliation Fine Gael leader Alan Dukes, raised the stakes. In an attempt to exploit the clear disarray in Fianna Fáil and in the process to try and shore up his own leadership, Dukes put down a motion of no confidence in the government. "I have put down a motion of no confidence in the government because it is now clear and beyond any doubt that lies have been told this week by the Tánaiste, Mr Lenihan, and that those lies have been supported by the Taoiseach and three other ministers," he said in a statement.

The motion was designed to test the unity of the coalition. The Progressive Democrats had not come out in favour of any of the candidates in the presidential election. Though most of the party's supporters favoured Mary Robinson, the parliamentary party felt it would be provocative towards their coalition partners to back her, so they stayed out of the campaign though individual members campaigned for Robinson.

Party leader Des O'Malley flew out to Luxembourg on official business less than two hours after the publication of the Duffy tape but he was already aware that the government had a political crisis on its hands. The Assistant Government Press Secretary, Stephen O'Byrnes, had received a copy of the Lenihan tape transcript soon after the press conference. He immediately went to consult O'Malley and show him the transcript. They were joined by Mary Harney.

The consensus between O'Malley, Harney and O'Byrnes was that they would now have a real problem in voting confidence in the government.The PD leader than rang Haughey to express concern at the development and he asked the Taoiseach not to say anything which would commit the government as a whole in relation to the motion of confidence that was pending.

In a move to signal the party's position publicly O'Malley told O'Byrnes to issue a statement on his behalf saying he found the situation "very disturbing". The PD leader then left for Luxembourg before the six o'clock news and Lenihan's "mature recollection" statement. After that broadcast the strong mood of the PD organisation was that they could not support Lenihan in any vote of confidence.

A factor which complicated the situation was that the Taoiseach, Des O'Malley and Bobby Molloy were all out of the country for periods during the crucial days which followed so that misunderstandings had time to develop. O'Byrnes met Haughey the day after the tapes fiasco to stress the gravity of the situation. The meeting was amicable but the Taoiseach's attitude was that the affair was a matter pertaining to Fianna Fáil rather than the government as a whole. He could see no reason why the PDs wanted to make it a government matter and found it difficult to understand why they were getting so excited.

That night O'Malley returned home and a crucial meeting took place in Michael McDowell's house. Also there were Mary Harney, the party's sole MEP Pat Cox, David O'Keeffe and Ray Gordon. Bobby Molloy flew up from Galway to join them and after a thorough examination of the issues the unanimous view was that they could not vote confidence in the government if Lenihan remained a member.

"This is a make or break issue for us. A central reason for our existence is our refusal to accept low standards in high places so there is no way we can go along with Fianna Fáil on this," said one of the participants after that meeting. It was quite an emotional gathering as the younger PDs were very conscious of the sacrifices they were asking their senior ministers to make. O'Malley and Molloy had come back to government a little over a year earlier after so many years in the political wilderness, but that night's decision threatened to put an end to their political power. O'Byrnes paid tribute to the two ministers before the meeting ended.

At 9 a.m. the following morning O'Malley met Haughey at Kinsealy before the Taoiseach flew off to Rome for an EC summit meeting. He again emphasised the seriousness of the situation as far as the PDs were concerned and said that it was not a problem of their making but one for Fianna Fáil. He told Haughey that the problem facing the government had been created by Fianna Fáil and it was up to them to respond to it. O'Malley did not say that Lenihan would have to go but the clear implication of his remarks was that the PDs could support the government only if he left the Cabinet.

After the meeting at Kinsealy, Haughey gave a press conference at the airport before leaving for Rome. He said the meeting with O'Malley was mainly about the current GATT talks, but he also said that an election on the confidence issue at this stage would be "absolute lunacy".

O'Malley met leading PD members in Michael McDowell's house, including his two ministerial colleagues Bobby Molloy and Mary Harney. They were taken aback by Haughey's claim that the meeting with O'Malley had centred on the GATT talks and they felt he was not taking them seriously, so they decided to issue their own statement on the meeting between O'Malley and Haughey:

"The purpose of this meeting was to discuss the implications for the coalition government of recent events. O'Malley made it clear that these implications were not of the Progressive Democrats' making. O'Malley presented to Haughey the PDs' analysis of these events. The parliamentary party of the PDs will meet early next week to consider the matter further in the light of the response from Mr Haughey. That meeting will also decide the parliamentary party's voting intentions on next week's Dáil order of business."

In order to issue a public signal Pat Cox went on Rodney Rice's "Saturday View" programme that lunchtime. On radio, Cox began to spell out the seriousness of the situation and the public were alerted for the first time to the fact that the PDs had made it a crisis issue. He said the PDs would make up their mind on what to do on the vote of confidence in the light of how Fianna Fáil responded. There was a question in relation to the credibility of the government but that question of credibility had nothing to do with the PDs but with Fianna Fáil. "A problem does arise which impinges on the credibility of the Fianna Fáil side of the government," he said. At this stage the PDs believed that Lenihan would probably resign to save the government.

The Minister for Justice, Ray Burke, and the Fine Gael deputy leader, John Bruton, were also on that programme and both were taken aback by Cox's attitude. Afterwards Bruton suggested to Cox that the PDs could satisfy honour by finding an alternative to pulling out of government. Another senior Fine Gael figure contacted Stephen O'Byrnes the same day to suggest that a way out for the PDs would be to come out with a public declaration of support for Robinson.

The following day the Sunday newspapers were full of speculation that the government would collapse and that a general election was on the cards. Senior Fianna Fáil people now knew that the government's existence was under threat. Haughey returned from Rome that night to find that a full-scale political crisis had developed.

The following day at noon O'Malley travelled out to Kinsealy for another meeting with Haughey. The Taoiseach was now keenly aware of the extent of the crisis that threatened to bring down his government. He called a special meeting of the Fianna Fáil members of the Cabinet that afternoon to discuss the situation and shocked ministers heard Séamus Brennan and Ray Burke spell out what they saw as the threat to economic stability posed by the political crisis. Brennan in particular emphasised the movements on the Dublin money market which he said already indicated that higher interest rates were on the way if an election was caused.

Neither Lenihan or his sister, Minister for Education Mary O'Rourke, was informed of the meeting. The ministers who did attend discussed the options facing them and there was broad agreement that Lenihan's resignation was the only course of action that would save the government. Haughey decided that he would have to meet his Tánaiste to sort out the situation and late that evening newsdesks at RTE and the national newspapers were informed anonymously that Lenihan had been summoned for a meeting at Kinsealy the following morning. P.J. Mara and Labour Minister Bertie Ahern spent much of the day at the Taoiseach's house planning the next move.

When Lenihan arrived by helicopter at Kinsealy the following morning Haughey told him that O'Malley and the PDs wanted his resignation and he bluntly told his Tánaiste that he should resign from the government. In his book *For the Record*, Lenihan recounts how he resisted this pressure and countered by offering to resign if he lost the election.

Haughey asked Lenihan to meet his ministerial colleagues as he himself had to go to Dublin airport to greet Queen Beatrix of the Netherlands who was beginning a state visit to Ireland. After the Taoiseach left, Lenihan was driven to Leinster House where he was confronted by a group of senior Fianna Fáil ministers.

In the room were Bertie Ahern, Pádraig Flynn, Ray Burke, Albert Reynolds and the party chief whip, Vincent Brady. The issue of resignation was raised and strong pressure was applied to Lenihan. Vincent Brady in particular was insistent that the Tánaiste would have to resign from the Cabinet by 5 p.m. that afternoon and he demanded that the rest of the day's electioneering in Longford and Westmeath should be cancelled.

Haughey, meanwhile, was being interviewed by reporters at the airport and he rejected suggestions that he would fire his Tánaiste. He said that Lenihan had not offered his resignation nor had it been sought. The question of resignation was entirely a matter for his friend of thirty years. "I want to make it clear that anything of that nature is entirely a matter for my old friend Brian Lenihan himself. I would not exert any pressure of any kind on any of my colleagues," the Taoiseach told the journalists and his comments were carried on the lunchtime news bulletins.

Back at Leinster House the Tánaiste again met Haughey who had returned from his lunch with Queen Beatrix. The Taoiseach repeated his request to Lenihan to resign and gave him a three-page resignation statement which had been prepared by one of Haughey's staff. The resignation statement expressed regret for the embarrassment caused to the government by Lenihan. "Accordingly, I have today tendered my resignation as Tánaiste and Minister for Defence in order to enable the Government to continue with its successful programme." To add insult to injury the statement went on: "This decision is mine and mine alone. I have not been subject to pressure from any quarter."

Lenihan refused to sign on-the-spot and asked for time to consider his position. He insisted on going ahead with the day's campaigning and shortly after 2 p.m. he left by helicopter for Granard in County Longford with Albert Reynolds. At Granard the Lenihan family – his wife Ann, their children, and his sister Mary O'Rourke – were waiting to set out on the campaign trail for the day.

The family immediately took Lenihan into what amounted to protective custody and told him not to be pressurised into doing anything he didn't want to do. Reynolds gave him similar advice as the bus headed across Longford. At every stop along the way there were phone messages from the Taoiseach's office but the cordon of protection around Lenihan kept the callers at bay. The crowds were getting bigger at each town and by the evening, when he crossed into Westmeath, people were shouting "don't resign" when he alighted from the campaign bus at each stop.

A very surprised Lenihan heard a radio report at 5 p.m. that Junior Minister Michael Smith had issued a statement welcoming his resignation. The Lenihan family believed that Smith's statement was a deliberate attempt to put pressure on him and if anything it swayed him against resignation.

As darkness fell and Lenihan's entourage drew near Athlone to bigger and bigger crowds, he made up his mind firmly that he would not resign, come what may, and he gave a television interview rejecting the option. In Moate two Cabinet ministers, Pádraig Flynn and Bertie Ahern, were spotted in the crowd.

"Am I welcome to Westmeath?" called out Flynn above the hubbub. "No you are not," replied his Cabinet colleague, Mary O'Rourke, who told him to clear off back across the Shannon.

The cavalcade swept on into Athlone and Lenihan retired to the house of old family friends, the O'Callaghan's, where he rested before the big rally in the town that night. Meanwhile Flynn and Ahern, who had been unable to speak to the Tánaiste in Moate, drove on to Athlone where they had a meeting in an upstairs room of the Prince of Wales Hotel with Albert Reynolds. Public relations consultant Frank Dunlop, who had become very active in the Lenihan campaign, joined them and there were rumours of a press conference to announce the Tánaiste's resignation. The emissaries from Dublin never met Lenihan however. Mary O'Rourke arrived at the Prince of Wales hotel and was asked if she would be prepared to meet the three in room 67. She agreed but a fierce argument developed between her and Flynn. The Environment Minister was again told that he wasn't welcome and left for Dublin without being able to speak to the Tánaiste.

The Lenihan family were deeply indignant at the pressure. Reynolds was the only senior Fianna Fáil figure who stood by them and continued to insist that the Tánaiste should be allowed to make his own decision in his own time. Ann Lenihan stuck at her husband's side and refused to allow him to be put under any pressure by Haughey's messengers. After the rally the family returned to the O'Callaghan's house with a group of thirty or forty supporters, and Lenihan went to bed around midnight.

Meanwhile in Dublin that evening the PDs were also facing the crunch. They had expected that Lenihan would resign that day and when it became clear that he was not going to take that course of action they decided that their ministers would have to resign the following morning before the Dáil debate on the motion of no confidence.

Haughey and O'Malley met again that evening at a state banquet in Dublin Castle for the Dutch queen and both of them became resigned to the fact that Lenihan was not going to step down. Haughey tried to persuade O'Malley to agree to allow the presidential election to run its course and that Lenihan would resign whatever the outcome, but the PD leader refused to accept this.

The 9 p.m. television news carried a report from the Lenihan campaign and the Tánaiste appeared saying he was not going to step down. Stephen O'Byrnes rang O'Malley at Dublin Castle to tell him the news and it looked as if the government's fate was sealed.

The following morning Mary Harney was woken at 7.30 a.m. by a phone call from Charlie McCreevy who urged her not to take any action until after the meeting of the Fianna Fáil parliamentary party that morning. He hinted that the meeting could change the picture and advised that there was no need for the PDs to take any decisions until it was over. Haughey met O'Malley and Molloy at 8.30 a.m. The Taoiseach told the PD ministers that there was no change in the situation and it didn't appear as if Lenihan would resign, but he asked them not to make any immediate announcement and to give every-body more time.

The PDs met around 9.30 a.m. and decided not to make any public statements in case the situation changed. However, O'Byrnes got to work drafting letters of resignation for O'Malley, Molloy and Harney and they all mentally prepared themselves to leave office and face into a general election. The Dáil debate on the no confidence motion was due to begin at 10.30 a.m. and they would see how the situation might change before then.

That morning the pressure on Lenihan also resumed. Shortly after first light a helicopter piloted by the Taoiseach's son, Ciaran Haughey, came into view over Athlone and circled ominously above the house where he had spent the night. Inside the house members of the Lenihan family received a stream of phone calls appealing to the Tánaiste to consent to board the aircraft for a journey to Kinsealy to meet the Taoiseach.

Fianna Fáil Deputy General Secretary Michael Dawson and Press Officer Niamh O'Connor called at the door of the house. As angry exchanges raged along the telephone line, the helicopter clattered around in circles overhead, young Haughey waiting to see if Lenihan would consent to make the journey to Dublin for a final showdown with his father.

Lenihan's family, particularly his wife Ann, angrily rejected the appeal for a meeting at Kinsealy and eventually the helicopter turned and flew off back to Dublin, leaving the family to consider their position. The telephone calls continued, however, but Mrs Lenihan refused to let anyone from the Taoiseach's office speak to her husband. He remained incommunicado in Athlone all morning.

Meanwhile in Dublin Haughey was in consultation with P.J. Mara and McCreevy and they urged him to do the unthinkable – to sack Lenihan. The Taoiseach had been adamant that he was not going to take that course of action but Mara and McCreevy argued that it would be madness not to as the alternative was a general election. An opinion poll in that morning's *Irish Independent* showed just how badly the whole affair had damaged Lenihan's presidential hopes, and while Fianna Fáil was holding up well, an election called on the tapes affair would inevitably tarnish the party.

Haughey was still agonising when the Fianna Fáil parliamentary party met at 11.30 a.m. to consider the position. Gloomy deputies and senators heard the Taoiseach begin the meeting by saying: "As of now there will be a general election." He went on to state just how serious the position facing them was, as it seemed that there was no way they could win a vote on the motion of no confidence.

Bertie Ahern induced even more gloom when he outlined the prospects facing the party in both the presidential election and a possible general election. He told the TDs that the party's private polls put Mary Robinson on 45 percent of the vote with Brian Lenihan trailing behind on about 39 percent. The IMS poll published that morning painted an even gloomier picture, putting Robinson a massive 21 percent ahead at 52 percent to 31 percent. While Ahern said that the poll predictions looked a lot better for a general election, he felt that an election in the circumstances would see a big slump in party support and another hung Dáil where nobody would be able to put a government together.

As the Fianna Fáil meeting was in progress, Lenihan, who had refused to take any calls from the Taoiseach, was driven to Dublin with barrister friend Esmonde Smyth. He stayed for most of the day with a group of supporters in the Rathgar home of Peg Fogarty, a family friend of long standing.

There was soon a procession of intermediaries between Rathgar and Leinster House but still the Tánaiste refused to come in and meet the Taoiseach or to speak to him on the phone. The Fianna Fáil parliamentary party meeting, which had been adjourned at lunchtime to give time for contact to be established with Lenihan, resumed in the afternoon, but the Taoiseach has still not been in touch with his Tánaiste.

Liam Lawlor, Lenihan's constituency colleague from Dublin West, told his parliamentary colleagues that he had just come back from a meeting with Lenihan and he read out a statement by the Tánaiste. It outlined the work Lenihan had done for the party over thirty years and the times he had gone out to defend Haughey when he was in trouble. "I do not propose to resign as Tánaiste and Minister for Defence," it concluded.

After some discussion about the need to avoid an election, Haughey intervened to ask the TDs if he had their approval to take the necessary steps to ensure an election was avoided. He pointed out that the last time he had been in this position and had negotiated coalition with the PDs, a number of TDs had gone around the country dissenting from the decision. This time he said he wanted people to be clear about what would have to be done to avoid an election.

Young Kildare TD Seán Power responded by saying that they were now discussing sacrificing Brian Lenihan's head and he demanded to know if the Taoiseach would give the same advice in six months if his head was the only thing that would save the government. A number of TDs, including M.J. Nolan and Noel Dempsey, supported Seán Power against Haughey.

The Taoiseach then spoke again. "Lest there be any doubt about what is at stake here I cannot contact my Tánaiste; he won't talk to me." He said a cold decision had to be made and he asked for the support of the parliamentary party. Chairman Jim Tunney summed up by saying that it was the feeling of the meeting that it should be left to the Taoiseach to do his best to avoid an election. Tunney didn't call a vote but simply ended the meeting on that note shortly before 5 p.m.

As the parliamentary party meeting was in progress the PDs continued to hold off an announcement of their decision to pull the plug. Resignation speeches for all three PD ministers had now been typed up and were ready for release to the media. O'Malley was due to go in on the confidence debate but he kept putting off his speech until the position became absolutely clear.

O'Malley and Molloy spent most of the afternoon in the PD leader's ministerial office. O'Malley had all his constituency files packed into cardboard boxes, on the assumption that he would have to clear out of his office that evening after his resignation from the government. There was a great deal of embarrassment on the ministerial corridor as members of the Lenihan family were in the Tánaiste's office with his private secretary, Brian Spain, during that afternoon.

Over at PD headquarters the party general secretary, David O'Keeffe, rang around a number of printers to get costings for election literature and a number of activists from around the country were summoned to make preparations for a general election.

The atmosphere suddenly changed at 5 p.m. After the Fianna Fáil meeting the Taoiseach rang O'Malley and asked him to come to his office. There he solemnly told the PD leader that he had decided to terminate Lenihan's membership of the government. The meeting between Haughey and O'Malley, like all their meetings since the crisis started, was correct and formal with no hint of the emotions that were seething under the surface.

With messages continuing to flash to and fro between Haughey's office, the Dáil and Rathgar, Lenihan eventually picked up the phone and rang the Taoiseach just after 5.45 p.m. Haughey formally asked his Tánaiste to resign and Lenihan refused. The Taoiseach then said it was with great regret that he was terminating Brian Lenihan's membership of the government. Brian Spain, the minister's private secretary at the Department of Defence, was dispatched to the house with a letter signed by President Hillery, removing Lenihan from office.

Lenihan made his way into the Dáil before 6.30 p.m., entering the visitor's bar with a group of family and friends. He was greeted there by Seanad Cathaoirleach Seán Doherty, whom Lenihan had backed when he was under pressure in the Seanad. There were emotional scenes in the bar and in the chamber when he made his way there to listen to Haughey read out his formal dismissal. There were tears in the eyes of many Fianna Fáil deputies as they marched through the lobbies to vote confidence in their government.

After the vote Haughey, his face like a mask, sat stonily on his seat, many of his colleagues avoiding contact with him. Afterwards he asked Lenihan to meet him and the two old friends had an emotional and unacrimonious get-together for a few minutes in the Taoiseach's office. In the corridors of Leinster House there was more emotion than anger, but some of the pent up feelings spilled over. Conor Lenihan, the ex-Tánaiste's son, who is a radio reporter with 98 FM, approached O'Malley, shook hands and said: "Are you happy now, Des, you got your pound of flesh?"

The ex-Tánaiste didn't have time for recriminations and after his meeting with Haughey he immediately set off for a press conference to get his presidential campaign back on the road. He had just six days to try to salvage something from the disaster of the previous week which had left him trailing by 21 percent according to the polls.

Lenihan staged a big rally in the last days of the campaign. Two good television performances managed to haul back some of the lost ground and the wave of public sympathy after his sacking put him back in contention. An opinion poll carried out by Lansdowne for the *Sunday Press* on the day after Lenihan was sacked, and published on the Sunday before the poll, showed that he had cut Robinson's 21 percent lead before his sacking to just 5 percent after it. If the trend continued he would overtake her by polling day. The big question, though, was by how much, because the *Sunday Press* poll also showed that there was now a massively solid transfer of second-preference votes from Currie to Robinson.

Another incident took place that weekend which had a bearing on the result and which damaged the Lenihan campaign just when the swing was coming his way. Environment Minister Pádraig Flynn was on RTE's "Saturday View" programme with PD chairman Michael McDowell and Brendan Howlin of Labour. Flynn spoke of how Robinson had remodelled her image for the election campaign. "She was pretty well constructed in this campaign by her handlers the Labour Party and the Workers' Party. Of course it doesn't always suit if you get labelled a socialist, because that's a very narrow focus in this country. So she has to try and have it both ways. She has to have new clothes and her new look and her new hairdo and she has the new interest in family, being a mother and all that kind of thing. But none of us you know, none of us who knew Mary Robinson well in previous incarnations ever heard her claiming to be a great wife and mother."

McDowell immediately pounced on Flynn, calling his attack on Robinson disgusting and demanding its withdrawal. McDowell's vitriolic attack created the public perception that Flynn had accused Robinson of being a bad mother. There was outrage up and down the country, particularly among women. Flynn was forced to issue a fulsome apology and the episode had a damaging effect on Lenihan's campaign. Flynn has always maintained that his comments were not intended to reflect on Robinson in a personal way but were designed to highlight the manner in which she had reinvented her image for the election. In the final days of the campaign, however, it was the perception and not the precise wording that counted. By pouncing on Flynn, the chairman of the PDs helped to bury Lenihan and the Fianna Fáil campaign.

Fianna Fáil tried a last major effort to grab the headlines with a campaign rally in the National Stadium on the last Sunday before polling. There was visible hostility between the Lenihan family and the Taoiseach in the hospitality room before the speeches began and Haughey was booed by some sections of the audience when he appeared on the platform. He kept his cool nonetheless and launched into a strong criticism of Robinson, saying that she could not escape from her backers – Labour and the Workers' Party. The Marxist Workers' Party would have an influence in the Aras if she was elected he told the audience and he also cited her *Hot Press* interview where she had threatened a confrontational presidency.

Fianna Fáil took up the same theme in newspaper advertisements in the final days, asking "Is the left right for the Park?" but the attack was too simplistic and anyway they had left it too late. The election took place on 7 November and while the poll findings of a swing back to Lenihan were confirmed he failed to get the vital 2 percent or so that would have made the difference. Lenihan got just over 44 percent of the vote on the first count with Robinson following with just under 39 percent and Currie trailing badly on 17 percent. However, the strength of the Currie transfers gave Robinson an easy victory in the end and she won by 86,000 votes on the second count.

Lenihan's defeat marked the first time in the history of the state that the presidency had passed out of Fianna Fáil's hands. It was another electoral disaster to add to Haughey's five unsuccessful attempts to win an overall majority in the Dáil and questions about his leadership now began to be asked again.

17 – Death of a Thousand Cuts

Haughey's authority over his own TDs was badly shaken by the trauma of Lenihan's sacking and defeat but Fianna Fáil's problems were immediately overshadowed by an upheaval in Fine Gael. Alan Dukes was removed as leader in a neat surgical operation just days after his party's miserable showing in the presidential election. John Bruton took over as Fine Gael leader, promising a more vigorous style of opposition.

Uncomfortable questions about Charles Haughey's leadership of Fianna Fáil were pushed out of the headlines but they persisted nonetheless. The leadership question was put on to the agenda in an oblique fashion by heir apparent Albert Reynolds, Minister for Finance, on the day of the presidential count. Speaking to reporters in Cork he said that he would be a contender for the leadership of the party when a vacancy arose. While he did not challenge Haughey, or express any disloyalty, the fact that he mentioned the leadership issue raised the whole question of Haughey's future.

The Fianna Fáil inquest into the presidential election did not get under way for a few weeks and when it took place on 28 November 1990 it was a typically damp squib. The parliamentary party met for four and a half hours, heard speeches from thirty-five TDs and senators but only one, Liam Lawlor, said openly that the question of Haughey's leadership should come up for consideration.

The Taoiseach had prepared himself very carefully for the meeting. He delivered a fifty-minute speech outlining the problems facing the party in terms of organisational structure, its capacity to fight elections and the perception of its policies. He told them that a special commission to examine the whole operation of the party would be set up and he assured them that not only would the government last but that Fianna Fáil would be in power for the next ten years.

After the meeting Haughey went to the Dáil chamber where he skipped down the steps, paused for a moment, clasped his hands together and held them aloft like a winning prize fighter. Fine Gael's Ivan Yates, who was speaking at the time, stopped in surprise. "I see you have survived yet again, Taoiseach," he remarked. Haughey smiled broadly in return.

The Taoiseach's sense of relief showed that he had been more worried than he had appeared to be at the parliamentary party meeting. Despite his evident high spirits just after it, those worries would never leave him for the remainder of his political life. Haughey regarded Reynolds's expression of ambition on the day of the presidential election count as the opening shot in a bid for the leadership and he began to treat his Finance Minister with great caution. Reynolds had gradually been building up to a challenge to Haughey. At the beginning of the year he had called the coalition with the PDs a "temporary little arrangement" and then in September he had toyed with the idea of backing John Wilson against Lenihan. Slowly but surely he was raising the stakes though it was clear he was not pushing for an immediate showdown.

As for Haughey, caution seemed to paralyse him as 1990 drew to a close. Brian Lenihan's Cabinet post was vacant and while the Taoiseach promoted the sixty-seven-year-old Wilson to fill the honorary position of Tánaiste, there was no move to fill the vacant Cabinet position. Some close friends like Senator G.V. Wright advised him to go for a big reshuffle, promote younger people and build a new power base for himself in the party. Haughey, though, was more concerned about the danger of making enemies among the older people who would have to be demoted or dropped.

In the face of the options he dithered. Despite Opposition taunts in the Dáil he kept putting off the shuffle. The delay did have the advantage of keeping people in line for fear they would ruin their chances of promotion or prompt their demotion. Haughey had always used appointments like this to keep his TDs under his control but the process dragged on so long it looked like indecisiveness.

Haughey was worried on two fronts. The budding challenge of Reynolds posed a longterm threat to his position but more immediately Lenihan appeared to be shaping up for some sort of confrontation. Motions of no confidence in Haughey's leadership were passed by some units of Fianna Fáil and speculation developed that Lenihan would challenge him for the presidency of the party at the Ard Fheis in March 1991. Such a move would have been devastating and would have caused bitter division in the party among its two most senior members who were long-time political allies.

In Dublin West a meeting of the constituency organisation fuelled the media speculation about a possible heave. Government press secretary P.J. Mara responded to the rumblings by threatening to meet any challenge head-on and he also raised the possibility of an early general election if Haughey lost the leadership, on the basis that whoever replaced him would do so on a platform of hostility to the PDs. This counterblast had the effect of calming things down for a little and meanwhile Mara tried to sort matters out with Lenihan. The two men met for lunch with Australian Ambassador Brian Burke, in a repeat of the lunchtime meeting that had marked the beginning of the Lenihan campaign. This was a sadder occasion, though Lenihan did reassure Mara that he would not proceed with the challenge to Haughey.

Meanwhile Albert Reynolds waited in the wings. In a number of interviews he carefully avoided pledging loyalty to Haughey but used a formula of words which stressed that while there was no vacancy for the leadership he would be a candidate whenever that vacancy did arise.

Other members of the Cabinet remained silent initially, but gradually began to come out in favour of Haughey. John Wilson described all the media speculation about the leadership as "much ado about damn all". More significantly, Foreign Minister Gerry Collins took a very decisive stand in Haughey's favour and let it be known through the organisation that he was strongly against any attempt to change the leader. Reynolds tried to assure people that a change of leader did not necessarily involve an election as Haughey's supporters were suggesting. On radio he stressed that despite his remarks about "a temporary little arrangement" the coalition government was in office on the basis of a five-year programme and that would be adhered to.

As the heave forecast by some sections of the media failed to materialise Haughey relaxed somewhat. In Rome for the EC summit in mid-December he was even able to poke a little mischievous fun at his Finance Minister. Giving his final press conference flanked by Reynolds and Collins, the Taoiseach was asked a question about

British financial policy and the effect it would have on the development of the Community.

"We all know that Chancellors of the Exchequer and Ministers for Finance are neurotic and exotic creatures whose political judgement is not always the best," replied Haughey while Reynolds sat stony-faced beside him. Haughey rubbed salt into the wound by delivering a paean of praise to EC Agriculture Commissioner Ray MacSharry for the "wonderful" job he was doing for Ireland and the Community.

The Taoiseach had not recovered enough confidence to proceed with his Cabinet reshuffle before Christmas 1990. More importantly, Haughey's insecurity damaged his ability to make the right decisions on fundamental economic issues. Because of his weakened authority and his uneasy relations with Reynolds, Haughey allowed his spending ministers to increase their budgets for 1991 by too much. Reynolds, because of his own ambitions and his distrust of Haughey, did not exercise his restraining authority, while PD leader Des O'Malley also allowed political considerations arising from the sensitivities of the Lenihan sacking to interfere with his political judgement. The result was that the framework for the 1991 budget went astray with the publication of the estimates in December 1990.

This process was compounded in the first month of 1991 as Haughey pulled out all the stops to get a deal with the social partners on a new programme for national recovery. The negotiations took place in the newly refurbished government offices in Merrion Street, with Haughey, his Departmental Secretary Padraig O hUiginn and Labour Minister Bertie Ahern in attendance at crucial stages to ensure that agreement was reached. The Taoiseach's all too obvious desire to get an agreement gave the government a bad negotiating hand and the deal that was eventually struck imposed intolerable strains on the exchequer.

While the settlement kept pay increases in the private sector in line, at just under 4 percent a year for three years, only marginally above the rate of inflation, the increases for public sector workers were much higher. Between the general round and special pay awards deferred from the previous deal, public pay was set to rise by nearly 10 percent a year for three years.

Both Albert Reynolds and Des O'Malley argued strongly against the deal, which horrified some of the officials in Finance. They tried to at least get a commitment from the unions to end the spiral of public service special pay awards as the price of the deal. The unions refused and Haughey insisted on going ahead in any case. All Reynolds managed to have inserted in the deal, called the Programme for Economic and Social Progress (PESP), was a loosely worded clause making the arrangement subject to a continued reduction in the national debt.

The PESP and the budget, which cut the basic rate of income tax to 29 percent, were dependent on the continuation of high growth rates in 1991 but economists warned immediately that such growth was unlikely. Recession in Britain and in the United States, allied to the uncertainty created by the Gulf War, did nothing for confidence and within a few months it became apparent that, after four years of success on the economic front, Haughey was drifting back to some of his old ways.

The government itself became more unstable with a number of ministers jockeying for position in the still-deferred reshuffle.

Bertie Ahern, who had played an important role in getting the PESP together, expected a reward for his efforts and for his long patient service to Haughey. Ahern, who was widely spoken of in the party as a potential future leader, wanted badly to get experience in a different department.

After the conclusion of the PESP, rumours began to circulate that Ahern wanted to move to Environment but that Pádraig Flynn was refusing to be moved sideways to accommodate him. Other ministers mentioned for a possible move were Rory O'Hanlon and Mary O'Rourke. Meanwhile there was also talk of wholesale changes in the ranks of the junior ministers and up to ten individuals were said to have been promised jobs by Haughey.

The situation got out of hand in the days following the budget and there were newspaper headlines about Ahern angling for Flynn's job. The rumours, which emanated from the Cabinet, were a direct result of Haughey's indecision and the longer he prevaricated the wilder they became. To the public it appeared as if Flynn and Ahern were jostling for position and the Taoiseach seemed to have opted out of the process. Eventually, in the face of newspaper headlines suggesting that Flynn was refusing to be moved, Haughey released a statement on 1 February saying that he proposed to leave both Ahern and Flynn in their existing departments.

He followed that up a few days later with a minimal reshuffle which brought Brendan Daly back into the Cabinet and promoted Tallaght TD Chris Flood to the ranks of the junior ministers. Ahern was badly let down, not simply by the failure to get promotion, but by the fact that he was made the scapegoat for the Taoiseach's indecisiveness. The line from the Taoiseach's office was that Bertie had caused all the trouble by leaking stories of his possible move to the press.

"I've been set up," Bertie told Cabinet colleagues, but there was nothing he could do except lick his wounds and watch as Haughey settled back into his old routine.

Things settled down after the reshuffle. Haughey appeared to have ridden out the crisis caused by the presidential election defeat and as the Fianna Fáil Ard Fheis came closer Lenihan made it clear that there would be no challenge to the leadership. Instead he indicated a willingness to accept an olive branch from Haughey in the shape of the chairmanship of the new Oireachtas Foreign Affairs Committee.

Haughey felt confident enough of his position to say in an interview in the *Sunday Press* that it was his intention to lead Fianna Fáil into the next general election, whenever that might be. He also defended his recent record and described the PESP as a "pearl of very great price". He took the initiative in the run-up to the Ard Fheis and let it be known that he proposed to outline a new vision of a liberal, pluralist future to the party faithful. Ray Burke had already been instructed to prepare a White Paper on marital breakdown and to decriminalise homosexuality.

Then a little over a week before the Ard Fheis the issue of contraception burst onto the political agenda again. British millionaire Richard Branson, with his usual penchant for publicity stunts, involved his Virgin Megastore in Dublin in a conflict with the law through the illegal sale of condoms from a stall in the shop, run by the Irish Family Planning Association. Prosecuted in the District

Court, the IFPA was convicted and on appeal to the Circuit Court on 26 February the fine was doubled.

The response from Haughey was almost immediate. P.J. Mara told political correspondents the following day that the legal position under which condoms could be sold only through chemists shops was "daft". He gave heavy hints that the law would be changed as part of a new approach by Fianna Fáil to such issues. Mara's view, and by implication Haughey's as well, was that Fianna Fáil was taking a continual hammering from the media, particularly RTE and *The Irish Times*, for its perceived illiberal attitudes. To cover that flank once and for all they intended to deal with the liberal agenda and give their critics no further cause for complaint on that particular score.

As for the reaction of Fianna Fáil's own supporters whose innate conservatism on social issues had been encouraged and exploited by Haughey in the past, their views did not count for much in the calculation. "Fuck them, they have nowhere else to go," was how one of the architects of Haughey's new-found liberalism summed up the attitude towards the traditionalist views of the majority of party followers.

The ordinary Fianna Fáil supporters, however, were not to be dismissed as lightly as that. This latest U-turn took them totally by surprise and also provoked a hostile reaction from Catholic Church leaders who were equally astonished at Haughey's conversion to liberalism. The Archbishop of Dublin, Desmond Connell, publicly asked why there was not one party in the Dáil which reflected the views of the Catholic population of the country.

Still, at the parliamentary party meeting two days before the Ard Fheis, only Senator Des Hanafin, the anti-divorce and anti-abortion campaigner, stood up to challenge Haughey. He followed that by putting down a motion for the following week's parliamentary party meeting calling for the retention of the eighteen-year age limit for condoms in any new legislation.

The issue dominated the Ard Fheis which opened on 8 March. It overshadowed Haughey's keynote speech which outlined his plans for a more liberal approach to issues like family planning, divorce and homosexuality. The attempt to deal with the liberal agenda was a clear response to the Robinson victory in the presidential election and marked a dramatic change of gear for Haughey, considering his record on such issues. Under his leadership Fianna Fáil had supported the anti-abortion amendment to the Constitution in 1983, opposed the liberalisation of the family planning laws in 1985 and campaigned strongly against divorce the following year, despite a token claim of neutrality.

The situation was particularly ironic in view of the fact that Des O'Malley had been expelled from Fianna Fáil in 1985 because he refused to oppose a liberalisation of the family planning laws. If Haughey had taken a liberal approach in 1985 the PDs would never have been founded and O'Malley would probably still have been a minister in a Fianna Fáil majority government.

Over the weekend of the Ard Fheis, as pressure mounted from within Fianna Fáil, it also emerged that the PDs were not even united in favour of the measure. Bobby Molloy went on radio to state that he personally was not in favour of lowering the condom age limit to sixteen. This increased the determination of Fianna Fáil TDs to oppose it as well.

At a Cabinet meeting on 12 March the issue was discussed for the first time and only two ministers, Ray Burke and Séamus Brennan, backed Haughey. Some, like John Wilson and Michael O'Kennedy, were adamantly opposed to lowering the age limit to sixteen, while senior figures like Albert Reynolds and Bobby Molloy were equally vehement. Bertie Ahern proposed a compromise of seventeen and was supported by Mary O'Rourke, Pádraig Flynn and Brendan Daly. While Rory O'Hanlon kept his feelings to himself it was no secret that he was also in favour of retaining the eighteen-year limit.

The Taoiseach's rebuff by his Cabinet was a gentle one, to the extent that a number of ministers indicated that they were prepared to accept an age limit of seventeen, but the following day the parliamentary party, fired up by the mood of the Ard Fheis, let Haughey know in no uncertain terms that they wanted no change in the law. Out of the 103 members of the parliamentary party only a handful backed the Haughey line. Junior Minister Máire Geoghegan-Quinn, despite her previous differences with Haughey, was one of them, while from the backbenches Dr James McDaid, Charlie McCreevy and Senator Eoin Ryan supported the Taoiseach.

The contraception debacle was not very important in itself but it indicated how far Haughey's authority had been eroded. Backbenchers now had no compunction about standing up at party meetings to disagree with him, something they would have been terrified to do even a year earlier. Des Hanafin, a senator without any formal position in the party, had effectively scuttled his condoms proposals and there was nothing Haughey could do about it. The liberal agenda was dropped as quickly as it had been adopted. The omens for the future were now beginning to look bleak. Gerald Barry, political correspondent of the *Sunday Tribune*, summed up the mood by forecasting a "death of a thousand cuts" for the Taoiseach.

One major issue which helped to stabilise Haughey's position was the opening of talks about the future of Northern Ireland. After many months of speculation the talks got under way at the beginning of May. The plan was that the Irish government would get involved in the second strand of the talks, after the Northern parties had been meeting for five weeks or so, but obstructionist tactics by the Unionist parties ensured they never got to strand two. Nonetheless the prospect of the Irish government talking to the Unionists helped to reinforce Haughey's position, as nobody wished to rock the boat at such a delicate stage.

At around the same time, however, another old issue came back to haunt Haughey – his association with beef baron Larry Goodman. A "World in Action" television programme transmitted by ITV on 13 May, carried what purported to be an exposé of the practices which operated in Goodman's meat plants. There was a furore in the Dáil the following day but hamfisted tactics on the part of the government only made matters worse. Instead of responding to special notice questions or scheduling an adjournment debate, Haughey stonewalled and there was uproar in the Dáil chamber. With the Opposition parties in full cry, the government was forced to hold a debate on the issue the following day.

It was a debate that nearly brought the government down and ended up with Fianna Fáil again being forced through the humiliating procedure of having to back down in the face of pressure from the PDs. The problem arose because of the wording of the motion drafted by Government Chief Whip Vincent Brady, to cover the Goodman debate: "That Dáil Eireann reaffirms its confidence in the regulatory and control procedures for the Irish meat Industry." It was shown to Des O'Malley the night before the debate and he expressed no objection, but by the following morning things had changed.

Key people in the PD leadership, like Stephen O'Byrnes and Michael McDowell, were unhappy at the situation, particularly as Fine Gael leader John Bruton was putting on the pressure by demanding a judicial inquiry into the meat industry. McDowell and O'Byrnes discussed the problem with O'Malley and got him to agree that in view of their party's record in highlighting the Goodman issue in the past and the political problem they now faced, the government motion was not good enough. The PD leader contacted the Taoiseach to tell him that his party were unhappy with the wording of the motion.

What followed was a day of huffing and puffing, a pattern which was now becoming familiar. The PD parliamentary party met, took a tough line on the issue and issued an ultimatum to Haughey which was delivered by their two ministers. The Taoiseach asked for time to consider the matter, consulted his Agriculture Minister and then gave in to the PDs by agreeing to a judicial tribunal. It was another embarrassing climbdown in the face of PD pressure which left Fianna Fáil TDs seething, but there was nothing they could do about it. A week later in the debate on the setting up of the tribunal Haughey hit back at his critics, but his response was too late.

"For a number of years now one of the most persistent and venomous political campaigns ever has been waged in an attempt to discredit the government over the affairs of the Goodman companies. The whole basis of this attack is, by innuendo and association, to create the impression that Mr Goodman and his companies enjoyed some unique, ill-defined, protective relationship with the Fianna Fáil government of 1987-89, a kind of relationship that they did not have with the previous Fine Gael-Labour coalition government. Nothing could be further from the truth as the records clearly show."

The Taoiseach's belated counter-attack won back some credibility among his own TDs but there was no disguising the steady erosion of his authority. At one stage in the Goodman debate on 24 May, Haughey responded to Opposition sniping by saying angrily: "I don't care; I just don't care anymore." It seemed as if he was resigning himself to some inevitable fate.

The results of the local elections in June appeared to accelerate that process with Fianna Fáil's vote slipping to 37.8 percent. It was the party's worst performance in a local election for decades. As had happened in the previous two general elections and the presidential election, high poll ratings for Fianna Fáil collapsed once an election contest got underway.

This further electoral failure appeared to put the kibosh on Haughey's prospects of leading Fianna Fáil into the next general election, but if his enemies in the party thought he was about go voluntarily they had another think coming. Death of a thousand cuts it might be, but Haughey had no intention of relinquishing his position without forcing his adversaries to show the whites of their eyes. The old Kinsealy fox had a few lessons to teach his enemies before the game was up.

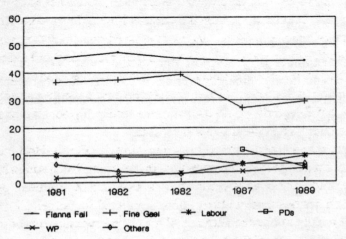

Party performance
1981 to 1989

206

18 – Reynolds Moves

By the summer of 1991 Albert Reynolds was gearing himself up to move against Haughey. From the time of the 1989 election, when Haughey concluded the coalition arrangement behind his back, Reynolds had been preparing the ground for his own leadership challenge. Initially these preparations were carried out, not with the intention of confronting Haughey but in readiness for the day when the Taoiseach stepped down.

By the middle of 1991, however, Reynolds and his supporters were coming around to the view that the only way to ensure a change of leadership was to pressurise Haughey into stepping down. The key people in the Reynolds camp since 1989 were dubbed the "Western Alliance" or the "Country and Western Brigade" by opponents in the party. The core of that group was made up of Pádraig Flynn, Máire Geoghegan-Quinn, Noel Treacy and Michael Smith. They met regularly, often in Reynolds's Dublin apartment, where they planned their strategy.

Reynolds regarded Bertie Ahern, the other negotiator of the coalition arrangement, as vital to his plans. Ahern had pledged his support to Reynolds when the leadership came up for grabs. Apart from being on good terms the two men needed each other. Reynolds wanted a strong urban backer to broaden his western base. Ahern, who regularly headed opinion polls as the most favoured choice by the public to be Haughey's successor, felt he was a little too young and needed experience in a key department like Finance or the Environment, before going for the top job. There was also an understanding between the two that Reynolds would take over the leadership for five or six years and nominate Ahern as his successor.

Ahern, though, had a prickly relationship with Flynn. Both men were still smarting from their encounter in the spring when Ahern had let it be known that he wanted Flynn's post in Environment, and Ahern had serious doubts about Flynn's political judgement. Flynn was still widely blamed in Fianna Fáil for his intervention on the last weekend of the presidential election and few accepted his protests that the remarks about Mary Robinson's family life had been taken out of context. RTE's satirical radio show "Scrap Saturday" rubbed salt into the wound by inventing a set of characters called the Flynn-stones which lampooned the minister from Mayo.

Flynn had been a loyal supporter and friend of Haughey's for more than a decade. The Taoiseach had very few close political friends but Flynn was one of them. He regularly strolled in to the Taoiseach's office to have frank discussions with him and was also a regular caller at Kinsealy. Relations had cooled since the election of 1989 and after the presidential election Flynn felt that he was being scapegoated for the failures of Lenihan and of Haughey himself. By the summer of 1991 Flynn had decided that the Taoiseach's time was up. Just as he had made no secret of his views about Jack Lynch back in 1979, he had no compunction now about stirring up trouble for Haughey.

Travelling around the country during the summer, Flynn canvassed the views of TDs about Haughey and sought their support for Reynolds. A newspaper interview by former President Patrick Hillery, hinting that he might be prepared to go public about the "long night of the phone calls" to the Aras on 27 January 1982, added to the air of instability so that by the time ministers came back to their offices at the end of August, jittery nerves were in evidence again.

The first Cabinet meeting after the summer holidays was a stormy affair. Reynolds trenchantly told his colleagues that the PESP would have to be renegotiated because the country could not afford to pay the increases due to the public service. In July Reynolds had announced extra spending cuts to limit a developing budget overrun. Now he said action would have to be taken on public service pay if the 1992 budget was to be kept in line. O'Malley supported Reynolds but Haughey was cautious about changing the terms of the PESP.

A week later Reynolds took the bull by the horns in an interview with Seán O'Rourke of RTE and openly expressed the views he had given to his Cabinet colleagues, telling the country bluntly that the PESP increases could not be paid. Haughey was furious and P.J. Mara issued an unprecedented public rebuke from the Taoiseach to Reynolds, dismissing his remarks as "the usual Department of Finance rhetoric". At a Cabinet meeting the next day Haughey tore strips off Reynolds for going public on the issue and he warned his Finance

Minister not to do it again.

At that stage in early September there was a clear breach between Haughey and Reynolds and it was only a matter of time before it came out into the open. A front-page story in the *Sunday Press* suggesting that Haughey was preparing himself for a challenge from Reynolds was dismissed by government sources, but the simmering discontent at every level in Fianna Fáil was now becoming obvious.

Another problem was the two-year review of the Programme for Government agreed with the PDs. Fianna Fáil had expected a token progress report but the PDs made it clear that they wanted a much more fundamental renegotiation and they were particularly insistent that the problems with the national finances should not stand in the way of tax reform to be funded from within the tax system itself. The old teams of Molloy and Cox on the one hand and Reynolds and Ahern on the other made only desultory progress and the two leaders had to intervene to push things along.

To add to his woes, Haughey came under pressure on another front. On 1 September the *Sunday Independent* carried a lead story about the affairs of the newly privatised Irish Sugar Company, now called Greencore. The nub of the story was that Greencore managing director Chris Comerford was taking legal action to establish his part-ownership of a Jersey holding company called Talmino which had sold its stake in a company, called Irish Sugar Distributors, to Irish Sugar. The story, by Sam Smyth, was not written in that journalist's usual crisp style but had clearly been rewritten by lawyers. The legalistic wording made the story obscure to the general reader but the effect on Greencore was shattering. Comerford was forced to resign within days at a hastily convened board meeting and the company secretary, Michael Tully, followed soon afterwards. Pressure then came on company chairman Bernie Cahill, a friend of Haughey's and chairman of Feltrim Mining, a company set up by Haughey's son Conor.

This was the first in a series of business controversies which were to rock the political system for the rest of the year. Hot on the heels of the Greencore resignations came the Telecom affair. The issue here was the purchase by Telecom of the old Johnston, Mooney and

O'Brien site in Ballsbridge for £9.4 million. The key question about the transaction concerned the role of financier Dermot Desmond in the process. Desmond had been a close associate of Haughey's since 1986 and there had already been allegations from Opposition parties that his stockbroking firm NCB (National City Brokers) had been getting an inordinate share of government contracts.

A property company established by Desmond, called UPH (United Property Holdings), had initially bought the site, but had sold it on to other developers who in turn sold it to Telecom. When it emerged that Telecom chairman and Ireland's top businessman Michael Smurfit had an interest in the property company, the political storm really gathered force, particularly as the *Irish Independent* in February 1990 had carried a series of apologies for an article about the transaction, one of which stated: "Dr Smurfit does not have and never had an interest, directly or indirectly, in the site."

As pressure grew on Smurfit, Desmond and the government, Haughey summoned a "council of war" at his Kinsealy home on 21 September in advance of a major radio interview the following day. At the meeting were Bertie Ahern, Séamus Brennan, P.J. Mara and Padraig O hUiginn, who helped devise a plan aimed at extricating the government from further political damage as a result of the saga.

They decided that if Smurfit had not taken steps to disengage from Telecom by the next day the Taoiseach would ask him to step aside from his post as chairman until the investigation was complete. In view of the growing controversy Haughey decided to ask the former chairman of the Revenue Commissioners Séamus Paircéir, who also had an involvement with UPH, to step aside from his position as chairman of the Custom House Docks Development Board.

When Haughey made this announcement out of the blue in the course of a radio interview with Seán O'Rourke the following day, it came as a complete shock to all concerned. Paircéir reacted immediately by giving a television interview to say he was going to resign in protest at the way he had been treated. Smurfit took a bit longer to react but two days later he arrived at Government Buildings to inform the Taoiseach that in view of the fact that he had been asked publicly to step aside without any prior consultation, he had decided to resign as chairman of Telecom.

In the same radio interview Haughey also stored up trouble for himself when he repeated his intention to lead Fianna Fáil into the next election. "Some of these Chinese leaders go on till they are eighty or ninety – but I think that's probably a bit long," he said jocosely. The remark was not treated as a joke by some of his TDs and it only added to the problems created by the "step aside" segment of the interview.

With rumours now circulating about plots being hatched by the Reynolds faction, other ministers reaffirmed their support for Haughey in an attempt to head off the Reynolds challenge. Mary O'Rourke was increasingly being mentioned in the succession stakes as an alternative to Reynolds, but she believed she needed more time to organise and she came out with a strong expression of support for Haughey. Other ministers, like John Wilson and Michael O'Kennedy, also backed the party leader.

It was all too much for four Fianna Fáil backbenchers who took the bull by the horns and issued a statement expressing their unhappiness at the Taoiseach's handling of recent issues. The four – Noel Dempsey, Liam Fitzgerald, M.J. Nolan and Seán Power – had met in northern Cyprus during the summer and found that they were all frustrated at the drift of things in Fianna Fáil. All were agreed that Haughey had to go before the next election. There was some irony in the situation because the fathers of Power and Nolan had both been strong Haughey supporters and were given Cabinet office by him in the early 1980s. On 27 September the four came together with a public statement designed to increase the pressure on the Taoiseach to step down.

"We have watched with growing disquiet the events of the past three weeks in the semi-State sector. We fully endorse the actions of the relevant ministers in instituting full and wide-ranging inquiries into these affairs and the commitments made by them that the results of these inquiries will be made public. For our part, we will be insisting that this happens.

"We are particularly concerned at the manner in which these matters were dealt with by An Taoiseach in his radio interview last week. We find it incomprehensible that the Taoiseach should suggest on air that someone of Séamus Paircéir's integrity should 'step aside' while he ignored the role of Mr Bernie Cahill, chairman of Greencore, in the Sugar Company affair."

Haughey moved to deal with the situation by asking Jim Tunney to convene a meeting of the parliamentary party the following Wednesday, a week earlier than planned. Of the 101 TDs and senators present, forty-two spoke, though no minister contributed. There was outright criticism of Haughey from just two – Seán Power and Noel Dempsey – but many others delivered coded messages. Power, a straight-talking young TD from Kildare, didn't beat about the bush and bluntly told Haughey he should go. "The people of Ireland are disgusted with the scandals and the relationship you, Taoiseach, have with some of the people at the centre of those scandals," he said, astounding many his older colleagues with his outspokenness. He also told the meeting about what he regarded as Haughey's insulting treatment of him in the past.

He instanced an occasion when, early in the life of the government, he had expressed concern at the return of stroke politics in the shape of a deal which Haughey had done with Roscommon Hospital TD Tom Foxe. Power told the meeting he had been called over to Haughey's office where the Taoiseach had immediately attacked him and said that anybody who had got through a Fianna Fáil convention in Kildare was in no position to complain about stroke politics. Power was still indignant nearly two years after the event at the dismissive way he had been treated.

Senator Don Lydon tried to reassure the meeting that Power had not been singled out for special treatment. Lydon recalled that a few years earlier he had made a controversial speech on Northern Ireland in the Seanad. Haughey called him over to the Taoiseach's office, berated him in strong language for the speech and told him to remember that in Fianna Fáil the leader decided Northern policy and nobody else. Lydon was then dismissed from Haughey's presence but he couldn't find the door in the Taoiseach's wood-panelled office. Haughey looked up from his desk a couple of minutes later to find the forlorn senator still in his presence!

"What are you still doing here?" he demanded.

"I can't find the door, Taoiseach," responded Lydon.

"Then why don't you jump out the fucking window," snapped Haughey.

Many of the older TDs and senators who had known Haughey's brutally tactless style down the years thought Lydon's story highly amusing but younger deputies like Power and Dempsey didn't see any funny side to it. They had no intention of putting up with that kind of attitude from their sixty-six-year-old leader and they were no longer intimidated by it.

That was the key message from the party meeting of 2 October. A majority of the parliamentary party didn't necessarily want Haughey to go, but they were no longer intimidated by him. The days when TDs quaked at a summons to the Great One's office were over; from now on it was down to pragmatic decisions for each individual about their own future and how that related to the timing of a leadership change.

Haughey's back was to the wall and it seemed to many in Fianna Fáil that there was no way of escape this time. A Lansdowne opinion poll showed a big drop in his satisfaction rating, while Fianna Fáil were down 11 percent. Rumblings within the party about his leadership continued, negotiations with the PDs were stalled and a host of further controversies had developed.

Fine Gael leader John Bruton then disclosed that a confidential report, carried out by Dermot Desmond's NCB for Celtic Helicopters, a subsidiary of Aer Lingus, had somehow found its way to the Taoiseach's son, Ciaran Haughey, whose own company Irish Helicopters is a rival of the state firm. Further controversy developed around the installation by the ESB of a wind generator on Haughey's holiday island home of Inishvickillane, and to cap it all the Carysfort land deal, which had been in the news nearly a year earlier, resurfaced as a political issue. As a response to all the controversies, Fine Gael put down a motion of no confidence in the government for the resumption of the Dáil on 16 October.

All in all was a very difficult situation, but Haughey showed yet again that he was at his best in difficult situations. The first thing that had to be done was to get agreement with the PDs and Haughey hoped to have this concluded before the Dáil resumed. This didn't happen because Fianna Fáil again underestimated the determination of the PDs to win substantial concessions or to pull out of government if they didn't get them. The PD hard-line was reinforced by the view among some senior party members, like chairman Michael McDowell and Junior Minister Mary Harney, that they should get out of government before they were dragged down by the controversies besetting Haughey.

As before in the Fianna Fáil–PD bargaining sessions, the talks were pushed to the brink and were only concluded hours before the deadline. The confidence debate in the government began on 16 October and was scheduled to finish with a vote at 4 p.m. on 18 October. That vote became the deadline for the conclusion of the talks when the PDs made it clear they would not support the government unless they got agreement by then.

The final days of negotiation were nerve-wracking. Haughey and O'Malley thought they had an agreement on 16 October but Albert Reynolds dug his heels in and refused to sign, on the basis that as Finance Minister he couldn't stand over the deal. Most Fianna Fáil TDs were initially delighted at what they regarded as Reynolds's decision to stand up to the PDs once and for all, and Haughey got a very poor response from his parliamentary party when he suggested that he should be given a mandate to conclude the talks on his terms. As the deadline for agreement loomed, however, and the prospect of a general election came menacingly closer, the mood of the TDs began to change. Haughey supporters began to accuse Reynolds of using the delicate situation for his own leadership ambitions.

The situation was fraught with dangers for everyone, particularly Haughey, because if the government collapsed and the country was plunged into an election there was little likelihood of Fianna Fáil being in a position to form a government afterwards and no prospect of Haughey surviving as leader. Equally there were dangers for Reynolds because if he forced a collapse of the government and Fianna Fáil were hammered, his leadership ambitions could be destroyed.

Bertie Ahern was the key figure in getting everybody off the hook. Like Haughey he had been prepared to put his name to the original deal and was surprised at Reynolds's refusal to go along with it. On the final night of negotiation, when things looked intractable, he managed to talk Reynolds, O'Malley and Molloy into putting their sundry reservations aside and hammering out the basis of an agreement.

Getting that agreement was the first hurdle Haughey had had to overcome, and he had no doubt that the credit lay with Ahern. The following day Ahern was briefing a few journalists about the deal in the Taoiseach's Department after it had been formally announced, when Haughey put his head around the door.

"He's the man," said the grinning Taoiseach, pointing to Ahern. "He's the best, the most skilful, the most devious and the most cunning," he added.

"God, that's all I need," said Ahern when Haughey withdrew, but there was no disguising the important role he had played in saving Haughey's bacon.

As for the deal itself, it was essentially another triumph for the PDs in terms of its tax commitments. Fianna Fáil ministers had been arguing for months that tax was not the priority and that the national finances and social services should take precedence over tax reform. In the negotiations the Department of Finance had argued that the PD plans for tax reform were impracticable and would cost the exchequer money. In one early session the Taoiseach maintained that all the tax allowances and reliefs were there for very good social reasons and should not be changed. The PD position, on the other hand, was that a substantial proportion of the £1.5 billion in shelters and reliefs could be eliminated to fund tax cuts and they argued that the reliefs totally distorted the economy by forcing people to spend money in certain ways in order to qualify for reliefs.

In the event the PDs won the argument with Fianna Fáil and Finance and got their commitments on the reduction of personal taxation to a basic rate of 25 percent by 1993 written into the agreement. They also got a lot of their policies incorporated in the rest of the document though many of the same commitments had been included in the 1989 Programme for Government but never implemented.

The reaction of Fianna Fáil TDs was surprising. Despite the wholesale concessions to the PDs, they accepted the document as a positive development to which they were as committed as the PDs. With the agreement finalised on 18 October the way was clear for the PDs to vote confidence in the government which they duly did. Haughey had crossed one major hurdle in the battle to retain his leadership.

While the majority of Fianna Fáil TDs were relieved at the prospect of stability, Pádraig Flynn and the other members of the "Western Alliance" tried to convince Reynolds that the time was ripe to throw down the gauntlet to Haughey. Only three days after the new Fianna Fáil-PD pact was agreed, a rumour that a backbench deputy would put down a motion of no confidence in the leader travelled like wildfire through the ranks of the Fianna Fáil parliamentary party. Haughey, desperate to stave off a challenge, went to his TDs on 23 October and, in an emotional speech, told them he would know when it was time to go. He outlined an agenda of work – the PESP talks, the Maastricht summit and the budget – which he wished to complete, and conveyed a clear impression that having completed that agenda he would stand down.

Even this clear signal that despite all previous utterances he would not be leading the party into the next election failed to calm the situation. The Reynolds camp was in a frenzy, with Flynn and Máire Geoghegan-Quinn pressing for an immediate challenge. Backbench TD Michael Ahern, from Cork East, was said to have put his name to a motion of no confidence in Haughey which might go down any time. Justice Minister Ray Burke, in an attempt to buy time and head off a challenge, gave a television interview in which he said that the Taoiseach would step down before the next election. Reynolds dithered and eventually backed off, mainly because Bertie Ahern made it clear that he would stick by Haughey if the issue was pushed at that time. A number of respected TDs, regarded as the middle ground of the party, also told Reynolds that while they would support him as the next leader they didn't want a bloodbath at this stage.

216

The "Western Alliance" deputies were bitterly disappointed, particularly as Haughey failed to extricate himself from the business controversies which still plagued the Dáil and continued to weaken his position. Reynolds, in an attempt to reassure his supporters, made a huge tactical mistake by giving a radio interview in which he said that while he had backed off in the interests of the party, he would have had the numbers if the issue had gone to a vote. That claim would be tested sooner than he realised.

19 – Another Heave

Just two weeks after Reynolds backed off in November 1991, the fourth heave against Haughey's leadership formally emerged and this time there was no pulling back. The challenge took place against a background of the continuing business controversies. The Goodman Tribunal, which had opened in October, was hearing a steady stream of evidence about irregularities in the meat business which made a mockery of Haughey's defence of Goodman back in 1989.

Questions also persisted in relation to the allocation of exchequer funds to University College Dublin to purchase Carysfort at the end of 1990. The decision was controversial at the time and erupted again nearly a year later in the welter of business scandals. A central ingredient in this controversy was the manner in which "Pino" Harris, widely regarded as an associate of Haughey's, had made a profit of nearly £1.5 million on the deal in just six months.

On top of this the Greencore issue and Haughey's relationship with the company chairman, Bernie Cahill, was now causing uproar in the Dáil. Answering a question from Dick Spring, the Taoiseach initially denied meeting Cahill to discuss the privatisation of Irish Sugar. However, a report in the *Sunday Business Post* revealed that Cahill had in fact been summoned by helicopter in May 1990 to discuss the privatisation.

With further Dáil questions looming, P.J. Mara accused Spring of being the mouthpiece of Chris Comerford. He also remarked cryptically to political correspondents that if it was a case of guilt by association, what about Spring's link with London property developer Pat Doherty, a central figure in the Telecom controversy?

With the political temperature rising rapidly, Haughey was due to explain his meetings with Bernie Cahill to the Dáil on the afternoon of 6 November. That morning the Fianna Fáil parliamentary party met as usual in Leinster House and there were heated exchanges between Brian Lenihan, who was standing in as acting chairman, and Charlie McCreevy.

McCreevy, who had a curious love-hate relationship with Haughey since the heaves of the early 1980s, was now expressing the view that the uncertainty would have to be cleared up one way or another and he had suggested publicly that the Taoiseach should seek a vote of confidence from his TDs. At the meeting on 6 November he tried to raise this issue but was peremptorily ruled out of order by Lenihan who had suddenly reverted to his old role as Haughey's staunch defender.

Lenihan told the meeting that if they wanted to discuss the leadership somebody should put the matter on the agenda. There was a great deal of anger among some of the younger TDs at the way Lenihan conducted the meeting and Seán Power was goaded there and then to the decision to settle the issue by putting down a motion of no confidence in the leader.

Power had already become increasingly impatient with the way senior figures were refusing to move on Haughey and the party meeting that morning was the last straw. Haughey's performance in the Dáil that afternoon, in relation to the questions about Greencore, impressed some of his internal critics, even though the claim about Spring amounted to nothing. Nonetheles, Power went ahead and at 5 p.m. handed in the motion to the chief whip's office.

There was something remarkably strange about this, the fourth challenge to the leadership of Charles J. Haughey. Now it was his old friends, who had stood by him through the heaves of 1982-83, who were looking for his head while, irony or ironies, his old enemies, Des O'Malley and Bobby Molloy, were propping up the government. It was yet another irony that young Power who put down the no confidence motion was a son of Paddy Power, a diehard Haughey supporter in the early 1980s whose loyalty had been rewarded by a Cabinet post as Minister for Defence.

In response to Power's motion the chairman of the parliamentary party, Jim Tunney, summoned a special meeting the following Saturday to decide Haughey's future. Reynolds was in a dilemma but he had no choice except to back the no confidence motion. He was driving down to a function in Newtowncashel in Longford when he heard of the motion on the radio, though Power had informed him of his intentions earlier in the day. With speculation rife about his intentions, Reynolds moved within twenty-four hours, issuing a statement declaring his support for Power's motion.

"For some time now there has been considerable political instability which has led to an erosion of confidence in our democratic institutions. This uncertainty must not be allowed to continue. The well-being of our country requires strong and decisive leadership of Government and of the Fianna Fáil party," said Reynolds's statement.

"I am not satisfied that such leadership now exists. In the circumstances I will be supporting the motion tabled for the party meeting on Saturday next," it continued.

However, he did not resign from the Cabinet as O'Malley and Martin O'Donoghue had done in similar circumstances in 1982. Instead, Reynolds followed the Lenihan precedent and waited for Haughey to fire him. He didn't have long to wait. Within an hour the Taoiseach requested President Robinson to terminate the appointment of the Finance Minister and the battle for the leadership was on in earnest.

The following day the process was repeated when Pádraig Flynn came out in favour of Power's motion and was fired. Junior Ministers Geoghegan-Quinn, Treacy and Smith also came out against Haughey but they were not fired immediately because, technically, their appointments had to be terminated by the government as a whole and not just by the Taoiseach.

Those in the Reynolds camp were not sure they would win but they were confident that at least thirty of the seventy-seven TDs would vote against Haughey. The Taoiseach appeared to be on the ropes when the Fianna Fáil senators declined to take part in the vote as he wished. There were also renewed rumblings from the PDs about their willingness to continue on in a government led by a man who had lost the confidence of two of his own most trusted followers.

Significantly, though, the rest of the government held firm. Ahern again refused to support Reynolds against Haughey and told the ex-Finance Minister that he just didn't have the numbers. While this was not unexpected, considering his advice of two weeks earlier, it was still deeply disappointing for Reynolds. Brendan Daly, who was close to the "Western Alliance" ministers, came out with a public statement in Haughey's favour. Mary O'Rourke and Brian Lenihan gave strong backing to the leader. O'Rourke's decision to support Haughey came as no great surprise, as everyone by now assumed she had an interest in creating an opportunity for herself in the future. Lenihan's motivation for backing Haughey so strongly was puzzling, given the events of a year earlier. While he had always maintained a policy of loyalty to the leader of the day, Lenihan went above and beyond the call of duty, just as he had done in the early 1980s, to the horror of the very same TDs who had sided with him a year earlier.

Other ministers too rallied to Haughey. Gerry Collins gave a bizarre television interview in which he appealed to Reynolds to back off. By the morning of the meeting the Reynolds camp knew the game was up. A number of TDs on whose support they were relying, including some who had encouraged Reynolds to make a challenge two weeks earlier, now made it clear that they were not going to vote against Haughey.

For the two days before the meeting Haughey had summoned a steady stream of TDs and ministers to his office. While he made no outright promises, many left his office believing they had a strong chance of promotion, in view of the two Cabinet posts and the three junior ministries that had become vacant following the departure of the "Western Alliance".

The meeting itself began at 11.30 a.m. on 9 November and continued until after 2 a.m. the following morning. When Haughey got his way by 44 votes to 33 on having the decision by an open roll-call vote, rather than a secret ballot, the worst fears of the Reynolds camp were realised. In the late afternoon Reynolds made a speech in which he said a campaign of misinformation had been conducted against him. He blamed Government Press Secretary P.J. Mara for this and he also claimed that a prominent business associate of Haughey's had been trying to dig up dirt on his business affairs in the midlands. Reynolds also complained about surveillance of his house in Longford from a white Hiace van and said a man had been seen acting suspiciously near his Dublin apartment.

Parliamentary party chairman Jim Tunney intervened to suggest that a special commission be set up to examine the Reynolds allegations, as well as those of two backbenchers, Noel Dempsey and John Ellis, that their phones were being tapped. These allegations were withdrawn when Ray Burke assured the meeting that the Gardaí were not tapping the phones of any TDs, but they indicated the level of mistrust which was now prevalent in the party.

The claims made by Reynolds provoked a mixed reaction from the meeting. His strong supporters regarded them as evidence of the trouble that had been taken to discredit him but some middle-ground TDs believed that Reynolds had gone over the top and they refused to believe that he could be serious. The mood of the meeting at this stage was dictated by the knowledge that Haughey was going to win the vote regardless of what was said. A number of TDs who had been complaining bitterly about Haughey behind his back, in conversations with other deputies and with journalists, now vied with each other to speak in praise of the leader.

"How can you speak like that when you can't say a good word about him in the Dáil bar?" piped up a voice as one TD expressed his impassioned support for Haughey.

As the meeting moved towards its inevitable conclusion the principal Reynolds supporters insisted on stating their case for the record. Máire Geoghegan-Quinn made one of the longest speeches but by general agreement the most riveting of the day came from Pádraig Flynn who, in characteristic style, referred to himself throughout in the third person as P. Flynn. He spoke of the mounting problems facing Fianna Fáil, including the prospect of bankruptcy with debts running at £2.3 million, the poor performances in the general election, the presidential contest and the local elections. He said the Taoiseach must take responsibility for all of those problems and for breaking Fianna Fáil's sacred principle of not entering coalition.

"P. Flynn would be doing himself a disservice if he did not support the motion to discontinue the leadership forthwith of Charles J. Haughey," said Flynn.

It was nearly 2 a.m. on Sunday morning before Haughey stood up to reply to the debate. He had spent almost fourteen hours in the Fianna Fáil party room, with just one break for tea and sandwiches. His stamina impressed everybody even if his speech was quite subdued. He told his TDs that he would not be around forever but he repeated that there was very important business coming up, particularly the issue of European union, and he wanted to be around to deal with it.

He also said he was genuinely impressed by many of the contributions he had heard during the long day and he mentioned the loss to Cabinet, particularly of Pádraig Flynn, which had been caused by the whole episode. When he sat down to general applause all that remained to be done was hold the roll-call vote. Names were called out in alphabetical order with Bertie Ahern being the first to vote confidence in Haughey. The only surprise was that some TDs who had been regarded as strong Reynolds supporters ended up voting for Haughey.

Michael Ahern of Cork East, who had reportedly signed a motion of no confidence in Haughey two weeks earlier, now voted for him, as did Larry Kelly from a neighbouring constituency who was also regarded as a Reynolds man. Junior Minister Joe Walsh, who was also anti-Haughey, was another whose support for the Taoiseach on this occasion surprised many. While Haughey's victory itself was not a huge surprise, the margin was. He routed his opponents by 55 votes to 22.

The anti-Haughey faction was only the same strength as the "Gang of 22" who had opposed him nine years earlier. Only three of the new "Gang of 22" – Charlie McCreevy, David Andrews and Willie O'Dea – were survivors from the old Gang. Most of the old Gang who were still in the Dáil now backed Haughey, while most of the new Gang had been strong Haugheyites back in 1982. More than one of those involved recalled Margaret Thatcher's remark after her demise: "It's a funny old world."

As for Haughey, he was on top of the world. He gave a press briefing for political correspondents in his government office at 2.30 a.m. that Sunday morning. He shook hands with each one and insisted that bottles of champagne be opened to celebrate his victory.

"Well, you got it wrong now. Admit it. Didn't you?" he remarked good humouredly. But in fact nobody had dared to write him off this time, considering his ability to survive in the past, though a number of journalists, including this one, had made the mistake of over-estimating the likely level of support for Reynolds.

It seemed that morning that despite his age, his health, the welter of business controversies and the privately expressed desire of many of his closest colleagues that he shouldn't lead them into the next election, there was nothing to stop Haughey doing precisely that. Coming from a position of weakness he had managed to stamp his authority on his party again and the decisive margin of victory had put an end to any doubts the PDs might have had about continuing in government with him.

However, it didn't take Haughey long to rub some of the gloss off his victory. He ruminated for a couple of days about the shape of his new Cabinet, but when it was announced to the Dáil on 13 November it caused a sensation. Instead of doing the obvious, as he usually did in these situations, by promoting junior ministers like chief whip Vincent Brady and Food Minister Joe Walsh, the Taoiseach catapulted two backbenchers into the Cabinet. They were Noel Davern from Tipperary and Dr James McDaid from Donegal.

The Fianna Fáil benches were stunned at the announcement and many who voted for Haughey in expectation of promotion would gladly have wrung his neck. It was not that most Fianna Fáil TDs had anything against either of the two newly appointed individuals. In fact they were both popular with their colleagues. It was just that the promotions appeared so unfair to a number of backbenchers who had carried the burden of defending unpopular government policies and who had been given strong hints of promotion by Haughey. Vincent Brady was livid; a constituency colleague of Haughey, he had served him loyally as chief whip for the best part of a decade and had been promised promotion before. Joe Walsh was almost equally disappointed, while backbenchers like Dick Roche, Michael Martin and Liam Aylward were sore at being passed over yet again. Dermot Ahern and John O'Donoghue were promoted to the junior ranks and in view of their ability and loyalty few begrudged them their step up, but the Cabinet promotions rankled deeply.

If shock was the immediate reaction of the Fianna Fáil TDs, it soon became apparent that there was a much more serious objection to one of the appointments. James McDaid, the new Minister for Defence, had been involved in an extradition case in 1990 concerning a leading IRA man, James Pius Clarke. McDaid provided an alibi for Clarke and was present at the hearing on 14 March 1990 when the Supreme Court refused to extradite Clarke to Northern Ireland. After the hearing, McDaid was photographed with Clarke on the steps of the Four Courts in the middle of a group of anti-extradition campaigners.

The incident had received some publicity at the time and McDaid had written to the *Irish Press* to make it clear that he supported government policy on extradition. Despite the sensitive security implications Haughey saw no problem about offering McDaid the post of Defence. Haughey did inform Des O'Malley the night before the decision was announced, but the PD leader was unaware of McDaid's involvement in the extradition case and he didn't object to the appointment. When the announcement was made to the Dáil on 13 November few initially recalled the incident.

Michael Devine, the *Belfast Telegraph* correspondent in Dublin, immediately remembered it and wrote a lead story for his paper on McDaid's appointment and the implications for Anglo-Irish relations. In the Dáil, John Bruton and Dick Spring made no reference to it and it was Workers' Party leader Proinsias De Rossa who first raised the issue. Fine Gael picked up on it and the McDaid appointment suddenly became a very hot potato.

Former Fine Gael Justice spokesman Michael Noonan got to his feet and held up newspaper cuttings and photographs about the Clarke extradition case. Noonan said that McDaid would be perceived as a "Provo fellow traveller", then, looking directly across the Dáil chamber at O'Malley, Noonan asked why he had agreed to the appointment. He referred back to the veto over the security departments exercised in 1979 by the late George Colley.

Alarm bells now started to ring in the PD leader's head and he returned immediately to his office and asked an official to get him the newspaper cuttings from 14 March 1990. He also got Michael McDowell to check the law report of the case. Having considered all the reports and discussed the issue with Bobby Molloy, himself a former Minister for Defence, O'Malley then sought a meeting with Haughey to explain his concern about the appointment. The Taoiseach suggested that the PD leader should meet McDaid to discuss the issue directly.

The situation now had all the hallmarks of another Fianna Fáil-PD confrontation, with only one possible outcome. McDaid, however, preempted the issue. After meeting O'Malley and Molloy he sensed the potential for another government crisis and he went to Haughey and offered to withdraw his name from nomination. Haughey accepted and postponed the appointment for a day. There was uproar in Fianna Fáil when McDaid announced his decision to the Dáil and wild talk of a special parliamentary party meeting the following day. Brian Lenihan got Haughey to agree to such a meeting but party chairman Jim Tunney refused to convene it, judging correctly that a little time was needed for tempers to cool.

The central outcome of the affair was that Haughey, having yet again outfoxed his internal enemies only days earlier, single-handedly created a fresh political crisis. The issue led to renewed questioning of his judgement and put his leadership back on to the political agenda.

20 – The Ghost of GUBU

In the early days of December 1991, Haughey acted as if he hadn't a care in the world. John Major came to Dublin for the first formal Anglo-Irish summit between Haughey and a British prime minister for eleven years. The two men got on well and Major made a very positive impression on Irish ministers and officials. "He is one of the very few senior British politicians I have encountered who is in no way patronising in his dealings with us," said one senior Irish official. Haughey's handling of the post-summit press conference caused some comment because he took a back seat and allowed Major to do most of the talking.

That led to some renewed doubts about his stamina but Haughey dispelled them a few days later when he went off to the historic EC summit in Maastricht where he was an enthusiastic supporter of the decision to press ahead with European union. The summit didn't end until after 1 a.m. on 11 December but the Taoiseach insisted on flying home in the early hours, snatching just a few hours' sleep before going into the Dáil to answer a gruelling set of questions on the Carysfort land deal controversy. In spite of months of buffeting it appeared that he was gradually rebuilding his authority.

There were, however, some ominous straws in the wind. The Cathaoirleach of the Seanad, Seán Doherty, blew a gasket when Minister for Justice Ray Burke published the Phone Tapping Bill in early December. The commitment to publish the Bill was contained in the joint Programme for Government with the PDs but Doherty took it as a personal affront. He had carried the can for the phone tapping incidents of 1982 and his political career had suffered as a result. It was galling for him to see other key members of that ill-fated government managing to put the incident behind them and go on to political success.

Over the years Doherty had told friends that there was more to the story than people knew and he issued dark hints that he might some day spill the beans. Now with the publication of the Phone Tapping Bill he saw the prospect of the whole episode being dredged up to haunt him one more time. Doherty approached Burke and asked him to withdraw the Bill or at least stall its passage so that he would not face the embarrassment of having to deal with it in the Seanad. Burke rejected such a move and he also refused to countenance a request from Doherty to be allowed to look at the files in the Department of Justice relating to the controversial incidents of 1982.

Shortly before Christmas, Doherty met P.J. Mara in the bar of Jury's Hotel and the two had a bitter stand-up row until late into the night. It was clear to those who knew him that the events of 1982 were gnawing away at Doherty and that the Phone Tapping Bill could push him over the edge.

However, the issue faded out of everybody's mind when the Dáil broke for the Christmas recess. TDs of all parties were relieved to reach the holiday because the previous few months had been so full of accusations, controversy and bitterness. There was widespread hope that the New Year would bring a calmer political atmosphere and a general feeling that things would settle down.

Returning to work in the early days of January, Haughey felt refreshed and buoyant and was looking forward to dealing with the tricky political issue of the budget. P.J. Mara told the few political journalists back at work from the beginning of January that the Taoiseach was fighting fit and had no intention of stepping down for the foreseeable future. To Haughey's enemies in Fianna Fáil this was a red rag to a bull. They were now convinced that he had no intention of resigning voluntarily and they resolved to step up the heat.

As Albert Reynolds and Pádraig Flynn prepared a strategy to put pressure on Haughey events suddenly took a turn in their favour. The "Nighthawks" programme on RTE decided to do a special on Seán Doherty. The format of the programme involves guests talking to presenter Shay Healy in a relaxed pub-like atmosphere in a makeshift bar in RTE. For the Doherty programme the production team travelled to Roscommon and Doherty was interviewed among a group of friends and supporters in a local pub. The interview was easy-going but in the middle of it the Seanad Cathaoirleach was asked about the phone tapping affair of 1982.

"There was a decision taken in Cabinet that the leaking of matters from Cabinet must be stopped. I, as Minister for Justice, had a direct responsibility for doing that – I did that. I do feel that I was let down by the fact that people knew what I was doing."

Doherty's statement initially threw more heat than light on the situation. It had been known since 1983 that the Cabinet of which Doherty was a member had discussed leaks, but his comment that people knew

227

what he was doing opened up the possibility that somebody else was aware that he had authorised the tapping of journalists' telephones. Details of the "Nighthawks" interview were leaked to the *Irish Press* before it was transmitted, so that it became a big story when the programme went out on 15 January. A number of ministers who had served during 1982, including Des O'Malley, reacted to the interview by saying that the question of phone tapping had never been discussed at Cabinet. The question of who else might have known about phone tapping was left hanging in the air.

Seán Doherty said nothing for a few days after the interview while speculation, claim and counter claim raged. Some of his Fianna Fáil Seanad colleagues publicly rebuked him and indicated that they might not back him if the Opposition in the Seanad put down a motion of no confidence in the Cathaoirleach. Doherty kept his counsel for six days as various members of his own party said he should put up or shut up.

Then on 21 January the time bomb that had been ticking for nine years exploded. Journalists were summoned to a hastily arranged press conference in the Montrose Hotel near RTE. The venue had been selected because of a strike which had crippled the national broadcasting service and severely restricted news coverage. The Montrose, being so close at hand, was judged the best place to make an announcement. Doherty, arriving at the press conference with his wife Maura, walked rapidly across the small conference room, sat down and began to speak before the conversation among the assembled journalists had died down.

The talking stopped quickly enough after the first few devastating words. "I am confirming tonight that the Taoiseach, Mr Haughey, was fully aware, in 1982, that two journalists' phones were being tapped, and that he at no stage expressed a reservation about this action. Here are the details." Speaking rapidly, Doherty outlined the circumstances of the telephone taps in 1982 and the leaks from Cabinet which prompted him to authorise the head of security at the time, Deputy Commissioner Joe Ainsworth, to tap the phones of Bruce Arnold and Geraldine Kennedy.

"I did not seek nor did I get any instruction from any member of the Cabinet in this regard, nor did I tell the Cabinet that this action had been taken. Telephone tapping was never discussed in the Cabinet. However, as soon as the transcripts from the taps became available, I took them personally to Mr Haughey in his office and left them in his possession.

"I understand that the Taoiseach has already denied that this happened so I wish to reiterate it in specific terms. Mr Ainsworth forwarded to me the transcripts relevant to the Cabinet leaks problem, numbering some four or five out of the roughly twelve or thirteen total. Each and every one of those relevant transcripts were transported by me to Mr Haughey's office and handed to him directly. He retained all but one of them, making no comment on their content. At no stage did he indicate disapproval of the action which had been taken."

Doherty went on for about ten minutes. He referred to Haughey's statement, made when the phone tapping was revealed in January 1983, that he would "not have countenanced any such action" and that it was "an abuse of power". He said he felt pressurised by Haughey's immediate response to support his (Haughey's) stated position. "Not only did I take the blame but when Mr Haughey claimed not to have been aware of the tapping while it was in progress, I did not correct this claim, and indeed supported it. However, the truth is that the Taoiseach, as I've already said, had known and had not expressed any reservation during the several months in which he received from my hands copies of the transcripts of the taped telephone conversations." Doherty then announced that he would resign as Cathaoirleach of the Seanad. He left the room without answering any questions.

The effect of the Doherty statement was electrifying. A substantial raw chunk of the press conference was put out on television less than an hour later. The fact that there were no facilities to edit and package the statement added rather than detracted from its impact on an unsuspecting public. Immediately after the press conference Shane Kenny, one of the handful of RTE journalists still working, phoned Des O'Malley and played the tape of the Doherty press conference down to line to him. The PD leader expressed his shock and consternation to Kenny and then summoned an emergency meeting of his closest advisors.

Fellow Cabinet Minister Bobby Molloy, Junior Minister Mary Harney, PD Chairman Michael McDowell, Assistant Government Press Secretary Stephen O'Byrnes and Press Officer Ray Gordon went around to O'Malley's house after they had seen the 9 o'clock news on television. The composition of the group was identical to that which had advised O'Malley from the beginning of the Lenihan crisis over a year before and their advice this time around was exactly the same. There was no way that the PDs could now continue to serve in government with Haughey. Nobody at the meeting dissented from that view but they agreed to hold their fire until Haughey had a chance to respond. They met the following morning along with the other PD TDs and senators but again put off a statement until they heard what Haughey would say at a lunchtime press conference. However, the PD ministers gave an earnest of their intentions by refusing to attend a Cabinet meeting on the budget, so the writing was clearly on the wall.

Haughey at his press conference delivered another bravura performance under pressure. He read a detailed statement in which he rejected Doherty's claims as absolutely false, pointed to the fact that Doherty was now saying the opposite of what he said in 1983 and asked: "Are the Irish people more entitled to believe me, who has been consistent in everything I have said about this affair from the beginning, or someone who has been inconsistent and by his own words untruthful on countless occasions with regard to it?"

Unlike Doherty, Haughey answered questions from the assembled media and his response to the grilling was impressive. He dealt with all questions, no matter how aggressive, with a mixture of imperiousness and good humour. He made it clear that he regarded the Doherty statement as part of a plot by the disaffected elements in Fianna Fáil and referred to them dismissively as the "Country and Western Alliance". He made one fundamental error, though, as far as many Fianna Fáil TDs were concerned. Asked about the time-frame he reportedly had set for his departure the previous autumn, he said: "I didn't set a time-frame. That's another misstatement", and pressed about when he intended to stand down he added: "When I decide ... I received a mandate from the party to decide when it's time to go."

Many of his own deputies were worried by this indication that he had no intention of stepping down but the majority thought he had given a very good performance. Fine Gael's Michael Noonan accurately captured the mood by saying: "Charlie did enough to reassure his own crowd but not enough to win over the PDs."

Haughey's claim that the "Western Alliance" deputies opposed to him were behind the Doherty revelation also met with a mixed reaction. Many Fianna Fáil TDs didn't believe that Albert Reynolds had put Doherty up to it but some were suspicious about the affair, and suspicions were fanned by Haughey supporters. "Albert may not have put him up to it but the instability in the party created by Reynolds and Flynn provides the context for the whole thing," said one TD.

After Haughey's press conference most Fianna Fáil TDs naively hoped that the issue would just go away. Yet again they totally underestimated the PDs. The junior coalition party held another meeting in the afternoon and decided to hold off to await developments in Fianna Fáil. When it became clear later in the day that the Fianna Fáil parliamentary party would not even be summoned to consider the issue, the PDs met again and decided to act. Just before the 9 o'clock television news they issued a statement.

"It is not for the Progressive Democrats to decide as between the conflicting accounts given by both the Taoiseach and Sen. Doherty in relation to the telephone tapping affair. The plain fact is that this is but the latest – and almost certainly the most serious – in a long list of unhappy and politically unacceptable controversies which undermined the capacity of the Government to work effectively.

"The situation which has now arisen is one which we view with the utmost gravity. It calls for an immediate response in order that the credibility and stability of the Government be immediately restored. While the Progressive Democrats will not interfere in the internal affairs of another party, we are anxious to see that the acute dilemma facing the Government is speedily resolved."

The statement did not spell it out but it was clear that the price of their continued participation in government was that Haughey should step down as Taoiseach. The parallels with the departure of Brian Lenihan a little over a year earlier were uncanny and the wording of the statement bore a striking resemblance to the phraseology used on that occasion by the PDs.

To make sure there was no ambiguity about the issue, Bobby Molloy and Mary Harney arranged a meeting with Bertie Ahern to spell out what lay between the lines. Ahern later rang Brian Lenihan, who was at a *comhairle ceanntair* meeting in Dublin West, to tell him what had happened and to ask him to come in for a chat early the next morning. Ahern also passed on the message to Haughey, who hardly needed it to be decoded in any case. That night, Wednesday, 22 January, Haughey could well have recalled a remark made by Kildare deputy Seán Power during the Lenihan crisis. When the party TDs discussed sacrificing Brian Lenihan to avoid an election, Power demanded to know if the Taoiseach would give the same advice if his own head was the only thing that would save the government.

That night Haughey made up his mind that, come what may, he would not be the cause of an election. Over breakfast with his family in Kinsealy the following morning he told them of his decision and they fully approved. When Seán Haughey arrived in Leinster House for a meeting of senators later that morning, he met Maurice Manning and Avril Doyle of Fine Gael in a corridor. Young Haughey asked the Fine Gael senators if they intended to press ahead with a plan to try and debate a motion of no confidence in the Taoiseach. When the Fine Gael senators said yes, he responded by telling them that by the time it was debated it would all be very pointless. It was a clear signal that Haughey would step down.

Meanwhile over in the Taoiseach's Department, Bertie Ahern and Tánaiste John Wilson met Haughey to discuss the situation. They looked at the various options facing them and the prospect of a general election if the PDs' demand was not complied with. As the two Fianna Fáil ministers stood up to leave, Des O'Malley and Bobby Molloy came into the Taoiseach's office to outline their position. They told Haughey they would have to withdraw from government unless he resolved the situation. The Taoiseach in turn told the PD ministers that he would not be the cause of an election and clearly signalled that he intended to go. All he asked was that they should give him a short breathing space so that he could step down with some dignity. This would also prevent a complete souring of relations between the two parties in government – something which could happen if the PDs were openly seen to be looking for his head on a plate. There was no animosity between the PD ministers and Haughey. Since forming the coalition Haughey and O'Malley had gone out of their way to avoid personal friction. Haughey didn't have to be told that there was nothing personal in their ultimatum; it was just business, however brutal.

After that meeting the tension evaporated and they all went in to a Cabinet meeting on the budget. Incredibly, in the light of what had gone on, Haughey presided over this Cabinet meeting in his normal fashion and there was barely a hint of tension in the air as ministers wrapped up most of the loose ends of the budget. After the Cabinet meeting, chatting to a few ministers, Haughey gave a clue about why he had come to his decision when he sighed: "You can't keep on refuting allegations all the time."

Word now began to filter around Leinster House that Haughey might go. While there was a feeling of relief among many TDs that an election

232

would be avoided, many in Fianna Fáil couldn't believe what was happening. P.J. Mara still retained his composure and good humour under pressure. Briefing the political correspondents after the Cabinet meeting he was asked if Haughey had made a decision to step down. Mara replied that nobody had informed him of any such decision, but he added after a pause: "All I'll tell you is that I'm going to ring FAS this afternoon to enquire about retraining courses."

Many Fianna Fáil TDs were not so philosophical. "It's not much over a year since the PDs took out the Tánaiste. A few months ago they prevented McDaid becoming a minister and now they are taking out our Taoiseach. It's all just too incredible," said one disconsolate TD. Another Fianna Fáil deputy had a more sanguine approach to the issue: "We have shown ourselves to be incapable of dealing with the leadership issue. In political terms the PDs had no choice and it is pointless blaming them for it."

Haughey, amazingly, took a somewhat similar line. At a meeting of the Fianna Fáil national executive that night a number of speakers lashed the PDs for their stand but Haughey did his best to calm things down. "We have nothing to fear from our enemies without, it is the enemies within we must fear," he said at the end of the meeting.

In an extraordinary end to an extraordinary career Haughey's bitterness was now reserved for his old friends who had turned against him rather than his old enemies who were putting the gun to his head. Many people still couldn't believe that Haughey had decided to go. As he had survived so many attempts to take him out, people found it hard to believe that finally the hour had come. However, as Haughey himself saw it, he had a simple choice – either he stepped down or he caused a general election. The logic he had applied to the Lenihan case he now applied to his own and to the astonishment of a great number of people he bowed to the inevitable.

Many in his own party regretted that he hadn't gone on a better note. He probably could have done so if he had made it clear earlier than he would step down after the 1992 Ard Fheis but that was now water under the bridge. A Dublin Fine Gael TD struck a chord with many in Leinster House when he remarked. "I hate to see him go like this. You have to hand it to him, he's such a battler. In a way I'm sorry he didn't confound the lot of them just one more time."

Summary – The Haughey Legacy

A complete assessment of the career of Charles James Haughey will have to await historians. The main features of his political life contain so many contradictions and ironies that only the fullness of time will enable his contribution to Irish political life to be put in its proper context. There is also the problem that the full story of some central episodes of his earlier career, particularly the Arms Crisis, remains to be told.

The striking feature of his period as Fianna Fáil leader for just over twelve years and his occupancy of the Taoiseach's office for seven and a half of those, is the contradictory nature of his achievement. In his first term as Taoiseach his economic profligacy helped to bring the nation to the brink of bankruptcy. Yet in his later years he imposed firm economic management on a nation that was rapidly becoming ungovernable.

In his efforts to make a major contribution to solving the problems of Northern Ireland he made a great breakthrough in 1980 in his meetings with Margaret Thatcher but immediately squandered it and brought Anglo-Irish relations to their lowest ebb for a long time. He rejected the Anglo-Irish Agreement in 1985 and yet as Taoiseach he operated it conscientiously and honourably.

As leader of Fianna Fáil he presided over a period of unprecedented upheaval and turmoil and attracted trouble and controversy like a political lightning conductor. His victory in 1979 shattered the rigid discipline of the country's most powerful and best-organised political movement. The splits and divisions in the 1981-82 period were unlike anything that had happened in the country's political history and at one stage the tension literally almost killed some TDs. The Progressive Democrats were the product of that period and their formation effectively put an end to Fianna Fáil's chances of getting an overall majority while Haughey remained.

To cap that, having forced Des O'Malley out of Fianna Fáil, Haughey then astonished his own most loyal supporters by agreeing to coalition with the PDs in 1989. It was that decision that shattered the belief in their leader of so many of his strongest followers. Yet in spite of his own party's deep resentment at his abandonment of a Fianna Fáil core value he continued to govern and to ride out storm after storm. The sacking of Brian Lenihan, the loss of the presidential election, a series of capitulations to the PDs, the spate of business controversies and the revolt of old supporters like Albert Reynolds and Pádraig Flynn – it appeared that nothing could overcome his will to survive as Taoiseach.

It was that will to survive, his all-consuming desire to retain power and the political dexterity with which he so often managed to out-manoeuvre his enemies, which was the most outstanding feature of his career. Even his initial response to Seán Doherty's bombshell in January 1992 demonstrated this pugnacious will to survive and he gave in only because the alternative was a general election and he had made up his mind some time before not to lead his party into another election.

Haughey's main achievement in political life was to provide stable government on his return to power in 1987, and this helped to bring the country back from the brink of ruin. That achievement showed what he could do when his enormous political skill was properly harnessed in the nation's interest. The striking lesson about Haughey's handling of the economy is the effect of political decisions on economic well-being. Bad and weak-kneed government policies between 1977 and 1982 put the country into a deep recession when the rest of the Western world was booming. Firm leadership from 1987 helped put the country back on the right track. For all Haughey's criticism of economists as the "dismal scientists" and his ridiculing of the "Doheny and Nesbitt School of Economics", the fact is that the economists were right to point out the harsh realities and the politicians wrong to go for the soft options in the first half of the 1980s.

Judged as a party leader, Haughey's contribution has also been a contradictory one. He was elected in 1979 with the support of the backbenchers against the wishes of the party establishment. However, instead of opening up the party and broadening its appeal he imposed a dictatorial style on its operations. While the Fianna Fáil tradition has always stressed discipline and loyalty, Haughey emphasised those virtues, almost to the exclusion of everything else. There was little discussion of issues in the parliamentary party and any disagreement with the leader was taken as a personal affront. This led to the absence of any real internal debate in the party for a number of years. This suppression of debate did a great deal of damage and led to the various splits and divisions which have been a feature of Haughey's leadership. It also led to a paucity of new talent in the higher ranks of the party because promotion was, for the most part, based on loyalty rather than ability, so that Fianna Fáil became something of a one-man band.

Haughey's domineering style sometimes gave the impression that he was a decisive leader, but for long periods he was nothing of the kind. His normal approach to events was marked by great caution, whether in appointments to his Cabinet or in his choice of policy options. He was also inclined to put off decisions until the last possible moment. This sometimes led him into unnecessary crises and provoked needless media speculation about his intentions. He did this in relation to government appointments, the holding of elections and the announcement of important political decisions. Caution rather than boldness was his hallmark.

Vincent Browne summed up his approach: "Haughey's public image has been that of the 'strong man'. In reality he has been perhaps the weakest of those who have led governments in this country. Faced with almost all challenges, except leadership challenges, his instinct has been to back off or fudge, to go for the populist stroke, never the bold stroke." Browne, writing at the end of October 1991, shortly before the fourth heave against Haughey, continued: "His premiership has been a dismal failure. He has achieved almost nothing as Taoiseach. He has contributed to a political and business culture that is tarnished. He has done great damage to his own party."

This assessment emphasises the negative to the exclusion of everything else, but there was a positive side as well. True, Haughey's style was marked by caution, often excessive caution. But in politics the postponement of difficult decisions often means that in the course of events they never have to be taken at all. The great British Prime Minister, Asquith, was known for his "masterly inactivity". Sometimes inactivity or caution, rather than frenetic activity, is the best political option. For instance Haughey was always loath to shuffle his Cabinet, on the basis that any change could be destabilising. When the course of events and the sacking of Reynolds and Flynn forced him to a shuffle in November 1991, the McDaid fiasco showed how justified his normal caution was.

Caution sometimes paid, but Haughey was cautious almost all the time. Garret FitzGerald often said of Haughey that he was good on tactics but bad on strategy. Those who know him well agree that he was best in dealing with the pressing issue of the moment rather than planning a longterm strategy which might pay off down the road. The decision to go into coalition with the PDs was a classic example of his style. He refused to face the reality of the 1989 election result and deluded himself into thinking that he might be able to get agreement to continue on as a minority Taoiseach. Because of his bad tactics he allowed himself to be put into a corner by the Opposition parties and the media, where the only choice was coalition or another election.

However, once he decided that coalition it would have to be, his tactics were excellent. He pushed his Cabinet and his parliamentary party into doing something they didn't want to do but he kept them in the dark about his intentions until it was too late for them to do anything about it. His remark to Bobby Molloy that nobody but himself could have done it was probably right. Doing the deal on coalition, whether his party liked it or not, was not simply a remarkable feat on Haughey's part, it marked a crucial step in the modernisation of Fianna Fáil. Those who mourned a core value were living in the past; coalition showed how Fianna Fáil could continue to retain office and broaden its horizons for the future.

All of Haughey's electoral performances were a bitter disappointment for Fianna Fáil. His inability to win an overall majority in five elections in a row and his loss of the presidency were serious political failures. The polarisation of the community into those who loved him and those who detested him played its part in those election results, but it is by no means certain that another leader could have done any better. Both Lemass and de Valera in their time brought in worse election results than Haughey and the party has won over 50 percent of the vote only twice in the history of the state, in 1938 and 1977. Given the independent electoral commission and the large number of five-seat constituencies that now exist, winning an overall majority is a near-impossible task.

Looked at in another light, Fianna Fáil's electoral performance through the 1980s has been no mean achievement. Other parties have had their ups and downs during the decade. Fine Gael rose to the heights, winning almost 40 percent of the vote under Garret FitzGerald and then plunging down into the 20 percent range by the end of his career. They have still not recovered from the trauma. Labour were almost wiped out in the middle of the decade and have now bounced back as a growing political force. The Progressive Democrats have waxed and waned and the Workers' Party, after their big breakthrough in 1989, are now on the slide. By contrast Fianna Fáil under Haughey remained consistent as the dominant political force in the country and the party retained an astonishingly large and loyal core vote.

The chief attraction of Fianna Fáil to the majority voters for the past few decades has not been its desire for a united Ireland or the revival of the Irish language. Fianna Fáil's appeal has been that it is the party which knows best how to attain power and how to use power. It has always tried to give the voters what they want rather than telling them what they should want. This is a source of enormous strength even though it is derided by intellectuals and many in the media, who have always hankered after a left-right divide in Irish politics.

It will take some time for Fianna Fáil to adjust to the post-Haughey world and political life will certainly be much duller without him. His legacy is a mixed one; his party may have difficulty coming to terms with itself in the absence of his imperious presence but it is still in power and in a position to be the dominant political force of the 1990s as it was for every other decade of the state's existence since 1932.